BUSES
IN BRITAIN

STEWART J BROWN

Capital Transport

Foreword

This new edition of Buses in Britain follows the successful format of the original volume published in 1990 – but it is all new, both words and pictures. Its aim is to paint a broad picture of who is running what and where, and in a fast-changing world that is quite a task. The pages which follow describe the scene as it was towards the end of 1995.

The bus world is changing rapidly. A comparison of the vehicles illustrated in this volume with those in the original edition will serve to underline how true this is, as operators have changed hands, bought new buses and adopted new liveries.

Throughout this volume I have used the word minibus to describe truck-derived vehicles such as the Mercedes-Benz 709D, and purpose-built buses of broadly similar size and weight, such as Optare's MetroRider. The term midibus has been used for vehicles such as the Dennis Dart and Volvo B6, which slot in between the small front-engined types and conventional 11m and 12m heavy-weight single-deckers. This terminology holds good now, although not for much longer as new models from Optare and Dennis – the Excel and the Dart SLF – stretch, quite literally, the midibus concept.

Low-floor buses have conventionally included vehicles such as the Leyland National, which has a two-step entrance. New concerns about accessibility in the 1990s have seen a change in opinion and in this book the new meaning of low-floor – a single-step entrance leading to a step-free forward section of the bus – has been used.

Readers wanting to know more about specific fleets will find most of the information they need in the Bus Handbooks produced by British Bus Publishing and by Capital Transport, covering respectively the northern and southern parts of the country. The magazine Buses, published monthly by Ian Allan, gives good news coverage of both operators and their fleets, while for those interested in detail the comprehensive news sheets produced by the PSV Circle and its hard-working teams of volunteers are very useful.

No work of this type could be completed without some help. The photographers who supplied material are credited individually. Trying to ensure that it is as up-to-date as possible has been a mammoth task and drafts of sections of the text were read and commented on by David Donati, Keith Grimes, John Hobbs, Colin Lloyd, Allan Macfarlane, Iain MacGregor, David Little, Roy Marshall, Geoff Mills, Dave Stewart, Steve Warburton and Roy Wilson. Any errors are, of course, mine and not theirs.

Stewart J Brown, MCIT
Framilode, November 1995

ISBN 185414 181 3

Published by Capital Transport Publishing
38 Long Elmes, Harrow Weald, Middlesex

Printed by CS Graphics PTE Ltd

© Capital Transport Publishing 1996

Title page photo:
Stewart J Brown

These pages:
Cliff Beeton, Tony Wilson, Paul Gainsbury

Cover:
Stewart J Brown, Russell Upcraft, Barry Spencer

Contents

INTRODUCTION

There have been few periods in the history of the British bus industry when it has changed as quickly as it is changing now. Looking back there are key periods of change such as 25 years ago when NBC and the first PTEs were being formed. Or you can go back almost 50 years to the postwar nationalisation of much of Britain's transport. But to find change in the bus industry at a pace anywhere near that of the last few years you really have to go back to the early 1930s. That was when bus companies were expanding, with big groups consolidating their strength by the acquisition of small competitors. Does this sound familiar?

Since the first edition of Buses in Britain we have seen the disappearance of Caldaire Holdings, Proudmutual and Western Travel, and the privatisation of London Buses. The pace of change is such that almost as soon as pencil is put to paper (or finger to keyboard if you want to be really accurate) something else has happened. In the months during which this book has been written there have been some surprising changes. Badgerline and GRT Bus Group have combined to form FirstBus. British Bus has taken over Caldaire and Maidstone & District, swelling the group fleet to 5,000-plus. MTL Trust Holdings has acquired Liverbus and its associated London Suburban company. London United has taken over Westlink, FirstBus now owns People's Provincial, and the EYMS Group has bought the Stagecoach Manchester operations – and that suggests that further change is on the way in the North West.

When the first drafts were being prepared MTL Manchester was competing with GM Buses North, while GM Buses South was running blue-liveried buses as Birkenhead & District. Both of these operations ceased in the summer of 1995. And at the start of the year most of the big Sheffield independents were just that – independent. Now they are part of the Yorkshire Traction group of companies.

Changes like these are well-publicised and relatively easy to keep track of. More difficult to follow are the many small operators who suddenly disappear, either forced out of bus operation by pressure from better-established companies, or forced out of business altogether because their operating licences have been revoked. This has been happening to a growing number of small fleets – very often those running scruffy minibuses and whose operations in fact do the entire bus industry a major disservice. New small operators continue to spring up too – and it would be a braver man than I who would forecast which will succeed and which will fail.

During the two years since the first edition of Buses in Britain, there has been significant change in the established groups. All have extended their spheres of influence. And all have been investing in new buses. In 1994 Badgerline announced the biggest single bus order since the days when NBC and SBG made bulk purchases every year. Worth over £60 million it called for no fewer than 926 buses made up of 389 Dennis Darts, 187 Dennis Lances, 317 Mercedes minibuses and 33 Volvo Olympians. Delivery will extend into 1996 and is being shared between most of what were Badgerline's subsidiaries. They are, of course, now part of FirstBus.

GRT, the other part of FirstBus, has been placing more modest orders, but for higher-specification vehicles, often with air-conditioning and double-glazing. These have included Scanias and Mercedes O405s, but no double-deckers. The group showing most interest in double-deckers is Stagecoach, which in 1995 added Northern Counties-bodied Olympians to its operations in Cleveland, Hull and London. However here too the single-decker rules, and Alexander-bodied B10Ms are appearing in Stagecoach fleets throughout the country.

In the autumn of 1995 Stagecoach topped Badgerline's record 1994 order by announcing that it was buying 1,050 new vehicles, 880 of which were for its British fleets – 400 Mercedes minibuses, 240 Olympians, 140 B10Ms and 100 Dennis Darts. Ten of the B10Ms will be articulated coaches.

British Bus has been buying increasing numbers of Scanias, with new N113 double-deckers for Derby City Transport, Midland Fox, Midland Red North and Northumbria. It has also been buying Mercedes minibuses with Alexander and Plaxton bodies. And it has steered clear of a corporate group identity. One of the more recent British Bus acquisitions, Luton & District, has underlined this with new names and a new image which rank among the smartest in the business.

Expansion in the last two years has seen British Bus establish a significant Scottish operation, through its ownership of Clydeside Buses. The company has also significantly strengthened its position in the Midlands by buying Derby City Transport and Stevensons of Uttoxeter, and is now established in Yorkshire through the operations purchased from Caldaire Holdings. Two years ago GRT was a purely Scottish operation, but by the time it merged with Badgerline it owned Eastern Counties, Leicester Citybus and Northampton Transport. Similarly the Go-Ahead Group in 1993 was confined to operations in the North East. These it has expanded by acquisition – and it has also moved south, with the purchase of London Central, Brighton & Hove and City of Oxford.

The greatest expansion has been by Stagecoach. In the last two years it has become a major operator in the North East of England and has expanded in the Midlands, the South West and into Wales with its takeover of Western Travel. It is also a major player in London, owning two former London Buses subsidiaries.

Among the smaller groups, Blazefield has expanded in the south with its takeover of BTS Coaches which runs tendered services in London, while Yorkshire Traction has gained significant ground in South Yorkshire by buying up Sheffield operators.

While all this has been happening, new bus sales have been booming too – but with a steady change of emphasis. Single-deckers are gaining ground at the expense of double-deckers. Low-floor buses which allow easy access for pushchairs and shopping trolleys have been slow to take off, partly on the grounds of cost. But there are clear signs that change is on the way, with the Scania Axcess-ultralow (not the catchiest of names), the Volvo B6LE and the Dennis Dart SLF. The last-named in particular looks set to challenge what might already be seen as the first-generation of low-floor buses, the Scania MaxCi, the Volvo B10L and the Dennis Lance SLF.

This growing interest in accessibility may prove to be another nail in the coffin of the double-decker, despite the large numbers still in use and the healthy deliveries to Stagecoach, British Bus and companies such as Lothian. There are few new double-deckers in the FirstBus empire. And some major urban fleets – notably Mainline, West Midlands Travel, MTL, GM Buses North and GM Buses South – seem increasingly to be pinning their faith on single-deckers of one sort or another.

At the other end of the spectrum there are still plenty of elderly vehicles about. It may be 10 years since the last Bedfords entered service, but there are still a good number running on rural services. It's approaching 15 years since the last Fleetlines, Atlanteans and VRTs were built, but all are still a common sight in towns and cities throughout Britain, and look set to remain so for some time to come. Growing pressure for seat belts on school buses – and the spectre of legislation – might lead to the end of the road for such buses on school contract work. Not before time, many would say.

Ten years ago many enthusiasts feared that deregulation and privatisation would mean that the bus industry would become less interesting. This volume shows just how misplaced those fears were.

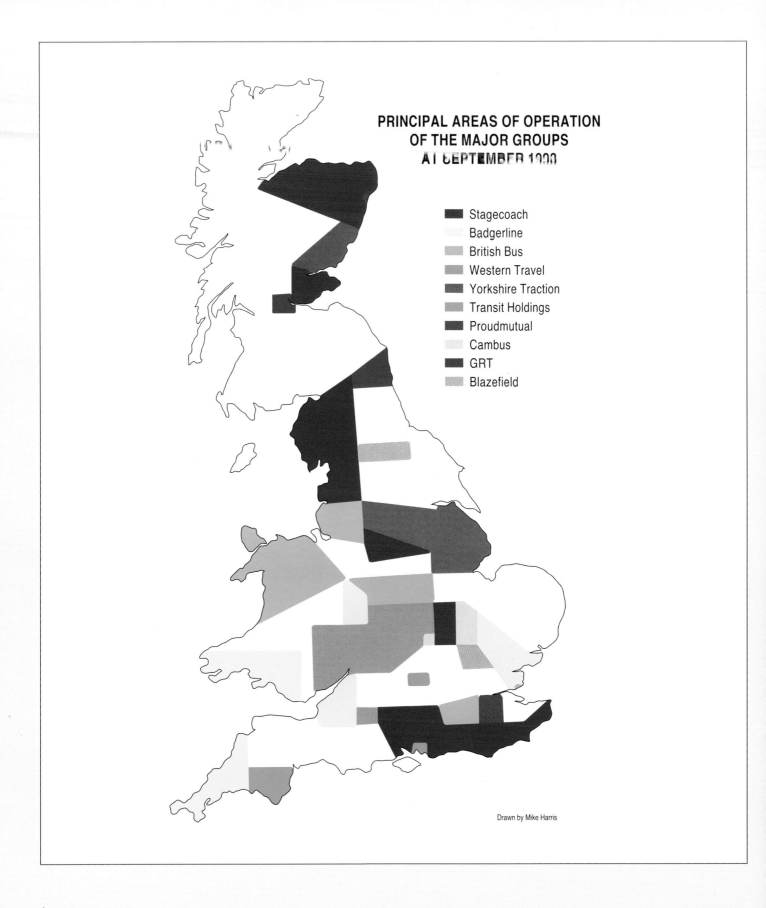

PRINCIPAL AREAS OF OPERATION
OF THE MAJOR GROUPS
AT SEPTEMBER 1990

- Stagecoach
- Badgerline
- British Bus
- Western Travel
- Yorkshire Traction
- Transit Holdings
- Proudmutual
- Cambus
- GRT
- Blazefield

Drawn by Mike Harris

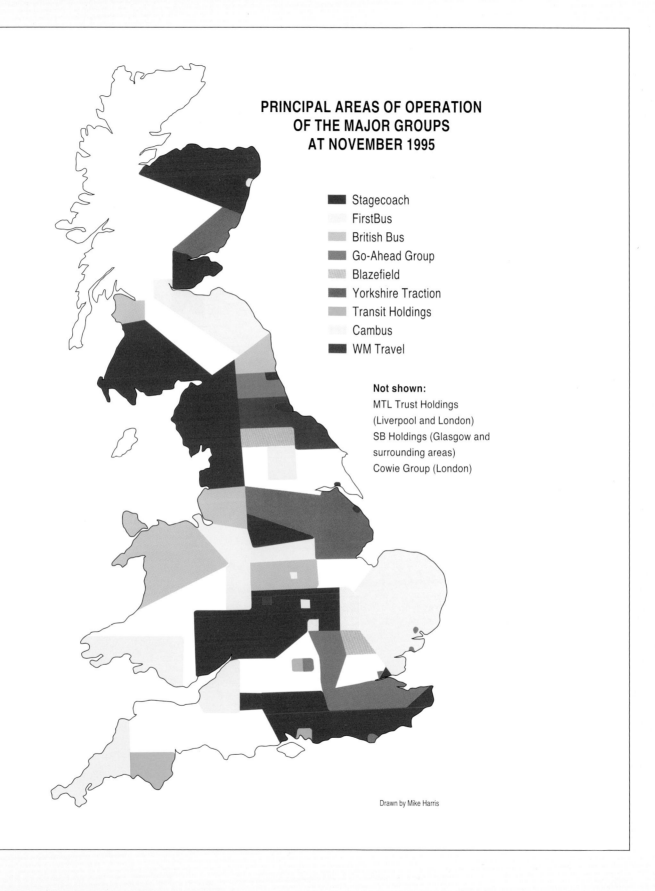

**PRINCIPAL AREAS OF OPERATION
OF THE MAJOR GROUPS
AT NOVEMBER 1995**

- Stagecoach
- FirstBus
- British Bus
- Go-Ahead Group
- Blazefield
- Yorkshire Traction
- Transit Holdings
- Cambus
- WM Travel

Not shown:
MTL Trust Holdings
(Liverpool and London)
SB Holdings (Glasgow and
surrounding areas)
Cowie Group (London)

Drawn by Mike Harris

SCOTLAND

Top **Stagecoach has invested heavily in new buses for all of its Scottish subsidiaries. The group's standard single-decker is the Volvo B10M with Alexander PS-type, as seen here in the Western Scottish fleet in Dumfries.** Malcolm King

Above **Surprise additions to the KCB fleet following its takeover by SB Holdings were a number of Atlanteans transferred from the Strathclyde Buses fleet. They were used to replace Dennis Dominators and Ailsas. This is a 1977 bus with Alexander body. Behind are a Strathclyde Buses Ailsa and an MCW Metrobus.**
Malcolm King

The ownership of Scotland's buses has undergone major change. Most of it took place in 1994 with two groups – Stagecoach and GRT – expanding largely by the purchase of privatised former Scottish Bus Group companies from their original management buy-out teams. But SB Holdings and British Bus have also played their part in what has been a quite dramatic reshaping of Scotland's bus business.

Starting in Glasgow, the country's main centre of population, SB Holdings is the major operator with three trading subsidiaries. The core city operation is in the hands of Strathclyde Buses, successor to the former Strathclyde PTE operation, and inheritor of the one-time Glasgow municipal operation. A smaller SB Holdings operation trades as GCT – which just happens to be the initials of Glasgow Corporation Transport. And the third SB Holdings operation is Kelvin Central Buses, serving an arc to the north of the city which sweeps from the north bank of the River Clyde on the west, right round to Lanark in the south-east.

Strathclyde Buses runs 750 vehicles in an orange and black livery which has been in use since 1983. The company was privatised in a management-led buy-out in 1993, beating a bid from Stagecoach. Its services run mainly in the city area, although it also has a reasonable presence in Paisley to the west and is the main operator in East Kilbride to the south. Both of these towns are served as a result of the company's post-deregulation expansion.

The Strathclyde Buses fleet is a varied one. It still includes 299 Leyland Atlanteans, the biggest fleet of the type north of the border and one of the biggest in Britain. Glasgow Corporation was the first Scottish operator to standardise on the Atlantean, as long ago as 1962, and the PTE was among Scotland's last buyers of new Atlanteans, with X-registered buses which were delivered in 1981. Alongside the Atlanteans there are significant numbers of Ailsas and underfloor-engined Volvo Citybuses. With 111 Ailsas in the fleet Strathclyde Buses is the biggest UK operator of front-engined double-deckers – just ahead of Tayside which has 102. And with 100 Citybuses it is also the biggest user of underfloor-engined double-deckers. There are also MCW Metrobuses, some with Alexander R-type bodies, and 73 Leyland Olympians. Most of these have Alexander bodies, but some of the earlier examples were bodied by Leyland Bus subsidiaries Roe and ECW, at a time when the PTE chose to spread its body orders around. There are also two with Leyland bodies.

The newest double-deckers in the fleet are four Volvo Olympians delivered in 1995. Two have Alexander Royale bodies, but the other two have Northern Counties bodies – the first new buses for Glasgow's main urban operator to come from the Wigan builder for just over 50 years. The Alexander-bodied Volvo Olympians are, incidentally, an all-Scottish product with bodies built in Falkirk and chassis manufactured at Irvine.

Top **Strathclyde Buses runs 299 Atlanteans, the biggest fleet in Scotland and one of the biggest in Britain of Leyland's classic workhorse. A 1980 example heads south from Glasgow's George Square for East Kilbride, an area which Strathclyde has served since deregulation.** Brian Ridgway

Centre **The last new Leylands for a British operator were 52 Olympians delivered to Strathclyde in 1993. These had lowheight Alexander R-type bodies. Strathclyde Buses and its predecessors had operated Leylands since 1924.** Stewart J Brown

Left **Four Volvo Olympians were added to the Strathclyde fleet for evaluation in 1995. Two were bodied by Alexander, the company's traditional supplier, and two by Northern Counties - the first Palatine IIs for a Scottish operator.** Stewart J Brown

Single-deckers are few and far between in the Strathclyde fleet. There are a couple of Scania N113s with Plaxton Verde bodies, acquired at a time of severe vehicle shortage after 60 buses were destroyed in a fire at Larkfield garage in 1992. Other odd acquisitions at that time – Atlanteans from Busways and Nottingham – are now in the GCT fleet. Small buses have all but vanished from the main Strathclyde Buses fleet. Eight MCW Metroriders remain; all others are now with GCT. Rarities in the single-deck fleet are three Volvo B10Ms with Caetano Stagecoach bus bodies. Only four vehicles of this type were sold in Britain. Strathclyde Buses bought its three in 1990 from Graham's of Paisley. The fourth is with Guildford & West Surrey Buses.

The GCT operation was set up in 1993. SB Holdings insists that it is not a low-cost unit, although its drivers are paid at lower wage rates... With its headquarters at Strathclyde Buses' Knightswood garage, GCT is a self-contained operation running some cross-city services and a number of suburban routes. Its livery, green and yellow, recalls schemes used by the original GCT, and its fleet is made up mainly of buses transferred from the parent fleet, along with a few other second-hand vehicles and three Scania K93 single-deckers with East Lancs dual-purpose bodies. These carry SB Travel livery, the identity used for the coach fleet and also worn by some Metroriders.

GCT's double-deckers are Atlanteans and a small number of ex-Kelvin Central Olympians, purchased while Kelvin Central was still independent from SB Holdings. One Atlantean, L-registered LA664, has been restored to what purports to be its original livery (though there is some argument about the shades of colour used) and is regularly used in service. The GCT fleet has Metroriders too. Those allocated to the fleet on its formation are in yellow and green, but a sizeable number were transferred to GCT in the spring of 1995 and still carry Strathclyde Buses' orange livery. These include two ex-demonstration Optare-built MetroRiders. GCT-owned Metroriders are immediately identifiable by their GM-prefixed fleet numbers.

SB Holdings has perpetuated the fleet-numbering system started by Glasgow Corporation almost 50 years ago, with class letters for different types of buses, as shown below. GCT buses use the same system but with the addition of a G prefix (eg GLA for Leyland Atlanteans).

A	Ailsa	LA	Leyland Atlantean
AH	Ailsa Horizontal	LO	Leyland Olympian
	(Volvo Citybus)	M	Metrorider
AS	Ailsa Single-deck	MB	Metrobus
	(Volvo B10M)	SS	Scania Single-deck
C	Coach	VO	Volvo Olympian

Top **Single-deckers play a small part in the Strathclyde Buses operation but include some unusual types, such as this 1986 Volvo B10M with Caetano Stagecoach body. It was new to Hutchison of Overtown.** Stewart J Brown

Centre **Glasgow Corporation's final livery, introduced in 1959 and used until the formation of the Greater Glasgow PTE in 1973, is carried by GCT's oldest Atlantean, a 1973 AN68. It is a frequent performer on service 100, linking the city centre with the Scottish Exhibition Centre.** Stewart J Brown

Right **The standard GCT livery does evoke memories of Glasgow Corporation. It is seen here on an ex-Nottingham Atlantean, acquired by Strathclyde Buses in 1992 to cover for a vehicle shortage following a major fire at Larkfield garage. It was transferred to the new GCT operation in 1993. It has an East Lancs body and is one of seven similar buses operated by GCT.** Brian Ridgway

Above **Some of the buses transferred from Strathclyde Buses to the KCB fleet received KCB red on the front, while retaining Strathclyde orange and black elsewhere. An ECW-bodied Olympian – which also has KCB cream wheels – illustrates the effect as it passes a Strathclyde Atlantean in Clydebank.** Stewart J Brown

Above **KCB's older single-deckers are generally Leyland Nationals. This bus was new to Central Scottish in 1980.** Stewart J Brown

KCB has taken over the services of a number of its small competitors and this has added various odd buses to its fleet. This 1982 Volvo B58 with Duple body was acquired from McKenna of Uddingston in 1992. Stewart J Brown

In 1994 SB Holdings made a significant expansion with the purchase of Kelvin Central Buses. KCB had had a difficult history. It was formed in 1989 by amalgamating two SBG subsidiaries – Kelvin Scottish and Central Scottish. Central was an old-established operation with roots stretching back to 1932, while Kelvin was a creation of SBG's deregulation strategy, having been formed in 1985 to take over the north Glasgow operations of Central, Midland and Eastern.

The fleet went through a number of identity crises before settling on a red and cream livery which had first been seen at the start of 1989 in the short-lived Lanarkshire Bus identity used by Central for part of its operations. This was initially applied in an unusual layout with diagonal bands of cream relief, but since late 1993 the company has used a conventional style with a single cream relief band. Both livery layouts are still in evidence. A new fleetname, KCB Network, was adopted early in 1994.

The fleet is pretty varied too, partly because of the mixed inheritance of its constituents. This means that KCB runs Leyland Olympians and MCW Metrobuses delivered to its SBG predecessors in the early 1980s. Variety was further increased by second-hand purchases, some of which were relatively short-lived, such as Bristol VRTs and ex-Merseyside Dennis Dominators. Both types have now left the fleet.

Leyland Leopards with Alexander Y-type bodies, most of which were inherited from Central, still dominate the single-deck fleet but there are various other models including former NBC Leopards with ECW B51 bodies (rare in Scotland), second-hand Nationals and half-a-dozen Dennis Darts which came with the services of Stagecoach's Magicbus operation in Glasgow when that was taken over by KCB in 1992. KCB is Scotland's biggest Leyland National operator with almost 70 in the fleet, including the only East Lancs Greenway in Scotland. Most are second-hand Mark 1s, many of which were acquired with the bus business of Morrow of Clydebank in 1992. Other older KCB single-deckers include Leyland Tigers and Dennis Dorchesters with Alexander T-type bodies. Few of the T-types carry their chassis maker's badges, so it takes an eagle eye to spot the difference between a Dennis and a Leyland. Some of the Tigers are unusual in having Gardner engines, installed by Leyland to meet the threat which the Dorchester posed to its business with SBG.

When SB Holdings took control of KCB in October 1994, it set about some rationalisation, withdrawing Dennis Dominators and replacing them with Leyland Atlanteans and Olympians from the Strathclyde Buses fleet. These were not any newer than the Dennises, but were said to be cheaper to operate. Some are running in Strathclyde's orange livery with KCB red fronts. The application of fleet livery to the fronts of otherwise unrepainted second-hand buses has been a KCB practice since the company's formation. The oldest of the Atlanteans are 1974 M-registered buses which makes KCB Network the only operator to have added double-deckers to its fleet in 1994 with both M suffix and M prefix registrations.

Before selling out to SB Holdings, KCB had in fact embarked on its biggest fleet upgrade since its privatisation in 1991. New additions to the fleet comprised a range of different combinations of Alexander bodies and Volvo chassis, including 23 Royale double-deckers on Olympians, six Dashes on B6s, and 10 Striders on B10Bs. KCB is the country's biggest operator of Royales. The latest deliveries have been to low-height specification and were the first lowheight Royales. Route-branding is relatively rare north of the border but some of KCB's Royales are used on the Goldline express route which runs non-stop on the motorway from Glasgow to Hamilton and then serves the Hamilton area. Lowheight Royales with a dark cream area between decks are used on this service.

Eighteen Stagecoach-style Volvo B10Ms with Alexander PS-type bodies were delivered to KCB at the end of 1994. Their arrival at KCB followed a threatened bus war in Glasgow, with Stagecoach having announced that it was launching cross-city services to compete with Strathclyde Buses. Strathclyde retaliated with plans to start operations in Perth, the Stagecoach heartland, and the scene was set for a major confrontation. At the last minute peace broke out, with Stagecoach buying a 20 per cent share in SB Holdings and abandoning its Stagecoach Glasgow operations. However the Monopolies & Mergers Commission has subsequently said that Stagecoach should sell its interest in SB Holdings. As part of the deal SB Holdings took over the 18 new B10Ms which are now serving Glasgow in the KCB fleet. A further 60 B10Ms with Alexander PS-type bodies are on order and will lead to the withdrawal of many older types. Some odd double-deckers bought by SB Holdings for use in Perth are also in the KCB fleet, including ex-Hull and ex-SYT Atlanteans.

KCB is the main operator along the north bank of the Clyde. A depot at Old Kilpatrick to the west of the city provides services in Dumbarton and Clydebank. This was previously Central SMT country. To the north, KCB runs in Milngavie, Kirkintilloch, Kilsyth and Cumbernauld, territory which was inherited from Alexander (Midland). There is little competition in this area, but in Cumbernauld a local service is operated by Canavan of Kilsyth using two new Plaxton-bodied Dennis Darts. In Kirkintilloch Ann's Coaches run a Mercedes minibus on a local service. It carries a KH depot code transfer in the style once used by Alexander (Midland). Eastwards KCB is the main operator in Coatbridge and Airdrie, and south to Motherwell, Hamilton and Lanark.

KCB's fleet numbering system can prove confusing to the uninitiated. The four-digit numbers consist of a prefix – 1 for buses, 2 for dual-purpose vehicles and 3 for coaches – with mini and midibuses being numbered below 099, single-deckers between 100 and 599, and double-deckers above 600.

Top **A number of second-hand Atlanteans have been added to the KCB fleet to speed replacement of non-standard types. They include buses which were new to Hull and, as shown here, South Yorkshire. Marshall built the dual-door body which carries the enigmatic notice "This is not a door" on the centre doors.** Malcolm King

Centre **The first lowheight versions of Alexander's Royale body were delivered to KCB in 1994. They are on Volvo Olympian chassis. One pauses in Kirkintilloch on its way from Glasgow to Campsie Glen.** Stewart J Brown

Right **The cessation of the short-lived Stagecoach Glasgow operations saw 18 new Volvo B10Ms being transferred from Stagecoach to KCB. They have Alexander PS-type bodies. A further 60 similar buses were ordered in 1995.** Brian Ridgway

To the south and south-west of Glasgow, the main operator is Clydeside Buses, as Clydeside 2000 was renamed in mid-1995. It's another company with a short but involved history, having originally been created from the northern area of Western Scottish. Suffice it to say that it was privatised in a management buy-out in 1991, with some financial backing from Luton & District. During 1994 L&D was taken over by British Bus, and at the end of the year British Bus bought Clydeside 2000.

The fleet which it acquired was not one of the most modern. The double-deckers are all Fleetlines with lowheight Alexander bodies, stylish buses but getting a bit long in the tooth. These originated with Western and Midland. Single-deckers include a fair number of Leopards with Alexander Y-type bodies. There are also large numbers of second-hand Leopards bought to help fight tough competition in Greenock. These came mainly from Cleveland Transit and Lancaster City Transport. The Cleveland Leopards have bus-seated Plaxton Supreme bodies while the LCT examples have Alexander Y-type bodies which don't look out of place in the Clydeside fleet. For those who appreciate the Leopard's distinctive roar Clydeside, with around 150 still in use, has Britain's biggest fleet.

In the 12 months prior to its sale to British Bus, Clydeside 2000 had embarked on a modest investment in new buses. At the end of 1993 a fleet of 15 Mercedes-Benz minibuses with Plaxton Beaver bodies entered service. These were followed in the summer of 1994 by seven Volvo B6s with Alexander Dash bodies which brought a brighter livery layout with white relief to separate the standard yellow and red. Most of these vehicles operate in and around Paisley, where competition has been intense.

After buying the company, British Bus quickly bought some new buses for it – and what an exciting mixture they were, introducing amazing variety to the fleet. First came 10 Dennis Lances with Plaxton Verde bodies, which entered service in white but were soon repainted in a variant of the bright new red, white and yellow livery first seen on the B6s. They were the first new full-size buses to join the Clydeside 2000 fleet since its privatisation. They operate mainly in the Glasgow-Paisley-Johnstone corridor.

Then came more full-size single-deckers, also for operation in the Paisley and Glasgow areas. These were Scanias with bodywork by Alexander, Northern Counties and East Lancs. These included L113s with East Lancs MaxCi-style bodies. All of the Scanias are based at Clydeside's Inchinnan depot and operate from Glasgow to Erskine and Glasgow to Paisley via Renfrew. Recent second-hand arrivals have been former London MCW Metroriders. They join a minibus fleet made up largely of Dodge S56s. The new livery with white relief is now being applied to older single-deckers in the fleet, and the '2000' is being dropped from the fleetname.

Top **British Bus acquired Clydeside at the end of 1994 and quickly injected new buses into the ageing fleet. Among the more unusual was this low-floor Scania MaxCi with East Lancs body.** Brian Ridgway

Centre **New Dennises were also delivered, including full-size Lances with Plaxton Verde bodywork. The Lance is still relatively uncommon north of the border.** Stewart J Brown

Right **Two Plaxton-bodied Dennis Darts added to the Clydeside fleet followed an earlier delivery of similarly-sized Volvo B6s with Alexander bodies. All operate in the Paisley area.** Stewart J Brown

With SB Holdings companies serving the city and the area to the north of the River Clyde, and British Bus running services to the south and west, there isn't much sign of small operators in the city. The main area where competition has sprung up in the mid-nineties is Govan, as immortalised by television's Rab C Nesbitt. The new operators run ageing minibuses, most of which look just a shade past their best. Puma Coaches have a Reeve Burgess-bodied Dodge S56, while Govan Mini Bus has 10-year-old ex-Greater Manchester Dodges with Northern Counties bodies. Hutchison of Renfrew links Renfrew and Govan in competition with Clydeside. The Hutchison fleet includes an Iveco Ford with Dormobile body.

In the central area HAD Coaches of Shotts run the inter-station service linking the city's two main rail terminals, normally using a Mercedes mini. Bridge Coaches run in from Erskine with new and second-hand minibuses which include ex-GM Buses Iveco Fords. The buses bought new are generally Mercedes 709Ds. McGill's Bus Service of Barrhead, the sole survivor of the established Paisley area independent operators of the 1970s (and earlier), operates Leyland National 2s on an hourly service to Glasgow from Barrhead.

In Paisley itself McGill's trunk route running south to Barrhead is also operated by Nationals, but added interest is provided by an ex-demonstration Leyland Lynx. McGill's also run Mercedes minibuses and a pair of Dennis Darts, but possibly of most interest is the fleet's only double-decker, an ex-London Routemaster which was acquired in 1994 and is frequently to be seen on the Paisley to Barrhead service.

New-generation independents in Paisley are generally minibus operators, usually with second-hand equipment. The biggest is Bellview, which started running local services in 1973. Its 17-strong fleet consists mainly of Robin Hood-bodied Iveco Fords which were new to Ribble. Others include Green Line and the imaginatively-named Shanks Pony, which runs second-hand Ivecos in a livery said to be that used by Paisley & District which was taken over by Western SMT the best part of 50 years ago. The colours are orange and cream with maroon relief. Neilston, to the south of Paisley, is home to Crawford, a coach operator whose express service between Glasgow and Ardrossan merits a mention because it is usually operated by an Alexander-bodied Volvo Citybus double-decker, bought new in 1989.

Top **A number of small operators have started services in south-west Glasgow, including Govan Mini Bus, whose fleet includes this Dodge S56 with Northern Counties body which was new to Greater Manchester Transport. It is seen in Govan bus station.** Stewart J Brown

Centre **The majority type in the McGill's fleet is the Leyland National. There are 16, most of which were bought new, although this National 2 came from Northern Scottish.** Brian Ridgway

Right **Among the new breed of small operators in Paisley is Green Line, running Freight Rover Sherpas on town services.** Stewart J Brown

Greenock has long been a hot-bed of competition, although tough action by the Scottish traffic commissioner has seen some order emerge from apparent chaos. But there are still at least seven small businesses running minibuses in the town, generally in competition with Clydeside which uses Leopards and minibuses. Key small operators serving Greenock are Harte Buses, with a fleet of five Mercedes minis, four of which were bought new and the fifth was a demonstrator, and Wilson's, running a fleet of predominantly second-hand minibuses. Harte's biggest bus is an ex-demonstration Optare Vecta complete with truck-style air horns mounted above the driving compartment. Look at a Harte fleet list and you'll spot that most vehicles have IIB registrations. The reason for this becomes clear when you see the vehicles on the road. A black retaining screw carefully positioned between the two Is gives the registration the appearance of HB for Harte Buses. Avondale, serving Greenock and Port Glasgow, also operates new and second-hand Mercedes minibuses. Roadrunner has 10-year-old Transits which came from Midland Red North, while Thistle Coaches has Northern Counties-bodied Dodges which were once part of the Alder Valley fleet. Westside Transport runs Ivecos and Mercedes. The biggest vehicle operated on Greenock local services by a small operator is a Leopard/Plaxton coach run by Lochview.

To the north of the Clyde, Allander Coaches provide services in and around Dumbarton and Balloch. Allander's bus fleet runs under the Loch Lomond Coaches name and includes ex-SBG Leopards and two new Alexander-bodied Volvo B6s. There are also a few rebodied buses – two East Lancs EL2000s, one on a Tiger and one on a B10M, and a Q-registered Leopard with a Plaxton body, the chassis of which originally operated in Singapore as a demonstrator. Weir's Tours, a long-established coach operator, runs Leyland Nationals in the Helensburgh area. Most came from Fife Scottish and McGill's.

Top **Greenock's most modern bus is this MAN with Optare Vecta body operated by Harte Buses. Note the air horns above the driver's side window and the registration letters designed to give the impression that they read HB.** Stewart J Brown

Centre **Weir's Tours operate in the Helensburgh area using Leyland Nationals. This bus was new to Fife Scottish in 1979. It joined the Weir fleet in 1992.** Paul Wigan

Left **Loch Lomond Coaches operate between Balloch and Clydebank, and also serve Dumbarton. A 1992 East Lancs body has been used to turn a 1981 Volvo B10M from a bus to a coach. The chassis was new to Western Scottish.** Stewart J Brown

To the east of Glasgow, Henderson Travel of Hamilton is a company which has expanded, mainly with new Alexander-bodied Mercedes minibuses. Its bigger buses include one Volvo B6, also bodied by Alexander, and a couple of Leopards rebodied with Willowbrook Warrior bus bodies. One of these has a Q-prefix registration; it was originally a Ministry of Defence bus with a registration mark in the military series. Henderson Travel started running buses in 1966 and now operates services in suburban Glasgow, and in the Hamilton and East Kilbride areas.

Also serving Hamilton is Whitelaw of Stonehouse. The fleet is varied, with one-time Green Line ECW-bodied Tigers, now fitted with bus seats and well past their first flush of youth, running alongside nine new Volvo B10Bs with Alexander and Northern Counties bodies. Wilsons of Carnwath also run to Hamilton, typically with Leyland Leopard coaches, some of which have been reseated as buses.

Hutchison of Overtown is the biggest of the traditional independent operators in the area to the east of Glasgow. This old-established company – its history can be traced back over 70 years – has long had a policy of buying new vehicles for both its bus and coach fleets. For many years Hutchison was a loyal Duple customer and its oldest buses are Volvo B10Ms with Dominant bus bodies, while the most numerous type is the B10M with the short-lived 300-series bus body. There are 13 of these in operation. Duple's demise has seen some new types appear – a pair of Volvo B10Bs with Northern Counties bodies, followed by a trio of MAN 11.190s with Optare Vecta bodywork. The only other Vectas in Scotland run for West Coast Motors and Essbee in Campbeltown, and Harte Buses in Greenock. The bulk of Hutchison's services run in the Wishaw and Motherwell area, but the company also runs a commuter coach service to Glasgow, using mainly Volvo B10Ms.

Another established independent serving Wishaw is Irvine of Law. Unlike Hutchison, the Irvine bus fleet is made up of second-hand stock, including two Duple Dominant buses. One is an ex-Hutchison B10M; the other an AEC Reliance which was new to AA of Ayr. A Leopard with Alexander Y-type body is operated by Irvine but this most typically Scottish bus was actually new to the South Yorkshire PTE. Bristol VRTs are used on school services. In Lanark local services are provided by Stokes of Carstairs, yet another firm with a long history of bus operation. Unusually for a small company, all of its buses have been bought new. They include four Tigers with Plaxton Derwent bodies, two Darts with Plaxton Pointer bodies, and four Mercedes 811Ds.

Top **Henderson Travel runs two Willowbrook Warriors in a fleet made up mainly of small buses. This bus has a 1991 body on a 1973 Leopard chassis which started life with Midland Red. It is loading in Hamilton bus station for East Kilbride.** Mike Harris

Centre **Among the modern buses in Whitelaw's fleet are three Volvo B10Bs with Alexander Strider bodies. The company also runs six Northern Counties-bodied B10Bs.** Iain MacGregor

Right **The Hutchison bus fleet is made up mainly of Volvo B10Ms with Duple 300-series bodies. The first of 13 in the fleet, a 1988 bus passes through Motherwell.** Stewart J Brown

If anyone doubted that Britain's bus industry was in the throes of change, the demise of the A1 Service co-operative in Ayrshire in January 1995 must surely have brought the message home. A1's varied fleet had been a magnet for enthusiasts for decades. The number of partners in the co-operative had dwindled as the years went by – there were 10 at the end – but Ayrshire without A1 seemed inconceivable.

A1 sold out to Stagecoach and there were soon signs of change. The most modern buses in the fleet, mostly Leyland Olympians, were quickly painted in Stagecoach white. A few older buses – Atlanteans and Ailsas – are still running in A1 blue, but not for much longer. New types have been drafted in from elsewhere in the Stagecoach empire. These have included Fife Scottish Leopards and Leyland Titans from London. Ex-London buses are no strangers to A1 – the last London Titans in the fleet were RTLs in the 1960s and early 1970s. The new arrivals, from Stagecoach's East London operation, are 13 dual-door T-class buses, some still in London red but most in corporate Stagecoach white. A few A1 duties are still crew-operated and there is a strange irony in the high-tech Titan (as it was in the 1970s) carrying a conductress. A major upgrade for the fleet came in the summer of 1995 with the delivery of 21 new Alexander-bodied Olympians to replace the oldest of the acquired 'deckers.

The centre of A1's operations is the Kilmarnock to Irvine corridor, with key services extending up the Clyde Coast to Stevenston, Saltcoats and Ardrossan. In a nice display of individuality the Stagecoach A1 buses, including the Titans, generally carry polished wheeltrims.

AA, the other old-established Ayrshire independent, used to be a co-operative but is now run by Dodds of Prestwick. Leyland Nationals abound in this operation. Some were bought new – rare for an independent in the 1970s – and these have in recent years been joined by second-hand examples from a variety of sources. There are 22 Nationals in use and they run alongside five Lynxes and seven Scanias, some with East Lancs bodies and some with unusual Jonckheere bodywork. The latter were new to Scancoaches of London and were originally operated on an LRT tendered service in the Hammersmith area.

The newest big bus in the AA fleet is a Scania L113 – a Scottish first – with Alexander Strider body. It was followed by AA's first midis, two Dennis Darts intended for the Ayr to Annbank service. Further Darts and Mercedes have been added to the fleet to run a Dalmellington service. The company used to run a large number of double-deckers but only two 1979 Fleetlines remain.

Top **To speed the withdrawal of elderly buses, a number of Titans were transferred to the A1 fleet from Stagecoach's London operations. An early Park Royal-built Titan passes through Irvine Cross.** Russell Upcraft

Centre **To modernise the A1 fleet Stagecoach injected 21 new Alexander-bodied Olympians in the summer of 1995. These replaced elderly Atlanteans, Fleetlines and Ailsas.** Gavin Booth

Left **AA Buses is the sole survivor of the established Ayrshire independents. The fleet includes a number of Scanias and the newest is Scotland's first L113. It has an Alexander Strider body and is seen heading south through Ardrossan on its way to Ayr. The initials of the two towns gave rise to the company's name.** Brian Ridgway

The third old-established Ayrshire independent was Clyde Coach Services. In the summer of 1995 it followed A1's lead and its commercial bus operations were taken over by Stagecoach. Clyde Coast was the established operator between Largs and Saltcoats and this service had been extended south to serve Irvine New Town. Clyde Coast minis also provide the Largs local service. Clyde Coast continues as a coach operator and still runs tendered services. Competition on the coast road comes from Greenock-based Ashton Coach Hire, with a fleet of new M-registered Mercedes running from Greenock to Ayr on the Coastline 585. These carry Coastline names such as Coastline Corvette and Coastline Comfort and most have WS Coachbuilders or TBP bodies. Clydeside 2000 also run between Greenock and Largs with anything from an ex-Lancaster Leopard to an ex-London Metrorider. In response to Ashton's service four established operators set up competition in the summer of 1995 branded as Coastlink 535 and using a very similar white livery with green relief. Following a court case against them, the copycat livery and similar name had to be dropped. They now compete using a white and red livery with the fleetname Clyde Coaster. The operators are Clydeside, A1, Clyde Coast and AA. Both A1 and Clyde Coast run Volvo B10Ms with Alexander PS-type bodies, diverted from a Western Scottish order.

In Irvine itself the biggest of the new-generation operators is Shuttle Buses, started in 1990 by two ex-Western Scottish employees. Its original Ford Transits have been joined by Freight Rover Sherpas and bigger Mercedes, and the company now runs almost 20 buses. Two of the smaller operators, Wynter M and Valley, withdrew services in 1995 following action by the Scottish traffic commissioner.

Further south, Keenan of Coalhall runs into Ayr. The company has three Atlanteans and a couple of Leopard buses for its service work. It also runs a coach fleet. Inland, Rowe of Muirkirk runs in and around Cumnock with new Mercedes minibuses or elderly second-hand Leopards. Rowe also has a service to Ayr.

Top **Clyde Coast's bus operations were taken over by Stagecoach in the summer of 1995, but initially with little sign of change. The standard bus on the company's Largs local service is a former United Counties Iveco with Robin Hood body. It loads in the town's main street.** Stewart J Brown

Centre **Coastline 585 is a recently-introduced operation by Ashton Coach Hire, running south from Greenock to Largs, Saltcoats, Irvine and Ayr. It is run by new Mercedes minibuses, including this 811D with TBP bodywork.** Brian Ridgway

Right **The appearance of Coastline 585 prompted a response from established operators along the route. The result was Coastlink 535, run by AA, A1 Clyde Coast and Clydeside 2000 in a similar white and green livery. This prompted legal action by Ashton Coaches which led to the rival service being re-branded from August 1995 as Clyde Coaster in a white and red livery, as shown on this Northern Counties-bodied DAF SB220.** Tony Wilson

The main operator in south-west Scotland is former SBG subsidiary Western Scottish. It was privatised in a management buy-out in 1991 and was taken over by Stagecoach in 1994. Its headquarters are in Kilmarnock, from where routes stretch north to Glasgow. But the bulk of its operations are to the south, with main depots in Ayr, Cumnock and Dumfries. It is also the only operator on the islands of Bute and Arran, having taken over Arran Transport in October 1994. The Arran fleet was made up mainly of Bedford buses but included a new Marshall-bodied Dart.

The old Western Scottish black and white livery is being replaced by Stagecoach stripes – and they do represent an improvement as a glance at a drab black and white Alexander T-type alongside a newly repainted one will show. The only Seddons in Stagecoach colours are to be found in the Western Scottish fleet. They are Pennine VIIs with Alexander bodies. The Pennine VII is often described as a Leopard with a Gardner engine, which is what some of SBG's engineers wanted to buy, but Leyland didn't want to build. Now they are disappearing fast.

Western's double-deckers are mainly Fleetlines with Northern Counties bodies bought new in 1978-79, and a few with ECW bodies which came from other SBG companies. There are also ex-Greater Manchester Atlanteans, introduced to the fleet in 1991 and giving the company its first taste of Atlantean operation. Leyland's original rear-engined double-decker was never purchased new by SBG companies. Most of the Atlanteans are running for A1, but still in Western colours.

Under its new ownership Western Scottish has seen new types appear – Volvo B10Ms with Alexander PS-type bodies, B6s with Alexander Dash bodies, and Mercedes 709Ds with Alexander Sprint bodies. The last-named have taken over town services in Dumfries. Until being acquired by Stagecoach, Western retained its traditional fleet numbering system with a two-letter prefix to its fleet numbers. The first letter was the depot code, the second the vehicle type code. This was traditionally based on using the first letter of the chassis make for single-deckers and the last letter for double-deckers. However this is one piece of Western tradition which is vanishing as the company's buses are repainted in Stagecoach white.

Gibson of Moffat runs to Dumfries, generally with a Leyland Leopard coach or a Leopard bus ex-Midland Red South. The Gibson fleet also includes Duple's bus-in-a-coach Dominant E, which featured the Dominant coach body shell fitted with bus seats. Gibson's example was new to Nottingham City Transport which was one of the main users of the type in the mid-1970s. MacEwan's of Amisfield run services from Dumfries to Kirkcudbright, Dalbeattie and Moffat with Leopard coaches and Mercedes minibuses. MacEwan's also operate a service to Edinburgh.

Top **There are not many Seddons in Stagecoach corporate colours. Most are run by Western Scottish, as shown by a Pennine VII with Alexander T-type body loading in Dumfries. It was new in 1979.** Stewart J Brown

Centre **Western's black and white livery is disappearing. The old order is illustrated by an ex-Greater Manchester Atlantean, one of a dozen taken into the fleet in 1991-92. Some, including this one, are running on hire to A1.** Brian Ridgway

Right **MacEwan's run local services in the Dumfries area using coaches and minibuses. Dormobile bodywork is fitted to this Mercedes, one of four similar buses delivered new in 1993.** Malcolm King

Western's services in southern Scotland generally cover the area to the west of the A74/M74 trunk road which runs north from Carlisle. To the east, the main operator in this sparsely populated part of the country is Lowland Omnibuses. Lowland was created by SBG in 1985 from the southern part of the Eastern Scottish company and was privatised in a management buy-out in August 1990, making it the first SBG subsidiary to move to the private sector. In November 1994 it sold out to GRT Bus Group and is now as a consequence part of the Anglo-Scottish FirstBus group.

Lowland runs 155 vehicles and has depots in each of the main towns in its area – Berwick-on-Tweed, Galashiels, Hawick, Jedburgh, North Berwick and Peebles. It also has bases at Haddington (acquired with the business of Ian Glass in 1991) and at Newtongrange, just outside Edinburgh, which came with the Lothian Transit business in 1994. The Ian Glass name has been retained for some of the company's coaches, while Lothian Transit's identity continues on assorted second-hand buses running around Dalkeith. Under Lowland ownership Lothian Transit took over the small Edinburgh Transport operation which GRT Bus Group bought from British Bus at the end of 1994.

Lowland operate trunk services from Carlisle and each of the major Borders towns to Edinburgh. Feeder services connect smaller centres of population with the trunk routes, and each of the larger towns supports a few local services.

The fleet is made up mainly of vehicles inherited from Eastern Scottish – Leyland Nationals and Alexander-bodied Seddon Pennine VIIs. Double-deckers play a small part in Lowland's operations and are used mainly on Edinburgh services and school journeys. Most are Olympians, including two bought new in 1987 which are the most modern 'deckers in the fleet. There are also second-hand Bristol VRTs and an ex-demonstration Leyland Titan which came with the Ian Glass business and was until the start of 1995 the only modern generation Titan in Scotland.

During its period under management ownership, Lowland bought small numbers of new buses. Four Leyland Tigers with Alexander Belfast Q-type bodies were diverted from an Ulsterbus order in 1992 and were the last new Tigers for a Scottish operator. Eight Optare MetroRiders were purchased in 1994.

The first sign of GRT Bus Group influence came in the summer of 1995 with the delivery of two Wright-bodied Scanias, originally intended for Midland Bluebird. These are used on a tendered service which runs between Galashiels and Berwick. Lowland's livery is being changed to a corporate GRT-style scheme with green bands of relief on a yellow base.

GRT's takeover of Lowland followed its purchase a few months earlier, in August 1994, of the adjacent Eastern Scottish company which Lowland had originally been part of. GRT also owns Midland Bluebird, giving it control of a broad swathe of former SBG territory from the English border at Berwick, up to Edinburgh and across through Falkirk and Stirling to Balfron, 25 miles north-west of Glasgow.

Lowland's last new buses before it was taken over by GRT were eight Optare MetroRiders. One is seen in Berwick, the southern extremity of Lowland's operations, at the end of a 2 hour 50 minute trip from Edinburgh. Tony Wilson

Lowland's oldest bus – apart from an open-topper – is a 1975 Daimler Fleetline with ECW body. It was new to Eastern Scottish, but joined the Lowland fleet in 1989 from Kelvin Central.

Below **The last new Leyland Tigers for a Scottish fleet were four diverted from an Ulsterbus order and delivered to Lowland Scottish in 1991. They have Belfast-built Alexander Q-type bodies, a type which is relatively uncommon in Britain.** Tony Wilson

Edinburgh-based Eastern Scottish was management-owned from 1990 and the first sign of its independence from SBG was the introduction of a new SMT fleetname. SMT – Scottish Motor Traction – was the company's forerunner with a history stretching back to 1905, although the SMT name had been dropped in favour of Eastern Scottish in 1965.

SMT's headquarters are in Edinburgh and it has depots in Dalkeith, Livingston and Musselburgh. Services are concentrated in the Greater Edinburgh area and eastwards along the M8 corridor as far as Bathgate and the smaller towns around it. Through services reach east to Glasgow and run north across the Forth Bridge into Fife.

New buses in the 1990s were mainly minis. Thirty Reeve Burgess-bodied Renault S75s were delivered in 1991, mainly to support the company's ongoing competition in Edinburgh with Lothian Region Transport. These were followed by 25 Optare MetroRiders in 1992/94, bringing the company's minibus fleet to a 125-strong peak. The earlier vehicles, Alexander-bodied Dodges, are now being withdrawn as competition between SMT and LRT has eased, but SMT is easily the biggest Renault/Dodge operator in Scotland. The only new big buses delivered in the '90s have been Volvo B10Bs. There are 13 in all – 12 with Alexander Strider bodies and one bodied by Wright.

The remainder of the fleet is made up largely of buses bought in SBG days. For single-deckers this means Seddon Pennine VIIs, of which 60 remain in service giving SMT the dubious distinction of running the world's biggest fleet of Seddon buses. There are also Leyland Tigers.

There's greater variety among the double-deckers with Ailsas, Fleetlines, Citybuses, Olympians and Lions. The Fleetlines and Olympians have ECW bodywork while the other types have Alexander bodies. The 13 Lions, with chassis built by Leyland DAB in Denmark, are the company's newest double-deckers. They entered service in 1986-87. The only other large fleet of Lions is owned by Nottingham City Transport, which also has 13. The first signs of GRT ownership have been a change of livery and the appearance of ex-Grampian Transport buses to replace the oldest Fleetlines. The livery change means that SMT buses are now in the same colours as those operated by Grampian. The ex-Grampian vehicles have introduced Atlanteans to the SMT fleet for the first time, along with some East Lancs-bodied Olympians which had been new to Northampton Transport. The new livery is being applied to modern types, but has so far excluded Fleetlines and Ailsas, all of which are still in pre-GRT livery and are thought likely to remain so. SMT, like other SBG companies, used letter prefixes to its fleet numbers to identify vehicle types. This is being abandoned as vehicles are repainted.

Top **SMT still has a substantial fleet of Seddon Pennines which are now being repainted in GRT-style colours. New in 1979, this bus has an Alexander Y-type body and, like all ex-Scottish Bus Group Seddons, a Gardner engine.** Gavin Booth

Centre **The acquisition of SMT by GRT has led to the appearance of a few unusual types in the SMT fleet. These include East Lancs-bodied Leyland Olympians, which were new to Northampton Transport.** Brian Ridgway

Left **Modern types in the SMT fleet include 12 Volvo B10Bs with Alexander Strider bodies. They were delivered in 1993.** Tony Wilson

The easing of competition between SMT and LRT means that Edinburgh is one of the few places in Britain where the scene looks pretty much as it did 10 years ago before deregulation. LRT provides the bulk of the city's urban services, and with a fleet composed largely of traditional double-deckers. The oldest buses are Atlanteans; the newest ones Olympians. Two batches of Olympians have ECW bodies; all the other double-deck buses in the fleet have Alexander bodywork. LRT has the country's biggest Olympian fleet with 294 Leyland-built buses and 67 Volvos.

The livery has hardly changed in living memory, and critics might add that the same could be said of the conservative body specification. Edinburgh is a sober no-nonsense city and this is reflected in its buses.

LRT is now the only UK operator sticking rigidly to dual-door buses. Even London and Nottingham, both bastions of the two-door layout, have accepted single-door vehicles for a growing proportion of services. Its insistence on two doors means that LRT operates the only dual-door Leyland Lynxes in Britain, 12 delivered in 1991. This gives it Scotland's biggest Lynx fleet. There are also 20 Nationals. The only buses in the LRT fleet not built by Leyland (or by Volvo as Leyland's successor) are 12 Dennis Darts. These are LRT's smallest buses. The company has steered clear of minibuses, even in the face of intense minibus competition from SMT, arguing that big buses offer more comfort. The scaling down of SMT's minibus operations suggests LRT may well have been right. LRT, working with the regional council, is advocating a major network of bus priorities known as Greenways. Trial stretches of road have already been given a green surface.

LRT runs sightseeing tours, with open-top Atlanteans for those hardy enough to brave the chill east of Scottish weather. On these it faces competition from Guide Friday. Six single-door Olympians are allocated to the Airport limited stop service. Their Alexander bodies have coach seats and wear an attractive new blue-based Airline livery designed by Best Impressions.

Below left **LRT and its predecessor, Edinburgh City Transport, have a long history of city tour operation. Recent years have seen the introduction of open-top tours and among the buses used on it are this Alexander-bodied AN68 with what might be described as compromise conversion – the roof has gone, but the top deck side windows remain in place. Competition on Edinburgh city tours is provided by Guide Friday.** Brian Ridgway

Below right **Alexander-bodied Olympians with coach seats are used by LRT for its service linking Edinburgh city centre with the airport. Until 1995 they wore the black and white coach livery, but this has now been replaced by a striking new Airline scheme.** Tony Wilson

A type still firmly associated with Edinburgh is the Alexander-bodied Atlantean. LRT still runs a substantial fleet of the type, the newest of which are X-registered buses which entered service in 1981. P Chancellor

Below **LRT then switched to its successor, the Olympian. Most have Alexander bodies, but early batches were bodied by ECW. This is a 1983 bus with non-standard electronic destination equipment.** Malcolm King

Midland Bluebird, GRT's Falkirk-based operation, has services running into Edinburgh. Midland Bluebird has been a significant beneficiary of GRT's investment in new vehicles, and the services which reach Edinburgh from Stirling are generally operated by Wright-bodied Scanias, including some with air-conditioning. These and similarly-bodied Mercedes O405s are also used on other long-distance services, including Stirling to Glasgow.

Midland Bluebird – previously Midland Scottish – is another former SBG subsidiary. It was bought by GRT in 1990 and was the company's first move outside its native Aberdeen. Midland Bluebird's main operations cover the Forth valley, with depots in Linlithgow (which was transferred from Eastern Scottish in SBG's 1985 reorganisation), Larbert, Bannockburn and Balfron.

The typical Midland Bluebird bus is that old SBG workhorse, the Alexander-bodied Leopard, running alongside Alexander-bodied Metrobuses. Daimler Fleetlines have been ousted from the fleet by Atlanteans transferred from Grampian Transport. There are 25 Atlanteans (at work in the Falkirk area) and almost 50 Metrobuses.

Leyland Nationals are being phased out – only 10 National 2s remain in service – as new buses arrive. Midland Bluebird is one of the few UK operators of full-size Mercedes buses, with six Wright-bodied O405s which were received in 1993 and soon joined by an O405/Alexander which had started life as a Mercedes demonstrator. The company also runs Mercedes minis, with bodywork by Alexander and Reeve Burgess. Leyland Tigers are used on some longer-distance services. The entire Midland Bluebird fleet is in corporate GRT livery; all traces of the previous SBG-style scheme have vanished.

Top **Typical of Midland Bluebird's older buses is this Leyland Leopard with Alexander Y-type body. A 1982 bus leaves Edinburgh for Linlithgow.** Russell Upcraft

Right **GRT's influence in the Midland Bluebird fleet is represented by modern rear-engined single-deckers, such as this Scania N113 with Wright Endurance body, one of 16 delivered in 1994. It carries GRT Advance livery, applied in preference to standard GRT colours to high-specification buses throughout the GRT group.** Stewart J Brown

Below left **Not many bus companies apply own-name registrations to their vehicles. This 1987 Midland Bluebird Metrobus carries a GRT number. It has Alexander bodywork and is passing through Kirkintilloch on the Falkirk to Glasgow route.** Stewart J Brown

Below right **Under GRT control Daimler Fleetlines were ousted from the Midland Bluebird fleet and replaced by Leyland Atlanteans. There are 25 in the fleet, all transferred from Grampian Transport in Aberdeen. They have Alexander bodies.** Stewart J Brown

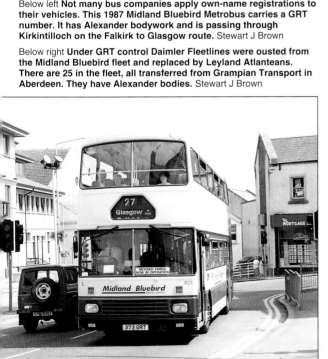

Midland Bluebird faces few competitors in its heartland. Woods of Falkirk provide local services with Alexander-bodied Mercedes minibuses in plain white. Bryans of Denny run into the town with an Omni sponsored by Central Region and painted in red Easy Boarder colours. This livery is also worn by two Midland Bluebird Stirling-based MetroRiders. Goosecroft Coaches runs locally in Stirling with minibuses, in particular second-hand tri-axle Talbot Pullmans. Fergusons Coaches run an Alexander-bodied 709D between Stirling and Fallin. Across the River Forth in Alloa, Mackie's is an old-established company whose claims to fame include being one of the few Scottish operators to have bought a new Leyland Lynx. It also has three second-hand Lynxes and a Willowbrook-rebodied Leopard. Mackie's run to Stirling and to Tillicoultry. The only other new Lynxes in Scotland went to AA Buses, Kelvin Scottish, Lothian and Whitelaw.

Above **Mackie's of Alloa was among the first Scottish operators to buy a Leyland Lynx, in 1986. It is the company's only new service bus, and has since been joined by three second-hand examples.**
Stewart J Brown

Left **Bryans of Denny operate into Falkirk on a contracted service run for Central Region. A low-floor Omni is used and it carries Central Region's Easy Boarder livery, also used on Optare MetroRiders operated in Stirling by Midland Bluebird.**
Stewart J Brown

Below **Moffat & Williamson's double-deck fleet includes 10 Leyland Atlanteans which were new in 1979 to Portsmouth Corporation. They were acquired by the Fife-based company in 1991, when Portsmouth's bus operations were being converted to minibuses by Transit Holdings.**
Stewart J Brown

Fife Scottish was bought by Stagecoach in 1991, and here too all traces of the company's previous livery have vanished. Fife Scottish serves Fife Region and faces little competition. Operators who have tried – noticeably Rennies of Dunfermline and Moffat & Williamson of Gauldry – have both cut back what were once quite extensive networks. Rennies ran in the south, around Dunfermline; Moffat & Williamson in the north, around Leven, Glenrothes and St Andrews. Both operators have retained some local services, but on a much reduced scale of operation. Moffat & Williamson runs both modern minis and elderly 'deckers. The former include Reeve Burgess-bodied Mercedes and Carlyle-bodied Ivecos; the latter are Alexander-bodied Atlanteans, which were new to Portsmouth, and Bristol VRTs.

The Fife Scottish SBG legacy is made up of Ailsas and Volvo Citybuses, a few Leyland Nationals, and a fleet of around 50 Leopards. Although all the Leopards have Alexander bodies, some have come from other SBG subsidiaries with a few even having spent time in England with Ribble before returning north. When it was bidding for Fife Scottish – in the face of strong local opposition which supported a management-led employee buy-out – Stagecoach said it would invest in the business. True to its word, there is a steadily growing number of new Stagecoach standard types in the fleet – Mercedes 709Ds, Dennis Darts, Volvo B6s, Volvo B10Ms and Leyland Olympians. The B10Ms have Plaxton Premiere bodies and are used on longer-distance services, in particular those to Glasgow and Edinburgh where they have introduced unaccustomed standards of comfort.

The intake of new buses over the last four years has been accompanied by the appearance of some second-hand ones, transferred from elsewhere in the Stagecoach empire. These have ranged from nearly-new B6s ex-Ribble, to quaint Willowbrook-bodied VRTs from East Kent. The Volvo Citybuses inherited with the company have been joined by three with Northern Counties bodies which moved north from Southdown. Other odd 'deckers are ECW-bodied VRTs.

Perth, the north-western limit of Fife Scottish operation, is the Stagecoach heartland. It was here that the company was formed to take advantage of coach deregulation in 1980, moving into bus operation with the purchase of local operator McLennan of Spittalfield in 1985. With the advent of bus deregulation in 1986 Stagecoach expanded its operations and it is now the main operator in Perth, having effectively ousted Strathtay Scottish. The Perth fleet, Stagecoach Scotland, is managed from the Aberdeen office of Bluebird Buses. Perth city services are run by double-deckers – ex-London Routemasters and ex-SBG Olympians, while out-of-town services are operated mainly by Leyland Leopards. There are also Mercedes minibuses.

Top **Fife Scottish runs 18 National 2s, some bought new, others acquired from Northern Scottish. This bus has always run for Fife and was new in 1980. It is loading in Dundee for the service across the Tay Bridge to St Andrews.** Stewart J Brown

Centre **SBG's legacy of Y-type Leopards will be around for some time to come. Fife Scottish has 56, including this 1982 bus which started life with Midland Scottish.** Stewart J Brown

Right **Routemaster operation continues in Perth under the control of Stagecoach's Aberdeen-based subsidiary Bluebird Buses. Stagecoach has been running Routemasters in Perth since 1987.** Iain MacGregor

Services to the north-east of Perth and in the area north from Dundee to Montrose are operated by Strathtay Scottish, a subsidiary of Yorkshire Traction. Formed in 1985 as part of SBG's deregulation strategy, Strathtay Scottish combined the Crieff, Perth and Pitlochry operations of Midland (all since given up) with the Dundee, Forfar, Arbroath and Montrose depots of Northern. The Strathtay operation is largely a rural one, with significant inter-town operation between the main centres of population. The new company adopted a striking blue and orange livery, since modified by the addition of white relief. It was bought by Yorkshire Traction in 1991.

Being an amalgam of two SBG subsidiaries meant that Strathtay started life with a varied fleet, and some of that variety lives on. The double-deck fleet is a mixture of MCW Metrobuses with Alexander bodies, Daimler Fleetlines and Leyland Olympians, all an SBG inheritance. The first new double-deckers since privatisation were a pair of Northern Counties-bodied Volvo Olympians which entered service in the summer of 1995.

The oldest single-deckers are the inevitable Leyland Leopards with Alexander Y-type bodies. These were followed by Tigers, two of which have been fitted with new East Lancs bodies and, like many of the company's other Tigers, have registrations transferred from London Routemasters – all of which have been withdrawn from service. The Routemasters had been used in both Perth and Dundee.

Renaults predominate in the small bus fleet. There are 11 bought new, with unusual Dormobile Routemaker bodies, and a number of second-hand examples, some of which were originally operated by London Buses. The company's first five Dennis Darts, delivered in 1993, are the only examples in Scotland with Wright bodywork. They were followed by Northern Counties-bodied Darts in 1995 which are used on crew-operated routes in the Dundee area and are probably the only crew-operated Darts in the country.

Yorkshire Traction owns another operator in this region, Meffan of Kirriemuir. The 17-strong fleet is managed independently of Strathtay and runs a few local services and contracts in the Kirriemuir area. Most of its vehicles are small Mercedes. Big buses include an ECW-bodied Ford which started life with Alder Valley and an ex-Strathtay Leopard/Alexander.

Top **The oldest double-deckers in the Strathtay fleet are Daimler Fleetlines. These include a pair of Alexander-bodied buses which were inherited with the Perthshire operations of Midland Scottish when Strathtay was formed in 1985.** Malcolm King

Centre **Strathtay's new Darts have Northern Counties Paladin bodies. Some carry conductors to keep journey times to a minimum on busy routes.** Tony Wilson

Right **New buses for Strathtay in 1995 have included Dennis Darts and Volvo Olympians with Northern Counties bodies. An Olympian prepares to leave Dundee city centre on its way to Kirriemuir.** Tony Wilson

In Dundee, the biggest town in the region, urban routes are run by Tayside Public Transport. Tayside was formed in 1975 to take over the Dundee Corporation Transport operation. It was privatised in 1991 in a management/employee buy-out. Prior to deregulation new bus purchases were predominantly double-deckers. Most of those running now are front-engined Ailsas, the oldest dating from 1979. There are just over 100 in operation – the second-biggest fleet in Britain – and they have bodies by Alexander, Northern Counties and, unique to Tayside, East Lancs. The Ailsas were followed by Volvo Citybuses, of which there are 20, the last being delivered in 1989.

There are no rear-engined double-deckers in the Tayside fleet. The company's oldest buses are 1979 Ailsas with Alexander bodywork. Stewart J Brown

The only other double-deck type operated by Tayside is Volvo's mid-engined Citybus. The newest were delivered in 1989 and have Alexander R-type bodies. Stewart J Brown

Since then Tayside has bought single-deckers of various types, abandoning the chassis standardisation of the 1970s and 1980s. Midibuses are represented by Volvo B6s and Dennis Darts, all with Plaxton Pointer bodies. Big single-deckers are five East Lancs-bodied Scanias, including a MaxCi which was Scotland's first low-floor bus and carries an apt registration, L3LOW. The company has also snapped up assorted demonstrators – a Lance/Northern Counties, a Lance/Plaxton and a B10B/Northern Counties. The Northern Counties-bodied Lance originally carried Merseybus livery. Tayside runs coaches under the Tayside Greyhound name (Greyhound was a local coach operator taken over in 1990), and also owns Wishart of Friockheim, another coach business.

The 1990s have seen Tayside buy a variety of single-deck types, including Scania N113s with East Lancs bodies. Stewart J Brown

The north-east of Scotland is largely Stagecoach territory except in Aberdeen, the headquarters of what was the GRT Bus Group before its merger with Badgerline to form FirstBus in the summer of 1995. GRT Bus Group was formed following the purchase of Grampian Regional Transport by its management and employees in 1989. Grampian was the successor to Aberdeen Corporation Transport, following the reorganisation of local government in Scotland in 1975.

The core business, Grampian Transport, continues as the main provider of city services in Aberdeen. Its fleet has traditionally been a double-decked one, although there are signs of change as GRT works to improve the image of public transport. However double-deckers still dominate the city scene. Most are Atlanteans (there are over 100), but the newest, delivered between 1984 and 1988 are 30 Olympians. All have Alexander bodies. The oldest Atlanteans date from 1979 while the newest entered service in 1983. They were the last new Atlanteans for a Scottish operator.

Recent deliveries have seen a marked change in policy. Fifteen Mercedes-Benz entered service in 1993. There were 14 O405s with high-specification Wright bodies which featured double glazing and air conditioning, and one O405G articulated bus with a similarly high-spec body built by Alexander. Almost 17.5m long, this was the first articulated bus built for service in Britain since South Yorkshire's Leyland DABs in 1985. Grampian also has more typical Mercedes products in the shape of 709Ds bodied by Reeve Burgess and Alexander. More O405s were delivered in 1995, but with bodywork by Optare. All are rigids. For the time being Grampian's artic remains a one-off.

Grampian Transport – now the northernmost operation of FirstBus – promotes some of its services under the Gold Service name as part of a quality drive. This new Mercedes-Benz O405 with Optare Prisma body is part of the Gold Service operation. Tony Wilson

The most modern double-deckers in the Grampian fleet are 30 Alexander-bodied Leyland Olympians delivered in the mid-1980s. A 1985 bus heads into Union Street. Tony Wilson

Services running out of town are provided by Bluebird Buses, which was previously SBG's Northern Scottish subsidiary. It was bought by Stagecoach in 1991. The entire fleet is in corporate Stagecoach white-with-stripes livery. The previous yellow, blue and cream has gone.

Bluebird Buses covers a large area with a number of significant towns from Stonehaven, to the south of Aberdeen, through to Elgin in the west. It also trades as Inverness Traction, operating in Inverness and northwards to Tain. Key centres of population served in the north-east corner of Bluebird Buses country include Peterhead, Fraserburgh and coastal fishing towns such as Macduff and Buckie. Bluebird has – so far – been able to escape the corporate Stagecoach fleetname. Its vehicles display the Bluebird name in shaded gold letters and accompanied by a bluebird symbol as carried on coaches operated by W Alexander & Sons from the early 1930s.

Although the company has only been in Stagecoach ownership for four years, such has been the pace of change that there are few signs of its SBG heritage. The most prominent are Alexander-bodied Olympians running mainly in Aberdeen, but also to be found elsewhere, and a small number of Leopards and Tigers, the latter usually with personalised registration plates which makes it difficult to identify genuine ex-Northern Scottish buses from those brought in from elsewhere. The most interesting of the Tigers are ten with Alexander's uncompromisingly square P-type body. This uses flat glass throughout and isn't to be confused with the more attractive PS-type which followed it. It was designed with export markets in mind.

Additions to the fleet under Stagecoach ownership have included Olympians, Mercedes minis and Dennis Darts, all bodied by Alexander. Many of the Darts are in the Inverness Traction operation, which is also home to some of the fleet's newest Olympians, which have Northern Counties bodies. There are also Bristol VRTs, brought in from other companies in the Stagecoach group to replace the last Fleetlines. Open-top VRTs in Guide Friday colours run between Inverness and Culloden in the summer. Long-distance services are operated in the main by Volvo B10Ms. These are either new Plaxton-bodied coaches, or Van Hool-bodied vehicles which were new to Shearings.

To the north of Inverness, double-deckers run as far as Tain which marks the northern limit of Stagecoach's operations. This is over 600 miles from the group's southernmost operations on the English south coast and even further from its true southern outpost – in New Zealand.

The dominance of Bluebird Buses in Inverness follows a series of bus wars. Inverness Traction was started in 1988 by a group of ex-Highland Scottish drivers. It soon ran into financial trouble – aided by Highland's competitive tactics – and was bought by Stagecoach at the end of 1990. When Highland Scottish was privatised in 1991 war broke out and Stagecoach flooded Inverness with buses transferred from various parts of its empire and driven largely by disgruntled ex-Highland employees. Highland capitulated, and is now relegated to a minor role in Inverness. It is still the main operator in the rest of the Highlands, although few bus operators would regard such unpopulated country as much of a prize.

Inverness Traction is the trading name used by Bluebird Buses for services in and around Inverness. This Tiger with Alexander TC body was new to Northern Scottish in 1987. The location is Inverness bus station. Stewart J Brown

There are over 70 Olympians in the Bluebird Buses fleet, making up the majority of the company's double-deckers. These include buses bought in SBG days, as well as examples added under Stagecoach ownership, as shown here in Aberdeen. Iain MacGregor

Bluebird Buses operates 10 Leyland Tigers with Alexander P-type bodies, inherited from the Northern Scottish fleet. Iain MacGregor

Highland Scottish must have been one of the least attractive SBG companies to potential buyers when privatisation was taking place. That it went to a local coach operator, Rapson's of Alness, rather than to one of the acquisitive southern groups serves to support this argument.

Inverness, population 43,000, is the largest centre of activity in the Highlands and the headquarters of Highland Scottish. The company is part way through a change of identity, shaking of the poppy red and grey which was used in SBG days and replacing it with a cream livery with maroon and green relief. From Inverness services radiate to other towns and villages in the region. Shorter routes are in the hands of Y-type Leopards while longer services are run by coaches. There is also a growing minibus fleet with a mixture of types including Renault S56s, an ex-MCW demonstration Metrorider and new Wright- and Alexander-bodied Mercedes.

Double-deckers play a small part in Highland's operations. Most are ECW-bodied Fleetlines but recent second-hand acquisitions have included an Alexander-bodied Fleetline which looks quite at home in Scotland but was actually new to Derby, and a pair of Bristol VRTs purchased from the United Kingdom Atomic Energy Authority at Dounreay. One of the latter is now based in Fort William, running alongside a former Lincoln City Transport VRT with Alexander body.

Local services are operated in Wick and Thurso and to John O' Groats, but Highland's business is generally in long-distance rural routes. In Fort William, there is local competition with Gaelicbus. This company runs Scotland's biggest fleet of AEC Reliance buses with six T-registered vehicles, all bodied by Duple and all ex-Hutchison of Overtown, once a staunch AEC supporter. There are four double-deckers too, three standard NBC-style ECW-bodied VRTs, and an ex-West Midlands Fleetline.

Further south, Oban & District runs just over 20 vehicles and is the successor to SBG's operations in the area. These were at different times under the control of Midland and Highland. At privatisation they were part of the Midland operation but, being remote from the company's main business, were sold by its new owners, GRT, in 1992. GRT has retained a stake in the company. The bulk of the fleet is made up of buses acquired from Midland, mainly Alexander-bodied Leopards. Recent additions to the fleet have been ex-Kelvin Central Leopards and new Transit minibuses.

Top **Highland's latest livery shakes off the old SBG red and grey in favour of a much brighter image. Alexander-bodied Leopards figure strongly in the Highland fleet. Most are second-hand, but this one was new to the company in 1982.** P J Chancellor

Centre **Gaelic Bus is the only Scottish operator still running AEC Reliances in any number, with seven being available for service. All have Duple Dominant bus bodies and were acquired from Hutchison of Overtown, a staunch AEC supporter in the 1970s. This bus was new in 1979 and is seen in Fort William.** Stewart J Brown

Right **Oban & District's full-sized buses are typified by this Alexander-bodied Leopard, one of the buses taken over from Midland Bluebird when Oban & District was created in 1992. It was new to Alexander (Fife) in 1981.** Paul Wigan

South from Oban, the only sizeable place is Campbeltown. Local services are run by West Coast Motors whose bus services run as far north as Ardrishaig, while the company's coaches run through to Glasgow. The company's oldest buses are Bedfords while its newest are Optares – two MetroRiders and a smart Vecta which was the first in Scotland. Competition came to this apparently quiet backwater in 1995 when Essbee of Coatbridge won most of the tendered services on the Kintyre peninsula from West Coast. West Coast responded by registering commercial services in competition which led to Strathclyde Region withdrawing much of its subsidy to Essbee. Essbee also has a Vecta (an ex-Optare demonstrator), but most services are run by Mercedes minibuses. Both operators continue – but for how long?

On the Cowal peninsula the only sizeable town is Dunoon, a resort on the Clyde. Here services are run by Western Scottish and by two associated local operators, Baird and Cowal Motor Services. The Cowal fleet features ex-Western Seddons, while Baird has recently introduced rear-engined buses, with a pair of 20-year-old ex-Ribble Nationals. Services link Dunoon with neighbouring small towns.

One major operator covers virtually the whole of Scotland with a 130-strong fleet – the Scottish Postal Board. Post Bus services were developed rapidly in the early 1970s and cover some of the most remote outposts, generally with Leyland DAF minibuses or Ford Sierra and Peugeot 405 estate cars. The only big bus in the fleet – and in this context big is comparative – is a Mellor-bodied Iveco Ford which runs between Laide and Achnasheen, connecting with certain trains on the Kyle of Lochalsh line. A more conventional country-wide service is provided by Scottish Citylink Coaches, a subsidiary of National Express. Scottish Citylink was started by the Scottish Bus Group in 1983. It has had its ups and downs. Now it concentrates on trunk services and, like National Express, uses coaches hired in from sub-contractors but painted in Citylink colours.

Top **West Coast Motors runs two Optare MetroRiders on its services on the Kintyre peninsula. This, the second bus, was new in 1994.** Iain MacGregor

Centre **Services in Dunoon are run by the associated businesses of Alexander Baird and Cowal Motor Services. Baird's fleet includes two ex-Ribble Nationals.** Brian Ridgway

Left **The Post Office runs bus services throughout the Scottish Highlands with minibuses, Land Rovers and private cars. The cars include Ford Sierra and Peugeot 405 estate cars. A Peugeot waits at Gairloch to take up a trip to Melvaig.** Stewart J Brown

NORTH WEST ENGLAND

Top **There are no obvious clues that Heysham Travel is part of MTL. Recent additions to the fleet have been National 2s acquired from Ribble. This bus was new to Cumberland.** Stewart J Brown

Above **North Western is among the growing list of operators running substantial numbers of Dennis Darts. Most have East Lancs bodies and those introduced to services in Liverpool in 1995 brought with them a bright new Cityplus livery.** Mike Harris

Although promoted as low-floor buses, the GM Buses North Superbus fleet is actually based on Volvo B10Bs with Wright bodies, so there is no direct access for push chairs or wheelchairs. However they are undeniably the most stylish new buses running in Greater Manchester and are built to a high specification which includes double glazing. Malcolm King

More conventional new buses for GM Buses North have been Volvo B6s and Dennis Darts with Northern Counties bodies. A Dart loads in Wigan bus station. Stewart J Brown

The last reminders of Lancashire United Transport are a handful of Leyland Leopards with Plaxton bodies which remain in service with GM Buses North. They can usually be seen in and around Bolton and Wigan. Stewart J Brown

The main centres of bus activity in north-west England are of course the two biggest conurbations, Manchester and Liverpool. But industrial Lancashire supports a healthy network of bus services supplied by a number of public and private sector operators. Of the latter, Stagecoach offers the widest geographical coverage, from the Scottish border down to Manchester, through its Cumberland and Ribble subsidiaries. British Bus also has a strong presence in the region, mainly through its North Western and Bee Line subsidiaries. FirstBus is represented by PMT operations – Pennine in Greater Manchester and Crosville and Red Rider in Cheshire.

In the Manchester area a long time seemed to pass with little change while the future ownership of Greater Manchester Buses hung in the balance. Now new owners and new buses have helped change the slightly tired look of the fleets of Manchester's major bus operator, GM Buses.

First, the company was split in two. Then – after some wrangling about the acceptability of outside bids – the two parts were sold to their respective management-led employee buy-out teams in the early part of 1994. GM Buses North, with its headquarters in Oldham, covers an area stretching west to Wigan and incorporating what was once Lancashire United Transport country. GM Buses South has taken over the southern area which includes part of Manchester itself, along with Stockport (where the company has its head office) and east to Glossop, once an outpost of the original North Western company.

Both GMN and GMS have in essence retained the orange livery whose history can be traced back through Greater Manchester Transport to the SELNEC PTE and its 1970 orange and white – which was revolutionary at a time when sombre liveries were the order of the day in most fleets. Each of the new GM Buses companies has modified the livery and added its own logo, GMN or GMS, although one wonders whether the man (or woman) in the street is aware that there are now two independent companies. But with a 25-year heritage to build on, their reluctance to abandon orange in favour of a totally new livery is understandable.

First off with new buses was GM Buses North, taking ten Northern Counties-bodied Volvo B6s to combat competition from MTL Manchester on the Bury corridor which, of course, is also served by the Metrolink from Altrincham. The B6s were followed by Volvo B10Bs with attractive Wright Endurance bodies – there are 20 in all, and they operate on services which penetrate central Manchester. GMN has added bright lettering to the sides of the B10Bs to promote their key features, although some might take issue with the low-floor claim in the light of recent advances which have produced notably lower floors than the B10B can offer. Further new vehicles are Dennis Darts which, like the B6s, have locally-built Northern Counties bodies. The first entered service in Wigan in the spring of 1995 in all-over white, while later deliveries arrived in fleet livery. The Northern Counties bodies for the two chassis differ; the B6s can be identified by their stepped window line.

These new buses have joined the fleet which GMN had inherited at its privatisation. This included most of the main types operated by its predecessor – Fleetlines and Atlanteans with standard PTE-style bodies from Northern Counties and Park Royal, MCW Metrobuses and assorted single-deckers such as a few Leyland Nationals and ex-Lancashire United Transport Leopards with Plaxton bus bodies. The last few ex-LUT Leopards are still in operation in the Bolton area, although probably not for much longer.

GMN has the North West's biggest fleet of Fleetlines, with just over 100. It also has the second largest fleet of Atlanteans in the country (after MTL), with 430. It rates high in the Olympian stakes too, with 164. All of GMN's Fleetlines and Atlanteans are original Greater Manchester PTE buses, although a few have come back from Yorkshire Rider which had acquired a number in the late eighties. All 30 of the former GM Buses Northern Counties-bodied Metrobuses run for GMN. They are the only examples built of this body/chassis combination.

MCW Metroriders bought new by GM Buses have been joined by a number of second-hand examples. The first came from London and were for operation in the company's heartland, but more soon followed from a range of other operators and were used in 1994 to introduce services in Southport under the Lancashire Gem name, competing with MTL's Southport & District operation in a tit-for-tat response to MTL's Manchester adventures. GMN withdrew its competitive services from Merseyside – in both Southport and Liverpool – in 1995 and MTL pulled out of Manchester. The GMN double-deckers which were used in Liverpool are now running in Greater Manchester once again and are identifiable by a bright yellow relief band above the lower deck windows.

GM Buses South has a fleet which, not surprisingly, is in general make-up similar to that of GM Buses North. Among the more interesting vehicles which it inherited were the 20 Northern Counties-bodied Dennis Dominos owned by GM Buses, most of which are still used on the frequent Manchester Centreline service, although they can also be seen on suburban routes from time to time. GMS also acquired the three Dennis Falcon double-deckers which were purchased by Greater Manchester Transport (the predecessor of GM Buses) in 1984. These had in fact been withdrawn some years ago, but have now been reinstated. One has been repainted and has acquired a Mercedes three-pointed star badge. The Falcons have Mercedes V6 engines and are the only Mercedes-powered double-deck buses (as distinct from coaches) in Britain. GMS also has the 30 Dennis Dominators which were owned by GM Buses. It is the region's biggest Dominator user.

Where GMN has been buying considerable numbers of new buses, GMS has been adding old ones to its fleet, in particular early Leyland Nationals whose considerable age has been partly disguised by re-registering some of them with dateless Ulster marks. Quite who that fools is open to question – but surely not the GMS passengers sitting in them as new GMN Wright Endurances glide by. Along with the second-hand Nationals GMS has reinstated some withdrawn GM Buses examples, one of which retains the brown-skirted livery used for the PTE-owned fleet from 1981 to 1988. The Nationals were needed to combat competition, mainly from Ribble's Stagecoach Manchester. This competition has since eased.

The first new buses for GMS entered service in the spring of 1995 and were 20 Alexander-bodied Volvo B6s on lease from erstwhile rival Stagecoach. Their Aberdeen registrations give the clue to their intended ownership and they can be seen on services running into central Manchester. Further new buses, Alexander-bodied 709Ds, followed later in the year.

Competition in Manchester continues to be intense but it has tended to be the more professional operators who have survived and most of those now to be seen in the city centre are running a mixture of new and used vehicles.

The most striking of the new vehicles are in the Walls fleet. Walls started running local buses in 1986 with ex-GMT Fleetlines. Since then the company has added new and used DAF SB220s to its operation, with Optare Delta and Ikarus 480 bodies. The second-hand Deltas include the first one built, which was new to Wigmore (now Northern Bus) of Dinnington, plus examples from OK Travel and Harris of Grays. The original Fleetlines have been joined by former NBC Bristol VRTs, but at the start of 1995 Walls made its most interesting and striking purchases yet with four new double-deckers. These are DAF DB250s with Northern Counties Palatine II bodies. The Palatine II uses the existing Northern Counties framing, but with a dramatically restyled exterior incorporating deep curved windscreens. The only other Palatine IIs in the North West are running for Blackpool Transport. Walls services operate from Piccadilly Gardens to the south along the well-bussed Wilmslow Road, and its fleet now numbers 40 vehicles.

Another DAF user is Stuarts of Hyde, running a pair of Ikarus-bodied SB220s bought new in 1992. These run on the Hyde Road alongside ex-West Midlands Fleetlines and a mixture of Atlanteans ranging from 1974 buses which were new to Grampian to 1981 buses built for South Yorkshire and unusual in having Marshall bodies. These have had a fairly basic conversion from dual- to single-door layout.

Stagecoach Manchester, part of Preston-based Ribble, introduced services running to south Manchester in February 1994, initially with Alexander-bodied Volvo B6s. These have since been replaced by bigger Volvo B10Ms with Alexander PS bodies. The Stagecoach Manchester services skirt the north-east edge of Piccadilly Gardens, starting from Newton Street. What started as head-on competition with GMS has since changed to peaceful co-existence and, as noted above, has now reached the point where GMS has upgraded its fleet with Volvo B6s on lease from Stagecoach. Alexander PS-types in Stagecoach livery are also operated by Ribble on routes from the Arndale bus station to Eccles.

Top left **GM Buses North operates the biggest fleet of Leyland Olympians in the North West. All have Northern Counties bodies. The yellow relief band carried on this 1988 bus shows that it was part of the fleet used to operate services in Liverpool until the spring of 1995, running in competition with MTL.** Mike Harris

Centre left **The first production Olympian for Greater Manchester is now running for GM Buses South, which took over 141 of the type when GM Buses was split into two companies at the end of 1993.** Malcolm King

Bottom left **The first new buses for GM Buses South were 20 Volvo B6s with Alexander Dash bodies. They had been built for Stagecoach hence the livery layout – and are on lease to GMS. Note the Aberdeen registration.** Malcolm King

Top right **Walls of Manchester have been regular customers for DAF's SB220 single-decker and in 1995 turned to the DAF DB250 for their first new double-deckers. There are four with Northern Counties Palatine II bodies.** Stewart J Brown

Centre right **Stuarts services are operated mainly by double-deckers. These include two ex-Grampian Atlanteans which were used to start the company's bus operations in 1987. They have Alexander-bodies and were new in 1974 – this bus originally had an M-suffix registration.** Stewart J Brown

Right **The standard Stagecoach single-decker is the Volvo B10M with Alexander PS-type body. Examples can be seen in various parts of the North West including Manchester, where they are operated by Ribble.** Stewart J Brown

MTL Manchester was set up in October 1993, grew rapidly in 1994 – and then pulled out of Manchester in the summer of 1995 after peace broke out between MTL and GMN. Its initial fleet of R-registered Atlanteans was expanded with Leyland Nationals (some transferred from MTL's Merseyside operations, others bought second-hand) and new Volvo B6s with Plaxton Pointer bodies. These brought a swift response from GMN in the shape of Northern Counties-bodied B6s which run between Manchester and Bury, although some have now been transferred to Wigan.

MTL's Lancashire Travel operation also ran into Manchester from the west, but it too withdrew from the city in the summer of 1995. As part of this complex realignment, GMN has taken over some of the former MTL fleet in Bolton, including those buses which were run by Bolton Coachways, an operation which MTL purchased in 1994. These are minibuses including four Mercedes, two with Optare StarRider bodies and two Plaxton Beavers. They are still running in the dark green livery which Bolton Coachways adopted when it bought the StarRiders from Athelstan of Malmesbury in 1990. Bolton Coachways run to Blackburn, and from Blackburn to Bury. The Bolton-based MTL buses now in GMN ownership are National 2s, a new type for GMN, and they carry GMN fleetnames on their MTL livery.

Ribble has long had a presence in Bolton, and runs Nationals, Olympians and Mercedes minibuses, all in corporate Stagecoach colours. The Nationals are, of course, a throwback to NBC days while the other types are new standard Stagecoach group buses.

The smallest operator running into Bolton is the Atherton Bus Company with an ex-Strathclyde PTE Atlantean which provides an hourly service to Leigh. An ex-NBC ECW-bodied Leopard is also operated. Timeline Travel of Leigh has a depot in Bolton and runs Volvo B6s, Leyland Tigers and Volvo B10Ms. Timeline was formed at the start of 1992 to take over the bus operations of Shearings, the Wigan-based coach holiday company, which dated back to deregulation in 1986. Timeline still uses what were Shearings colours, and much of the fleet with Alexander (Belfast) bodywork was taken over from Shearings. Timeline services also operate into Manchester city centre. In and around Leigh a smart fleet is operated by Jim Stones. The most interesting bus in the Jim Stones fleet is the Leyland-DAB Tiger Cub, one of only two built when Leyland was trying to develop a successor to the Bristol LH. The company also runs Dennis Darts and Mercedes minibuses.

The end of direct competition between MTL and the two GM Buses companies has seen some rationalisation of services and also some movement of buses between MTL and GM Buses North. GMN has taken over services and vehicles previously operated by MTL in the Bolton area, as shown by a National 2 in MTL livery but with GMN fleetnames. Stewart J Brown

The Atherton Bus Company runs one service, linking Atherton with Bolton. The usual bus is this Alexander-bodied Leyland Atlantean which was new to the Greater Glasgow PTE. Stewart J Brown

Timeline has a modern fleet and continues to invest in new buses. Recent deliveries have been Volvo B6s with Alexander Dash bodywork. Malcolm King

Typical of the smart fleet operated by Jim Stones are these two Mercedes 709Ds with Plaxton Beaver bodies. Jim Stones runs local services in the Leigh area. Malcolm King

Competition from smaller operators continues elsewhere in GMN territory. In Rochdale Bu-Val has a fleet of minibuses, Ivecos ex-GM Buses, Renaults ex-Merseyside and the latest a pair of new Ivecos with Mellor bodies. Mellor is a locally-based builder and its minibus body bears a strong resemblance to the Plaxton Beaver. Mellor was for a short time part of the Plaxton group. Pioneer is the other small operator in the town, running an interesting selection of buses. The biggest are a former SBG Seddon Pennine VII and a couple of Leopards, but of more interest are two rare Leyland Cubs with 31-seat Duple Dominant bus bodies. The front-engined Cub was built in Leyland's Bathgate truck factory and the Pioneer examples came from Lothian Region Transport which was the biggest psv user of the type. Of broadly the same size, but radically different in concept, are a pair of Optare-bodied Dennis Dominos from the batch built for South Yorkshire Transport in 1985.

Rochdale is served by Yorkshire Rider buses from Halifax. So too is Oldham, now GMN's headquarters town. Here Stotts Tours have built up a sizeable bus operation, run almost exclusively by double-deckers. These include ex-Greater Manchester Fleetlines, ex-South Yorkshire Fleetlines and Atlanteans, ex-Merseybus Atlanteans, and ex-SBG Dennis Dominators. The company's services also run to Ashton-under-Lyne. Pennine Blue, based in Dukinfield, runs to Ashton. This business was taken over by PMT in late 1993, and this has led to the arrival of Olympians, VRTs and Mercedes minibuses from the parent fleet to replace some of Pennine Blue's older buses. There are also new Marshall-bodied Darts. The change of ownership has seen some service rationalisation with GMN. Pennine Blue's livery – blue, obviously – is giving way to PMT red and yellow with the fleetname Pennine. PMT is now the name on the side as legal owner.

Top **Pioneer of Rochdale operate two Dennis Dominos with Optare bodies. They come from a batch of 14 built for South Yorkshire Transport in 1985.** Tony Wilson

Left **Stotts run local services in Oldham, generally using second-hand double-deckers. These include a number of Leyland Atlanteans, such as this 1981 bus which came from South Yorkshire Transport. It has Alexander bodywork.** Stewart J Brown

Below left **Under PMT ownership the Pennine fleet has switched from a blue livery to PMT's red and yellow. It has also received an influx of modern buses, including these Marshall-bodied Dennis Darts seen in Ashton bus station. The badger logos have since been removed following the merger of Badgerline and GRT to form FirstBus.** Malcolm King

Below **Bu-Val operate services in the Rochdale area with a fleet of 15 minibuses. These include Iveco Fords with bodywork by Northern Counties and, as shown here, Mellor.** Tony Wilson

Based in nearby Ashton is Dennis's, running services locally and into Manchester's Piccadilly Gardens. Most of Dennis's buses are new Mercedes – there are 19 in all – but the company also has three big buses which are regular performers on the Manchester service. Two are Leyland Nationals; the third is a DAF SB220 with Optare Delta body which was bought new in 1991.

British Bus has rationalised its operations in the North West and this has reduced the variety to be seen in Manchester. The C-Line operation has vanished, being taken over by Bee Line and Midland Red North. The Bee Line fleet has been upgraded, largely by the addition of MCW Metrobuses leased from West Midlands Travel. The arrival of the Metrobuses coincided with a rethink on livery. The first carried Bee Line's red and yellow in North Western-style layout, with a diagonal colour break separated by a silver band. Bee Line had adopted this style in the autumn of 1993. But during the autumn of 1994 this was abandoned in favour of a more traditional layout with simple horizontal colour breaks, and this has been applied to most of the company's Metrobuses. It has also been used for other routine repaints and can be seen on one-time Crosville and Ribble Olympians.

On the minibus front there are still a number of the D-registered Dodges which were used at the start of the Bee Line operation when it was launched by United Transport back in 1987. But these have largely been replaced by newer vehicles in the shape of Mercedes with bodywork by Carlyle and Alexander. Single-deckers have played only a small part in Bee Line's operations, but these now include Dennis Falcons with East Lancs bodies which have been transferred from North Western.

Top Most of the vehicles in Dennis's fleet are Mercedes minibuses bought new, but there are a few second-hand Nationals including this bus which was new to GMT. Stewart J Brown

Right For some 12 months in 1993-94 Bee Line buses were painted in a North Western style livery with diagonal colour breaks, as shown on two ECW-bodied Olympians in Manchester's Piccadilly Gardens. The bus on the left was new to Crosville while that on the right started life with Ribble. Stewart J Brown

Below Fleet modernisation at Bee Line has been achieved by the acquisition of MCW Metrobuses from West Midlands Travel. Their arrival from late 1994 coincided with the change to a simpler livery layout as demonstrated by this bus in Stockport, one of the original centres of Bee Line operation back in 1987. Russell Upcraft

Below right Bee Line took over some of the operations of Heatons Travel of Leigh in the spring of 1995, using Leyland Nationals which were given Leigh Line fleetnames and black window surrounds. This bus was new to London Country. Mike Harris

The other British Bus subsidiary running into Manchester is Stevensons of Uttoxeter which has taken over from Midland Red North what was previously part of the C-Line business in Cheshire. Vehicles used on the service from Macclesfield can range from an ECW-bodied Olympian in Midland Red North's drab all-over red retro-livery (one of the bus industry's less successful ventures into nostalgia) to Leyland Swifts with Wadham Stringer bodywork in Stevensons yellow. Stevensons took over the Macclesfield operations of Midland Red North at the end of 1994, just under 12 months after Midland Red North had absorbed C-Line. British Bus has since the spring of 1995 owned Star Line of Knutsford, which had expanded quite considerably in the South Manchester and Altrincham areas. The Star Line fleet is a modern one, with all but two of the vehicles in the 42-strong fleet having been bought new since 1990. Mercedes 709Ds with Reeve Burgess and Plaxton Beaver bodies form the mainstay of the Star Line operation, but there are also four Darts, one with Plaxton Pointer bodywork and three Northern Counties Paladins.

One of the smaller bus companies serving Manchester pre-dates deregulation in 1986 – and by a handsome margin. In 1995 Maynes were celebrating their 75th anniversary. Part of this celebration included the painting of two Scania N113s in an old-style livery of deep red with turquoise relief bands. It was a colour scheme which many thought quite unremarkable 30 years ago, but which looked distinctly old-fashioned in 1995. The Scanias have East Lancs bodies which are copies of Alexander's R-type.

The remainder of the Mayne fleet is in the bright red and cream which has been in use since the late 1970s. This includes more Scania 'deckers (there are eight in all), as well as second-hand Fleetlines, three of which are relatively unusual (in England) lowheight ECW-bodied buses which were new to the Scottish Bus Group. The other 10 are ex-London DMS-type Fleetlines, a fast-disappearing type. There are three 1993 East Lancs Dennis Dominators.

There is considerable variety in the Maynes single-deck operation. It is one of the few companies running both Dennis Darts and Dennis Falcons. Five of the Falcons came from Chesterfield Transport and have rather plain Marshall bodies, but there is in addition one former Alder Valley vehicle with rather more stylish Wadham Stringer Vanguard bodywork which, incidentally, is newer than the chassis – it was rebodied after a fire in 1987 while still in Alder Valley ownership. The four Darts were bought new and are Marshall-bodied. The newest fleet additions are the company's first Scania single-deckers, L113s with attractive Northern Counties Paladin bodies. There are also four mid-1970s Leopards with 1990 Willowbrook Warrior bodies.

Top **Reorganisation at British Bus has seen the appearance in Manchester of buses from the Stevensons of Uttoxeter fleet. This follows the transfer to Stevensons of the operations in Macclesfield, previously part of Midland Red North. A wide variety of types can be seen on the Macclesfield to Manchester service including Leyland Swifts with Wadham Stringer bodies.** Stewart J Brown

Centre **Old-established operator Mayne of Manchester has a mixed double-deck fleet with vehicles bought both new and second-hand. The former are mainly Scania N113s with bodywork by East Lancs or, as shown here, Northern Counties. This was Mayne's first Scania double-decker. There are now eight in service.** Mike Harris

Left **Mayne has recently introduced midibuses to its operations. It runs four 40-seat Marshall-bodied Dennis Darts. They are the smallest buses in the fleet.** David Barrow

Another pre-deregulation small operator was Citibus Tours. Citibus started running local services between Manchester and Blackley under the relaxed road service licensing system which existed just before deregulation, initially with a fleet of ex-Preston (via the Isle of Man) Panthers. More recently the company's services have been predominantly double deck operated, mainly by Alexander-bodied Atlanteans which came from South Yorkshire Transport. Ownership passed to Lynton Travel in 1993, but at the start of 1995 Citibus was taken over by GM Buses North. At first there were few outward signs of change, but in the summer of 1995 Citibus vehicles started to appear in GMN colours with Citibus fleetnames. The GMN livery looks particularly striking on the fleet's peak-domed Alexander bodies. However the Citibus name is now being abandoned and its operations absorbed into the GMN fleet.

J P Travel of Middleton operates into Manchester city centre. Its minibus fleet is of interest in that the majority of the 20-odd vehicles were bought new. Most are Mercedes-Benz, but there are also Iveco Fords and Northern Counties-bodied Renaults. The last-named include two ex-Stagecoach South vehicles which were new to Alder Valley. J P Travel trades as City Nippy. Another Middleton operator is Bluebird, serving Middleton, Heywood, Ashton and Manchester. The company's big buses are Leopards, but most of its fleet is made up of Iveco Fords – 10 bought new and six purchased from other operators including GM Buses and Strathclyde Buses.

Wilmslow Road, the haunt of GMS, Bee Line and Walls, is also served by other operators. Bullocks of Cheadle is one, usually with interesting double-deckers. These include ex-London Fleetlines, ex-SBG Alexander-bodied Metrobuses (a rare body/chassis combination), ex-Southampton Dominators and a number of new East Lancs-bodied Olympians. Among the newest are two long-wheelbase versions which were built in error for The Delaine of Bourne, who had ordered standard 9.5m-long buses. They were bought by Bullock, while Volvo and East Lancs built replacement buses for The Delaine. Bullock has on order low-floor Scania L113 single-deckers with Wright bodies for use on a Greater Manchester PTE tendered service. These will join a few existing single-deckers including ex-London Nationals, a couple of National 2s which were new to PMT, and an East Lancs rebodied Leopard.

Finglands, a subsidiary of the EYMS Group since 1992, operates to the south, with services in Manchester and Stockport. Most of its double-deckers are former Greater Manchester Atlanteans, but among those bought new is an Alexander-bodied Volvo Citybus. Not many small fleets run Citybuses, despite the model's close affinity with the popular B10M. Finglands also run five MCW Metrobus IIs which originated with London's Harrow Buses operation. This is another type not found in many small fleets.

Top **Bluebird's services are run primarily by new minibuses and second-hand big buses. Most of the minibuses are Iveco Fords, including 59.12s with Marshall bodies.** Malcolm King

Centre **New double-deckers first appeared in the Bullock fleet in 1993. More followed in 1994 including this Volvo Olympian with East Lancs body.** Malcolm King

Right **Most of Finglands services are operated by second-hand double-deckers. The company's first new 'deckers since 1989 were a batch of Volvo Olympians with Alexander Royale bodywork. They entered service in August 1995 and were the first N-registered double-deckers in the North West.** Malcolm King

Blue Bus of Horwich, near Bolton, runs Leopards in Bolton and from Bolton to Bury, Manchester and Wigan. Most have Alexander Y-type bodies and are ex-SBG buses, but there are T-type bodies on former Trent vehicles. Blue Bus also has Leopards fitted with new East Lancs EL2000 bodies, and new buses – two Dennis Darts with BLU registration marks. The oldest bus in the fleet is an L-registered Leopard with Willowbrook bus body. A small number of double-deckers are operated in Bolton. All are Atlanteans and again most have Alexander bodies and were new to either Grampian Transport or South Yorkshire Transport.

Left **Blue Bus of Horwich serves Bolton, Wigan and Manchester with a fleet made up mainly of 1970s Leyland Leopards and Atlanteans. This Atlantean has Alexander bodywork and was new to Aberdeen Corporation Transport in 1973.** Stewart J Brown

Below **Cutbacks by the Scottish Bus Group in the aftermath of deregulation saw many serviceable buses migrate south. Vale of Manchester operates four Seddon Pennines with Alexander Y-type bodies which were new to Eastern Scottish.** Stewart J Brown

A recent arrival on the city's streets is South Manchester, formed by ex-Pennine Blue directors and running assorted second-hand double-deckers including an ex-Northampton Alexander-bodied VRT and Atlanteans which were new to Greater Manchester and Merseyside. The ex-Merseyside buses still carry their original owner's fleet number plates beneath their new owner's green paint. South Manchester's livery is not dissimilar to that used by Tame Valley, which serves Manchester, Stockport and Hazel Grove running elderly Nationals and Atlanteans and some newer minibuses. Both companies share an operating base in Hyde. The Glossop-based Glossopdale fleet features new Mercedes and a new Dennis Dart, all bodied by Marshall, as well as second-hand Sherpas and Dodge S56s. Glossopdale run from Glossop to Stockport and Ashton.

The South Manchester fleet includes Leyland Atlanteans and a Bristol VRT. The original operator of this Willowbrook-bodied Atlantean seen in Manchester's Wilmslow Road was the Merseyside PTE. Malcolm King

Trent's operations stretch north to Greater Manchester. A half-hourly service runs from Stockport to Buxton using new Optare Vectas with modest route-branding – a list of places served being carried above the side windows. Equally interesting are the vehicles used on the R1 Trans-Peak service which links Manchester and Nottingham on a two-hourly frequency. This is operated by five smart Volvo B10Ms with Alexander Belfast Q-type bodies.

Buxton, in the Peak District, is the first sizeable town to the south of the Greater Manchester conurbation. Local services are operated by Trent using Optare Vectas and by Bowers of Chapel-en-le-Frith with Mercedes minibuses. Trent is the main operator of longer-distance routes in the area, but Whites of Calver have regular services to Buxton.

In Wigan GMN is the main operator and during 1995 it has introduced a fleet of Northern Counties-bodied Dennis Darts. There are two distinct batches. The white-liveried buses in the 11xx number series were dealer stock vehicles. The buses in fleet livery, in the 06xx series, were a separate order delivered direct from Northern Counties and incorporating items to GMN's specification. The Darts have been joined by some of the Northern Counties-bodied B6s displaced from the Bury services and repainted yellow and white. These carry Quality Choice branding. Other GMN vehicles in Wigan are mainly standard Atlanteans.

The Wigan Bus Company, which started in 1993 with four ex-SBG Leyland Nationals, has made considerable progress. The Nationals have gone and its fleet now includes two new DAF SB220s with Ikarus bodies and three Northern Counties-bodied Darts. These are in the rather sombre overall red fleet livery, which was chosen to evoke memories of the long-vanished Wigan municipal bus operation. The company also has a number of new Alexander-bodied Mercedes minis in a variety of colour schemes. Bellair & Dootson of Leigh also run into Wigan, with Iveco and Dodge minibuses, all second-hand.

Top **Trent's Buxton to Stockport service is run by MANs with Optare Vecta bodywork.** Mike Harris

Right **Quality Choice branding and a non-standard livery have been adopted by GM Buses North for some Wigan routes. Volvo B6s are used. They have Northern Counties bodies.** Mike Harris

Below **The Wigan Bus Company has been buying new buses as its operations have expanded. Its Dennis Darts have Northern Counties bodies.** Malcolm King

MTL operate into Wigan with double-deckers – usually MCW Metrobuses – and on the Warrington service face competition from Warrington Borough Transport with Dennis Dominators.

British Bus has a major presence in the town through its North Western subsidiary, running new Merc minibuses, ex-Ribble Nationals and a variety of double-deck types including Atlanteans and Dominators. North Western holds the contract to provide accessible bus services in Wigan and for this has three Plaxton-bodied Dennis Darts which have wheelchair lifts concealed under the entrance steps. A CVE Omni is also operated in Wigan by North Western and carries the same silver Easylink livery as the Darts.

Skelmersdale, the new town which lies between Wigan and Liverpool, is served by Little White Buses of Ormskirk, which started running local routes soon after deregulation. Its 14 buses are little and white (with blue relief) and are mainly Mercedes 811Ds and Dodge S56s. All of the S56s have locally-built Northern Counties bodies – not a common choice for a small operator buying new.

Former West Midlands Metrobuses have appeared in both the North Western and Bee Line fleets. A North Western Metrobus leaves Wigan for Warrington, a route on which the company faces competition from Warrington Borough Transport. Mike Harris

North Western provides wheelchair-accessible services in Wigan using Dennis Darts and an Omni. The Darts have Plaxton Pointer bodies with a chair lift built into the entrance area. Russell Upcraft

On Merseyside competition has characterised the area virtually since the start of local bus service deregulation in 1986. But there are signs that it is easing. MTL Trust Holdings, the successor to the Merseyside PTE bus operation when it was privatised in 1992, is still the dominant operator. Although MTL has invested in new buses, most notably 50 Volvo B6s and 45 B10Bs delivered in 1994, the fleet still contains a lot of old double-deckers. The oldest are L-registered Leyland Atlanteans, now in their 22nd year of operation. That buses of such an age can still be used in all-day service says a lot about the company's maintenance standards. MTL has the country's (the world's?) biggest fleet of Atlanteans but not all of the 450-plus still on the road are quite that old. Merseyside PTE was one of the last UK operators to put new Atlanteans in service and has the only B-registered examples.

Merseyside took bodywork from both Alexander and East Lancs, and to a unique specification. The end of Atlantean production brought an end to chassis standardisation and to Merseyside's insistence on non-standard bodies. Post-Atlantean double-deck types have been Leyland Olympians and MCW Metrobuses. There were some Dennis Dominators – all now withdrawn – and there are 15 Ailsas which are still running on Wirral area services.

More recently MTL has been buying second-hand 'deckers and there are some 170 ex-London buses in the fleet. The vast majority are Leyland Titans. There are in round numbers 150, which gives MTL the biggest Titan fleet outside London – not that it has much competition. The remainder are MCW Metrobuses, including some which started life with Tyne & Wear. The early Titan acquisitions are in the company's rather drab livery in which maroon predominates. More recent repaints wear the mainly cream livery adopted in 1994. A number of Titans are still running in London red. Vehicles in Liverpool generally carry Merseybus fleetnames.

A fleet of 12 low-floor Neoplans, funded by the Merseyside PTE, is operated in central Liverpool. These wear a distinctive yellow, grey and white livery. The Neoplans are big buses with low floors.

Top **MTL runs elderly Atlanteans in all-day service, with Alexander-bodied buses over 20 years old still in operation. The company has the country's biggest Atlantean fleet, with over 450 still in service.** Stewart J Brown

Right **Despite being a minority non-standard type, MTL's Ailsas have survived. There are 15 which were bought for evaluation by the Merseyside PTE in the early 1980s. All have Alexander bodies and are allocated to Wirral services.** Stewart J Brown

MTL bought Titans from London to update its fleet. These are still running in three liveries – London red, MTL maroon and, as seen here, the current corporate MTL cream-based scheme. Mike Harris

The Merseyside PTE has funded accessible bus services in Liverpool which are operated by MTL using a fleet of low-floor Neoplans. The only other Neoplan buses in Britain are operated by Mainline in Sheffield. Malcolm King

After deregulation Liverpool saw the establishment of three sizeable independent operators started by former PTE employees. All still exist – but none are independent. The first to fall was LiverLine, started with 10 Atlanteans in 1988. It had grown to 51 vehicles when it was taken over by North Western in 1993, and is still run as a separate operation. The company's two-tone blue livery was changed into a diagonally-divided North Western-style scheme, but this was abandoned in favour of a more conventional layout in the autumn of 1994. The LiverLine fleet is made up primarily of Atlanteans, but while still independent the company bought ten new Scania N113s with Northern Counties bodies and these are still in the fleet. Under British Bus ownership they have been joined by Plaxton-bodied K93s single-deckers from North Western. These and a few other ex-North Western buses retain North Western livery but with LiverLine fleetnames.

Next of the big three to lose its independence was Fareway. It was the first to start, introducing services from Liverpool to Kirkby in 1986. MTL took it over in 1993 and has retained the Fareway name. This fleet – 71 strong by the time it sold out to MTL – also bought a small number of new buses – 10 Northern Counties-bodied Leyland Olympians. But the bulk of the vehicles acquired by MTL were elderly Daimler Fleetlines, including former London DMSs. Under MTL control a few vehicles have been transferred from the parent fleet including further Olympians, with both elderly X-registered and more modern E-registered examples appearing in Fareway colours. Fareway also received some of MTL's intake of new buses in 1994, three Volvo B6s (in PTE livery) and four Optare MetroRiders. However after repainting some ex-Merseyside buses in Fareway's blue and yellow, the fleet is about to lose its distinctive look with the adoption of MTL red and white with MTL Fareway fleetnames. This first appeared on new Wright-bodied B10Bs delivered in 1995.

MTL's low-cost Mersey Rider business has had a number of different identities but it too is adopting the new MTL corporate colours, as shown on a 1976 East Lancs-bodied Atlantean, one of almost 50 allocated to the Mersey Rider operation.
Stewart J Brown

The most recent takeover by MTL involves Liverbus, which started up in 1990 and was acquired by MTL in the spring of 1995. Liverbus runs a predominantly double-deck operation with Atlanteans and Olympians.
Stewart J Brown

MTL took over one other, smaller, independent in 1994. It was Blue Triangle, running assorted second-hand double-deckers and two Dennis Darts. The Darts are now in MTL's Merseyrider fleet, set up in 1992 as a low-cost unit to counter the activities of the new generation of independents which were attacking MTL's business. The green livery used for Merseyrider is being replaced by the standard MTL cream and red, but with Merseyrider fleetnames. Much of the Merseyrider fleet is made up of Atlanteans transferred from the main MTL operation, along with second-hand Nationals. But there are also six B6s from the 50 delivered in 1994 and three B10Bs with Alexander Strider bodies, the only examples of this combination in the MTL group.

The last of the big independents to fall was the newest, Liverbus. This company was started in 1990 by a former Fareway director – and expanded into London on tendered operations in 1993. In April 1995 it was taken over by MTL. The fleet was founded on ex-Greater Manchester Atlanteans which are still in use. There are Olympians too – three ex-Highland Scottish buses, plus one delivered new in 1993 as part of a total order for 17, the remainder of which are in service in London. Single-deckers were introduced to the Liverbus operation in 1993 with the delivery of eight Volvo B10Bs with Northern Counties bodies which were among the first B10Bs on British roads. They were followed by second-hand Leyland Nationals. All of these are still running.

Merseyline is now one of only two independents with a significant number of double-deckers to be seen in Liverpool. Merseyline started running in 1993, taking over from the defunct City Fleet operation. It serves Garston with a remarkably standardised fleet – 14 Fleetlines which were new to West Midlands, plus two former Greater Manchester examples. The Merseyline livery is that used by West Midlands in the 1980s.

The other independent with double-deckers is Village Tours, also running Fleetlines to Garston. Here many came from Derby City Transport, but there are also five ex-West Midlands buses similar to those run by Merseyline and a number of Alexander-bodied buses from the A1 fleet, made redundant following the acquisition of A1 by Stagecoach. Blue and cream liveried Nationals and an ex-Whitelaw of Stonehouse Lynx are operated on a Liverpool local service by Bleasdale, who trades as Liverpool Citybus and also runs an Optare MetroRider on a service to Clatterbridge from Eastham Ferry on the Wirral peninsula.

The biggest independent operator on Merseyside is now CMT Buses, with a fleet of just over 50 Leyland Nationals. CMT started running coaches in 1973 and moved into bus operation in 1988. Its first new big buses entered service between Liverpool and Maghull in the spring of 1995 and were four Volvo B10Bs with Wright Endurance bodywork.

CMT's main operations are in Liverpool but its Nationals, which have come from a variety of sources around the country, are also strongly in evidence in St Helens, where MTL faces an astounding array of competitors. One of the first was Ogdens, which originally – and rather cheekily – used a North Western-style diagonally-striped colour scheme. Now Ogdens older buses, Nationals and Bristol REs, are dark red with a grey skirt, while its newer vehicles, four DAF SB220s and a Dennis Dart, are predominantly white. Two of the DAFs are Optare Deltas bought new; the other two have Ikarus 480 bodies and came from OK Travel. The Dart is an M-registered bus with Plaxton Pointer body.

South Lancs Transport operates locally around St Helens. Its fleet includes Plaxton-bodied Dennis Darts, Leopard buses and an assortment of Mercedes minibuses. Recent new deliveries carry SLT registrations. Another provider of St Helens local services is Town Flyers. The bulk of Town Flyers' operations are run by ex-GM Buses Dodges, but of more interest are a pair of Dennis Dominos which came from South Yorkshire Transport. Hatton runs a local service too, with anonymous Leyland Nationals in a predominantly red and blue livery. These include both Marks 1 and 2. Hatton also runs second-hand minibuses. St Helens is served by Timeline with minibuses, including a tri-axle Pullman. Halton Transport run between St Helens and Widnes with Leyland Nationals.

Top **Village runs over 20 Fleetlines which started life with no fewer than six different operators. Three have dual-door Roe bodies and were new in 1976 to Chesterfield Transport. They reached Village in 1994 by way of Pennine Blue.** Michael Fowler

Centre **Citybus is a small operation in Liverpool with five Nationals, a Lynx and a Bristol VRT available for service. Most duties are covered by Nationals, as illustrated by an ex-East Kent Mark 1 in Liverpool city centre.** Malcolm King

Right **The bulk of CMT's services are operated by Leyland Nationals, but in 1995 the company took delivery of its first new vehicles, four Volvo B10Bs with Wright bodies, similar to those running for MTL.** Malcolm King

South Lancs Transport's biggest buses are Leyland Leopards. It has four with Duple Dominant bus bodies, including this 1982 PSU3 which came from A1 of Ardrossan.
Stewart J Brown

Town Flyers run small buses on local services in St Helens. These include two Optare-bodied Dennis Dominos.
Mark Bailey

Another small company serving St Helens is Hatton, generally using Leyland Nationals. These include three ex-PMT Mark 2s with dual-purpose seating. They were new in 1984. Mike Harris

On the other side of the Mersey, MTL trades as Wirral Peninsula, an identity adopted in the spring of 1994. Among the non-standard types running here are the Ailsas and five DAF SB220s with Ikarus bodies. A fair number of MTL's Olympians are allocated to the depot in Birkenhead, the main centre on the Wirral side of the Mersey. PMT, trading as Red Rider and Crosville, has services on Wirral, operated by Mercedes minibuses, Olympian and VRT double-deckers and Dennis Darts. At the end of 1994 PMT took over the bus operations of Toppings. Four Leyland Lynxes, bought new by Toppings in 1988 and that company's most modern buses, are still running in Birkenhead with Crosville fleet-names added to their Toppings livery.

Among the area's smaller operators running from Birkenhead, Happy Al's fleet is one which has become firmly established in the early 1990s. Its buses are all second-hand double-deckers, mostly ECW-bodied VRTs and Olympians which were new to a range of NBC subsidiaries from Badgerline in the south to Ribble in the north. A number have been re-registered with ALS marks. The only double-deckers which were not new to an NBC company are two Ailsas acquired from Clydeside Scottish. Avon Buses of Moreton also has two Ailsas, which operate alongside two ex-London Titans, a National Greenway, and a National 2 which started life with the Scottish Prison Service – but has now been released.

Top right PMT acquired Crosville's Wirral operations in 1990. The Crosville name lives on, but the buses which carry it are in PMT colours. This ECW-bodied Olympian was new to Crosville in 1983. Stewart J Brown

Top right **PMT acquired Crosville's Wirral operations in 1990. The Crosville name lives on, but the buses which carry it are in PMT colours. This ECW-bodied Olympian was new to Crosville in 1983.** Stewart J Brown

Right **The bus services operated by Toppings were taken over by PMT at the end of 1994. The Toppings bus fleet included four Leyland Lynxes bought new in 1988 and these are still running in Toppings colours but with Crosville fleetnames.** Stewart J Brown

Below **The most common type in Happy Al's fleet is the Bristol VRT - 18 are operated. All have ECW bodies and started life with NBC subsidiaries. This one seen in Birkenhead was new to Bristol Omnibus in 1980.** Stewart J Brown

Below right **Ex-London Titans are an unusual choice for an operator as small as Avon Buses, which runs two in its six strong fleet. Park Royal built this bus in 1980.** Mike Harris

A smaller operation running smaller buses is A1A Travel of Birkenhead, operating local routes in Wirral with Mercedes and Freight Rover minibuses, most of which are second-hand. A1A shouldn't be confused with A2B of Heswall, also running Mercedes on services which reach as far south as Chester.

British Bus runs services on Merseyside, mainly through its North Western subsidiary whose head office is at Aintree. North Western was formed in 1986 to take over the southern part of Ribble's business and was bought by British Bus (or Drawlane as it then was) in 1988. Since then it has expanded south, taking over part of what was Crosville. There are still substantial numbers of ex-Ribble buses, mainly Leyland Nationals and Park Royal-bodied Atlanteans. More interesting Atlanteans are six long-wheelbase AN68/2s with Alexander bodies, purchased from Preston in 1987. Under its new owners North Western has received a steady influx of new vehicles. There are Dennis Dominators and Volvo Citybuses, both bodied by East Lancs. More recent acquisitions have included Dennis Lances with Plaxton Verde bodies, some of which have replaced Leyland Tigers on the tightly-timed Liverpool to Runcorn limited-stop operation. A few North Western Atlanteans carry Red Knight livery. This is a low-cost unit. Bright new Cityplus branding was adopted in 1995 for a fleet of East Lancs-bodied Dennis Darts serving Liverpool.

Top left **Bristol VRTs are a minority type in the North Western fleet. Those which it does have all came when North Western took over part of Crosville's operations in Cheshire in 1989.** Stewart J Brown

Left **More typical of the North Western double-deck fleet is the Leyland Atlantean, large numbers of which were inherited from Ribble when North Western was created in 1986. This ECW-bodied bus was new to Ribble in 1976, but did not join the North Western fleet until 1993.** Stewart J Brown

Below left **North Western also runs just over 20 Atlanteans which were new to Greater Manchester Transport. They have Northern Counties bodies.** Malcolm King

Below **A few Atlanteans in the North Western fleet carry Red Knight livery. These include this ex-London & Country PDR1A with Park Royal body which is one of the oldest buses in the fleet. It was new in 1972.** Mike Harris

North Western's services run north to Southport, where MTL's Southport & District fleet includes 19 Plaxton-bodied B6s, running alongside B10Bs, Nationals, Atlanteans and a few Olympians. An open-top Atlantean in the town carries the red and cream colours of Southport Corporation, whose bus operation was absorbed by the PTE in 1974. ABC Travel of nearby Formby provides the Formby local service and also has operations in Liverpool. These are generally run by minibuses, either Mercedes 709Ds or Optare MetroRiders. The company's longest route is from Preston to Skipton and for this it owns two Optare Deltas. Occasional journeys start from Southport.

Heading north from Southport the next major town is Preston, served by Preston Bus, the former local authority operation which was privatised in a management buy-out at the end of 1993. There have been no dramatic changes as a result of the new ownership. The bulk of the Preston Bus operations are firmly within the town's boundaries and are operated mainly by a mixture of Leylands and Renaults. At one time the fleet was 100 per cent Leyland, and there are still Atlanteans, Olympians and Lynxes in service. The small bus fleet is made up of Renault S56s with Northern Counties bodies and ten Optare MetroRiders, the latter the only additions to the fleet since privatisation.

Top right **MTL's Southport & District operation was launched in 1994 using a fleet of 19 new Volvo B6s with Plaxton Pointer bodies from a batch of 50 in course of delivery to MTL. The Southport & District name is carried by all MTL buses in the town.** Michael Fowler

Right **ABC Travel runs a smart fleet of minibuses on local services, including the Formby town service, seen here being operated by a Marshall-bodied Mercedes 709D.** Stewart J Brown

Below **Lancashire Rose operates a Preston local service using Dodge S46s which were new to Greater Manchester Transport. They have Northern Counties bodies.** Mark Bailey

Below right **The only survivors of Preston's once numerous fleet of Alexander-bodied Atlanteans are 10 delivered in 1980. Subsequent Atlantean deliveries were bodied by East Lancs.** Mike Harris

Most of the out-of-town services are run by Ribble, a Stagecoach subsidiary since 1989. All traces of Ribble's previous red livery have now vanished as old buses have been repainted or replaced. Stagecoach has invested sizeable sums in updating the Ribble fleet with B10Ms, B6s, Olympians and Mercedes minis. It has also added Dennis Javelin coaches for use on inter-urban services. The only Javelin buses bought by Stagecoach, three 1989 examples with Duple 300-series bodies, are also in the Ribble fleet, usually running in the Lancaster area. Older types to be seen in Lancashire include Nationals, Olympians and VRTs to standard NBC specifications. The VRTs are based in east Lancashire.

One sign of the times is that for a company long associated with the Leyland Atlantean (Ribble's first were delivered in 1959) there are now only 20 in the fleet. Of these 12 were acquired with the operations of Barrow Borough Transport in 1989 (two) and Lancaster City Transport in 1993 (ten). The other eight are ECW-bodied buses which were new to Ribble, but have spent some time in the Cumberland fleet. Ribble is, of course, the main operator in Lancaster following the demise of Lancaster City Transport in 1993 after a short bus war. MTL has an outpost serving Lancaster – MTL Heysham. Services operate to surrounding rural areas using Leyland Leopards and Nationals in a green and yellow livery. The operation, previously Heysham Travel, was bought by MTL in 1993. It retains the Heysham Travel fleetname.

Fishwick of Leyland continues to operate between Preston and Chorley with Lynxes and Nationals. And Fishwick's unusual green livery has remained immune to fashionable stripes, squiggles and designer fleetnames. Whatever else has changed in Lancashire's bus services, the Fishwick business in 1995 is still recognisably linked to that of 10, 20, 30 or even 40 years ago.

Double-deckers are now down to just nine and are used mainly for school journeys. The double-deck fleet still has Atlanteans bought new, including the only AN69 in Britain, which is fitted with a unique highbridge Titan-derived ECW body. New in 1983 this is the most modern double-decker in the fleet. However recent double-deck additions have been second-hand and – shock, horror – have introduced two Daimler Fleetlines and two Bristol VRTs to an operation which for many years has been synonymous with Leyland buses. These all have Gardner engines and ECW bodywork – standard NBC lowheight pattern on the VRTs and full-height bodies on the ex-Thamesdown Fleetlines. The company's newest buses are four Lynx IIs delivered in 1990-91. Minibus services are operated in Leyland using Mercedes 609Ds with Reeve Burgess conversions. They run as FishKwick.

Top **Ribble's fleet has changed quite dramatically during its six years in Stagecoach ownership. Standard Stagecoach types such as Alexander-bodied Volvo B6s are rapidly replacing older vehicles. This B6 was just a few months old when it was transferred to Ribble from Stagecoach's Fife Scottish operation.** Stewart J Brown

Centre **The Leyland Olympian was Ribble's standard double-decker in NBC days, but with ECW bodywork rather than Alexander, as specified by Stagecoach. This is a long-wheelbase Stagecoach-specification Olympian, easily identifiable by the short window in mid-wheelbase.** Stewart J Brown

Right **Fishwick, its depot within sight of Leyland's main factories, was long a staunch Leyland user. Its newest buses are two J-registered Lynx IIs.** Malcolm King

Down the Ribble estuary lies Blackpool, Britain's most famous coastal resort, complete with splendid tower, currently painted gold to mark its centenary in 1994. Blackpool Transport is still owned by the district council, and in a move which seems to defy the logic of the government's pro-privatisation policies, it expanded in 1994 by buying the neighbouring Fylde operation after it had been privatised in a management buy-out. Fylde was actually only in private sector ownership for five months between being sold by Fylde district council and being bought by Blackpool.

The Blackpool bus fleet was in the late 1980s and early 1990s standardised on Optare products, with 29 full-size Deltas running alongside 35 of the smaller CityPacers. Blackpool has the biggest fleet of both types in the North West, and the biggest CityPacer fleet in the country. The CityPacers are operated under the HandyBus name. The latest deliveries have seen a reversion to double-deckers, and a move away from Optare to Volvo and Northern Counties. Six Volvo Olympians entered service in 1994 and have Northern Counties' distinctive Palatine II bodywork.

The pre-Optare fleet is made up mainly of East Lancs-bodied Atlanteans, comparatively unusual long-wheelbase AN68/2 models with 86 seats. A dozen ex-London Routemasters are owned for use on summer services, although they were in fact last used in 1994. Blackpool Transport also runs the coastal tramway from Fleetwood in the north to Starr Gate in the south. There is a wide range of types, including 60-year-old double-deckers which although much rebuilt are still striking vehicles. The end-to-end trip takes just under an hour.

Top **The oldest Blackpool buses in regular service are East Lancs-bodied Atlanteans delivered between 1979 and 1984. A 1981 example passes the foot of the famous tower.** Michael Fowler

Centre **Blackpool's first new double-deckers for five years were delivered in 1994. They were six Volvo Olympians with Northern Counties Palatine II bodies, marking a double first for the company – its first Volvos and its first Northern Counties bodies.** Malcolm King

Right **Blackpool's minibus fleet was until 1995 made up of 35 Optare CityPacers in distinctive Handy Bus livery. Additions to the Handy Bus fleet in 1995 included this Renault S56, one of 21 broadly similar buses acquired with the Fylde business. This style of Northern Counties body is relatively unusual – most Renaults and Dodges bodied by the Wigan builder retained the chassis maker's bonnet. New Optare MetroRiders are also scheduled to join the Handy Bus operation.** Paul Wigan

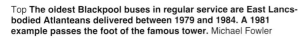

The acquisition of Fylde Borough Transport in 1994 finally put paid to any chance of more bus wars between the two operations. There had been occasional skirmishes and much sabre-rattling in the years since deregulation. Fylde's is an ageing fleet, which trades under the Blue Buses banner. Apart from three Optare Deltas purchased in 1991, the newest big bus is a 1984 Leyland Tiger. The newest double-decker is a 1984 Atlantean. Atlanteans form the bulk of the big bus fleet and are used on the trunk Lytham to Blackpool services. There are also elderly PDR1 Atlanteans, most of which are open-toppers. Fylde runs minibuses too – 21 Dodge S56s with Northern Counties bodies. The newer buses have the short-lived body design with a so-called "fast front" which replaces the original Dodge bonnet and attempts to give the vehicles something of the style of purpose-designed minibuses like the Metrorider.

However while Fylde may not have been buying many new buses, it has gone in for a considerable amount of re-building of Atlanteans. Some double-deckers have had new front ends grafted on to their existing Northern Counties bodies. More radical has been the fitment of new Northern Counties Paladin single-deck bodies to four heavily-rebuilt K-registered Atlanteans, the chassis of which came from Kingston-upon-Hull. The outcome is a modern-looking bus, belied by the retention of the original registration numbers. The rebuilt double-deckers have Ulster marks to disguise their ages. Signs of the change in Fylde's ownership have been the transfer from Blackpool Transport of two Deltas and several Atlanteans as part of an upgrade of the fleet. Fylde also runs coaches under the Seagull name, a Blackpool-based company which it took over in 1987.

Top In keeping with Blackpool's brash image some vehicles in the Fylde fleet carry garish promotional liveries, as demonstrated by this Northern Counties-bodied Atlantean which was new to AA of Ayr. It is seen outside Blackpool's most famous landmark, the 100-year-old tower. Mark Bailey

Centre The oldest closed-top bus in the Fylde fleet is a PDR1A Atlantean supplied to Fylde's predecessor, Lytham St Annes Corporation, in 1970. It has a Northern Counties body and was repainted in 1995 in the new livery adopted following the take-over of Fylde by Blackpool Transport. Paul Wigan

Left A number of Blackpool Transport buses have been transferred to the Fylde fleet, including Optare Deltas and East Lancs-bodied Atlanteans. The Deltas join three bought new by Fylde in 1991. This 1990 Delta was Blackpool's first. Paul Wigan

Inland there are still local authority-owned fleets serving Blackburn, Hyndburn, Burnley and Rawtenstall. Blackburn Borough Transport remains primarily an urban operator, serving Blackburn and neighbouring Darwen and Accrington. The older vehicles in the fleet are Atlanteans with East Lancs bodies. The East Lancs factory is in the town and has supplied Blackburn with most of its buses over the last 40 years. Recent deliveries from East Lancs have been National Greenways, of which there are 12, and single-deck Volvos. Five B10Ms in 1991 were Blackburn's last new full-sized buses; four B6s in 1994 are the company's newest vehicles and were the first B6s to be bodied by East Lancs. Blackburn was one of the many small municipal fleets which did not buy Nationals, which makes its conversion to the Greenway rebuild all the more noteworthy. There are 25 MCW Metroriders in operation. These were bought in 1987-88 after United Transport had established its Zippy minibus operation in Preston and was thought to have designs on other towns in the North West.

Blackburn operates a service to Manchester from Clitheroe via Accrington and Haslingden, normally using Volvo B10Ms. Other single-deckers include ex-SBG Leopards with Alexander Y-type bodies and ex-NBC Tigers with ECW's short-lived B51 coach body. Blackburn has had the front and rear ends of its B51s rebuilt by East Lancs – and has actually improved their appearance in the process. Most of the fleet is in the predominantly cream livery adopted in 1993, but a few Atlanteans retain the earlier style with green lower half and cream upper deck.

Ribble has a significant presence in and around Blackburn and has a depot in the town. Smaller operators include Darwen Coach Services, competing on the Darwen to Blackburn corridor with Freight Rover Sherpas. The first two came from Fishwick of Leyland and were put into service in Fishwick's colours. Subsequent additions have been repainted to match. Powercrafts also runs second-hand Sherpas and a Transit. White Lady operates a Darwen local service and runs into Blackburn with four Mercedes minis bought new. Two are van conversions; two have coachbuilt Reeve Burgess Beaver bodies. In Clitheroe, which is served mainly by Ribble, Town Car Hire operates a local service using Metroriders while Lakeland of Hurst Green provide a service to the town.

Top **All of Blackburn Borough Transport's double-deckers are East Lancs-bodied Atlanteans, with just over 50 in operation dating from between 1976 and 1983, a period when it was the fleet's standard bus. This one dates from 1980.** Stewart J Brown

Centre **The first Volvo B6s to be bodied by East Lancs were four for Blackburn Transport in 1994. They are 41-seaters.** David Barrow

Right **Darwen Coach Services started operations with two ex-Fishwick Sherpas and Fishwick's colours have been applied to subsequent acquisitions including this ex-Bee Line Carlyle-bodied Sherpa.** Stewart J Brown

Hyndburn Transport is Accrington's principal operator. Its services are concentrated in and around the town. Recent years have seen Hyndburn's buying policy favour small buses. Double-deckers now play a smaller role than in the past and all but two are Atlanteans. Four were delivered new in the late 1970s, while more recently the company has been buying used examples, from Ipswich, Merseybus, Preston and Ribble. The odd two double-deckers are the fleet's first Olympians, two Y-registered ECW-bodied buses purchased in 1994 from the West Riding group. The single-deck fleet has a good number of Leopards in it, generally with Duple Dominant coach bodies or East Lancs bus bodies. The two oldest Leopards are N-registered vehicles which came from Halton Transport and originally had East Lancs coach bodies, but were rebodied with new East Lancs bus bodies in 1983. The newest full-size single-deckers are two Dennis Falcons, dating from 1984-85.

New additions to the Hyndburn fleet since deregulation have been mini and midibuses. MCW Metroriders came first, but since MCW's closure Hyndburn has bought Iveco Fords, not that common a choice for bus operation. The midibuses are all Leyland Swifts. Seven are operated, giving Hyndburn one of the biggest fleets of Leyland's midi, and all have Reeve Burgess Harrier bodywork. One started life in 1990 as a demonstrator for VL Bus & Coach, at that time the sales organisation for Volvo and Leyland psvs. Hyndburn also operates a small coach fleet, including vehicles taken over with the business of Rigby's Coaches of Patricroft in 1993.

Competition for passengers travelling between Accrington and Blackburn comes from Pilkingtons, with Mark 1 Nationals, Raja Bros with a Dodge S56 and East Lancs Travel with Leopard coaches.

Top **All but two of Hyndburn Transport's double-deckers are Leyland Atlanteans, most of which are second-hand. Four are long-wheelbase AN68/2 models with Alexander bodies which were purchased from Preston Borough Transport in 1990.** Stewart J Brown

Centre **The Leyland Swift with Reeve Burgess Harrier body was a neat but short-lived combination. Hyndburn has five, which entered service in 1990. Most Harriers were coaches; Hyndburn's are unusual in being 39-seat buses.** Tony Wilson

Left **Pilkingtons operate between Blackburn and Accrington using Leyland Nationals and providing competition for the established operators on the route, Blackburn Borough Transport and Hyndburn Transport.** Tony Wilson

Burnley is the hub of Burnley & Pendle's operation which, like Blackburn and Hyndburn, remains in local authority ownership. Burnley & Pendle serves the adjoining towns of Colne and Nelson and also runs to Keighley and Accrington. Tendered services are operated in Bury. The oldest buses in the fleet are Leyland Leopards and Bristol VRTs, the latter including five ex-Tayside buses with Alexander bodies which served their original operator for just five years but have been with their present owner for 13. There are also six VRTs bought new which have standard lowheight ECW bodies. The only other 'deckers are 15 Volvo Citybuses – the biggest fleet (by one) in the north west. These have Alexander R-type bodies and were delivered between 1988 and 1991.

Burnley & Pendle's single-deck fleet includes B10Ms, the chassis from which the Citybus was evolved, and Leyland National 2s, including some second-hand examples. Minibuses, which operate under the Whizzard name (a pun on the Witches of Pendle, for those unfamiliar with local folklore), are Mercedes-Benz and Optare MetroRiders. Viscount Central is the name used for the company's coach business, built on the operations of an independent of the same name which was purchased in the mid 1980s. The only small operator of note in the Burnley area is Border, whose fleet is made up mainly of Atlanteans and Leopards acquired from a variety of sources. Border's oldest buses are M-registered Atlanteans which were new to Grampian Transport. Its newest is a 1981 Leopard.

Yorkshire-based operators serving Burnley are Yorkshire Rider from Halifax, Keighley & District from Keighley and Pennine Motor Services from Skipton, whose Leopard coaches are being displaced by Mark 1 Nationals.

Top **The newest full-size buses in the Burnley & Pendle fleet are Volvo Citybuses with East Lancs bodies. There are six, with the most recent dating from 1993.** Tony Wilson

Centre **Earlier deliveries to Burnley & Pendle were Alexander-bodied, with six P-types in 1988 being followed by seven of the more attractive PS-type in 1991. A PS lays over in Burnley bus station.** Tony Wilson

Right **Border of Burnley operate local services in Burnley and also run from Blackburn to Leyland. The fleet is made up mainly of Atlanteans and Leopards, including this former NBC coach with ECW B51 body.** Tony Wilson

To the south lies Rossendale Transport, whose services run north to Accrington and Burnley, south to Bury, Rochdale and Manchester, and east to Todmorden, although much of the company's business lies in and around Rawtenstall, Bacup and Haslingden, the main towns in the Rossendale valley. Services in Rochdale have expanded and over the last 10 years the Rossendale fleet has grown quite remarkably, from 46 vehicles prior to deregulation to 119 now.

Pride of place goes to the two newest vehicles, Volvo Olympians with Alexander Royale bodies which were delivered in 1994 and lay claim to being the country's first double-deckers with kneeling suspension. These join two Leyland-built Olympians with East Lancs bodies which came from Stevensons of Uttoxeter in 1993 but had been new to Eastbourne Buses in 1985 when that operator was running an express service to London. Most of Rossendale's double-deckers are rather more mundane Atlanteans, generally with East Lancs bodies and including both new and used examples.

The single-deck fleet includes some rarities too, such as the only Bristol LHSs to be bodied by East Lancs, four East Lancs-bodied Tigers, second-hand Tiger/Duple buses (from Hutchison of Overtown and Trimdon Motor Services), and assorted second-hand Leopards, most of which have recently been rebodied by East Lancs. There are five Dennis Darts, the two newest of which have Reeve Burgess Pointer bodies. Very few Pointers were completed by Reeve Burgess at Pilsley before production was moved to Plaxton. Minibuses are in the main MCW Metroriders, many of which are second-hand, to which have been added new Optare-built examples. In 1991 Rossendale took over Ellen Smith Coaches of Rochdale, and this has been retained as a trading name for the company's coach business. The most unusual vehicle in the Ellen Smith fleet is a 1985 East Lancs-bodied Volvo Citybus double-deck coach, bought from Wright of Wrexham in 1993 when that company was closing down.

Above left **Expansion by Rossendale Transport has been catered for by the purchase of second-hand Leopards and Atlanteans. The latter include seven Alexander-bodied buses which were bought from South Yorkshire Transport in 1991.** Tony Wilson

Left **Rossendale's minibuses run as Handyriders. The majority are Metroriders bought both new and secondhand. They include four Optare-built buses, one of which is seen in Bury Interchange.** Stewart J Brown

To the north of the region the main operator is Cumberland Motor Services, one of Stagecoach's original NBC purchases back in 1987. Cumberland's territory stretches from the Scottish border at Carlisle, where it meets Stagecoach's Western Scottish operation, south to Kendal, where it adjoins the Stagecoach Ribble company. The Cumberland fleet has undergone significant modernisation and standard Stagecoach Volvo B10Ms with Alexander PS-type bodies make up a significant proportion of the fleet. These have effectively ousted the Leyland National, many of which have moved south to Ribble. The only National remaining is a green-liveried B-series model for operation on the Borrowdale service. Routemasters have gone too. Now Carlisle passengers travel in the comfort of B10Ms. The only other single-deck buses are Leyland Lynxes, which are relatively rare in the Stagecoach empire. Five are operated, including one former demonstrator and an early C-registered production model which was evaluated on NBC's behalf by Ribble, but was destined to be NBC's only Lynx.

Small buses are mainly Mercedes, with a mixture of L608D van conversions dating from NBC days, to Alexander-bodied 709Ds which are the Stagecoach standard minibus. There are eight Volvo B6s which are based in Carlisle. The double-deck fleet is made up of Leyland Olympians and ECW-bodied Bristol VRTs. The Olympians include ECW-bodied examples (two bought new, four ex-Ribble) and Alexander-bodied buses. The latter are mostly standard Stagecoach buses, but there are five transferred from Bluebird Buses in Aberdeen, which are to SBG specification, and two of the Stagecoach group's trio of three-axle Olympian Megadekkas with 96 seats. Open-top VRTs, and a solitary open-top Atlantean, carry green Lakeland Experience colours. This livery is also carried by three Mercedes L609Ds. Cumberland operate coaches in a brown and yellow livery – in the process of being changed to red – with Coachlines fleetnames.

Top **Cumberland was the first Stagecoach company to run a large fleet of Volvo B10Ms with Alexander PS-type bodies, taking 90 in 1992-93. More joined the fleet in 1995 and like some of the earlier vehicles have coach-type seats for use on long-distance services.** Peter Newman

Centre **For a time Cumberland was the only Stagecoach subsidiary running Leyland Lynxes, although recent expansion has changed that. Cumberland has five. This one in Barrow forms part of a trio bought new in 1989. The others are a former demonstrator and an early production model which was originally operated by Ribble.** Paul Wigan

Right **Cumberland Motor Services has a high-profile presence in the Lake District, promoting its services to the many millions who visit the area every year. A number of Cumberland's tourist-oriented services are marketed as the Lakeland Experience and are run by green-liveried vehicles which include minibuses, a National and various open-toppers. The oldest bus in the Cumberland fleet is this 1966 Atlantean with Metro-Cammell body. It was new to Portsmouth City Transport.** Tony Wilson

Moving south to Cheshire, there are three local authority bus fleets, in Warrington, Halton and Chester. In Warrington the main operator is Warrington Borough Transport. It runs a varied fleet, with Leyland Atlanteans and Dennis Dominators representing the old order, and Dennis Darts representing the new. Most of the older vehicles in the fleet are double-deckers, including some second-hand examples such as Atlanteans from Eastbourne and Preston, Olympians from Derby and Dominators from Leicester. Double-deckers delivered new to Warrington are Atlanteans, the oldest of which date from 1978, Olympians, and Dominators. The newest deckers in the fleet are F-registered long-wheelbase Dominators, two of which carry CoachLines colours.

But the 1990s have seen a switch to midibuses, and there are now over 30 Darts in operation with a range of bodies and in two liveries. The first Darts carry blue MidiLines colours, but the most recent deliveries have been in red fleet livery. The bodywork on the Darts is by Carlyle, Marshall, Northern Counties and Plaxton. The Northern Counties bodies are of that builder's first style for the Dart chassis – a style of which few were built. The oldest buses in the fleet (other than a preserved PD2 Titan) are four 1976 East Lancs-bodied Bristol REs. It is rare to find REs still running for their original owner.

Bus wars broke out in Warrington at the start of 1995, with North Western launching services in the town using a fleet of 35 new Dennis Darts with Plaxton Pointer bodies which were later joined by Mercedes minibuses. They run as Warrington Goldline in an all-over white livery, and have prompted a spirited defence by Warrington Borough Transport. Additional Dennises of very different types joined the Warrington fleet as a result – new Darts and ex-Ipswich Falcons which had been new to Chesterfield Transport. Warrington now has services running to Liverpool and Chester.

Top **Warrington Borough Transport started buying Dennis Dominators in the early 1980s. Four East Lancs-bodied buses were delivered in 1983, forming the second batch of the type. One loads in Wigan.** Mike Harris

Centre **Growing competition in 1995 has seen the Warrington fleet expand to retaliate. Vehicles which have joined the fleet in 1995 include East Lancs-bodied Dennis Falcons from Ipswich Buses. They were new to Chesterfield Transport.** Mike Harris

Right **The competition in Warrington has come from British Bus, with its North Western company launching Warrington Goldlines, which started off with a fleet of new Plaxton-bodied Dennis Darts.** Mike Harris

Runcorn has one of the biggest networks of bus priorities outside London in the shape of the Runcorn busway. The key operators here are North Western, which has a depot in the town, and Halton Transport, based in Widnes on the opposite bank of the Mersey. The Runcorn busway was built in the 1970s and gives extensive coverage of the town. Where the busway crosses other roads there are traffic lights which are activated by an approaching bus, giving it priority over other traffic.

Halton serves Runcorn and Widnes with Leyland Lynxes and Nationals. Until early 1995 the 54-vehicle fleet was made up entirely of these two models, but the Leyland hold was then broken with the delivery of a number of Dennis's ubiquitous Dart model, starting off with two with Marshall bodywork. The North Western fleet in the area is more varied, ranging from new Dennis Darts with East Lancs bodies, to elderly former NBC Atlanteans. Halton also has a frequent service between Runcorn and Liverpool, operated by Lynxes.

Right **Halton Transport, like Warrington still in local authority ownership, has also expanded its fleet. The company's standard bus from 1986 was the Leyland Lynx and it now runs 36, of which 15 are J-registered buses delivered in 1991-92.** Malcolm King

Below **Until 1994 the Halton fleet was 100 per cent Leyland. That changed with the arrival of two Marshall-bodied Dennis Darts. More Darts have since followed.** Malcolm King

In Chester local services are provided by Chester City Transport. PMT, trading as Crosville, provides most of the out-of-town services. Chester has built up a substantial fleet of Dominators. There are 14 Northern Counties-bodied buses bought new in the early 1980s, but at the start of the 1990s this number was increased to 30 through judicious second-hand buying, and Dominators now account for just under one third of the fleet. The second-hand examples have come from Brighton, Eastbourne, Hyndburn, Warrington and A1 Service. All have East Lancs bodies.

A similar tale can be told about the company's Olympians. There are six which were delivered new and nine bought from other operators, in this case A1 Service, Derby, Highland Scottish and the West Yorkshire PTE. The oldest buses in the Chester fleet are Fleetlines, including ex-GM Buses examples. The newest are 16 Plaxton-bodied Dennis Darts. Chester City Transport operates open-top buses on city tours, as does Chester Bus & Boat on a combined bus and boat tour. The latter fleet includes Routemasters.

Local coach operator Lofty's operates minibuses on a service from Chester to Ince, on Wirral between Neston and Ellesmere Port, and in Heswall. Most of the vehicles are Mercedes, but there are two TBP Pullman three-axle minibuses, and three low-floor CVE Omnis. Also running into Chester is Huxley of Threapwood, near Malpas, generally operating on tendered services. Huxley's fleet is made up primarily of coaches, some of which are used on service, but also includes a couple of Mark I Leyland Nationals.

A number of operators run in from Wales – in particular Devaway and British Bus subsidiary Crosville Wales. These are covered in the Welsh chapter.

Top **Chester City Transport runs a number of Dennis Dominators, most of which it has bought from other operators. This 1983 bus with East Lancs body is one of six which came from Hyndburn Transport.** Capital Transport

Left **Acorn Travel runs minibuses in Chester, but of more interest is the company's open-top Routemaster used on a city tour.** Mike Harris

Below **There are two Mark I Leyland Nationals in the fleet of Huxley of Threapwood. These share the company's local bus operations with Leyland Leopard and Ford R-series coaches. A National arrives in Chester on the route from Bunbury.** Mike Harris

NORTH EAST ENGLAND

Top **The Go-Ahead Group runs a wide range of Optare products. Its newest deliveries are MetroRiders for the Coastline fleet.** Malcolm King

Above **Northumbria is one of a number of British Bus subsidiaries to have put new East Lancs bodied Scanias into service in 1995. This is an L113.** Malcolm King

Newcastle-upon-Tyne is one of England's great cities, its regional importance underlined by the magnificent cross-Tyne bridges which connect Newcastle on the north bank of the river with Gateshead on the south. The existence of the huge MetroCentre shopping mall in Gateshead doesn't seem to have hindered Newcastle's prosperity or diminished its importance as a key shopping centre, although it has drained the life from central Gateshead.

In Newcastle the principal operator is Busways Travel Services, created in 1986 to take over the former Tyne & Wear PTE direct bus operation. It was the second of the former PTE bus companies to be privatised, in a management/employee buy-out in 1989. The words "An employee owned company" were added below the Busways fleetname, to signify the operation's new status. However in 1994 it was all change, and Busways sold out to Stagecoach, giving the Scottish-based group its first operation in the north east of England – although more soon followed and in little more than six months the expansionist Stagecoach group became one of the North East's biggest bus operators, following a string of take-overs.

Part of the deal at Busways was that Stagecoach would initially retain the company's distinctive yellow and white livery. Its history can be traced back through the days of the PTE to Newcastle Corporation, whose buses in post-war years were yellow and cream. The Busways livery has local variations, with maroon relief for buses allocated to the Newcastle Busways operation, blue for South Shields Busways and green for Sunderland Busways. It's a subtle touch and a nice gesture to local interests. In the days before the PTE South Shields municipal buses were blue, while those in Sunderland were green.

Subtle or not, the Stagecoach takeover meant that the days of distinctive liveries were numbered and the stay of execution for Busways' attractive colours was, sadly, a short one. In mid-1995, barely 12 months after the take-over, Busways buses began to appear from the paint shops in corporate Stagecoach white.

Busways runs a smart and modern fleet. Recent deliveries have in the main been Dennis Darts, with body orders shared between Alexander and Plaxton. The former can be seen in Newcastle and Sunderland, while the latter provide a high proportion of the services in South Shields. Shortly before the sale of the company to Stagecoach, Busways ordered a fleet of single-deckers for evaluation, sharing its business between three chassis makers and four body-builders. This saw the delivery in 1994 of four Dennis Lances, three with Plaxton Verde bodywork in Sunderland, South Shields and Newcastle plus one with Optare Sigma body in Newcastle; four Scania L113s, two each bodied by

Top **At first glance this Busways bus looks like another standard Stagecoach single-decker with Alexander PS-type body. However it is in fact a Scania N113, one of 38 similar buses in the fleet. Most were supplied new, but this 1990 example was originally operated by Stevensons of Uttoxeter and was bought by Busways in 1993.** Russell Upcraft

Centre **Most of Busways' Alexander-bodied Darts are based in Sunderland, which has 33 out of the 47 in the fleet.** Mike Harris

Right **One of the last acts of Busways before it sold out to Stagecoach was to buy a number of different types of single-decker for evaluation. These included four Scania L113s, two of which have Northern Counties Paladin bodies. Note that the wording under the fleetname has been changed from "An employee owned company" to "Part of the Stagecoach group".** Roy Marshall

Alexander (in Newcastle and Sunderland) and Northern Counties (in Sunderland and South Shields); and two Alexander-bodied Volvo B10Bs which are also allocated to Newcastle. Quite what Stagecoach will make of this variety remains to be seen. Its favoured full-size single-decker is the straightforward Alexander-bodied mid-engined Volvo B10M. Busways' standard had been the rear-engined Scania N113, also bodied by Alexander.

Since privatisation in 1989 Busways has bought new Scania N113s with Alexander PS-type single-deck and R-type double-deck bodies, as well as Northern Counties-bodied Olympians. All of the Scanias operate in Newcastle and among the 38 single-deckers are two second-hand examples. One is an ex-Scania demonstrator while the other came from Stevensons of Uttoxeter. The Olympians include ten bought new and 21 which came from the Bexleybus operation in south-east London in 1991 when Selkent lost most of its London Transport tenders in the Bexley area. These buses were just three years old and have already served longer in the North East than they did in London. Most of the Northern Counties-bodied Olympians are based in Sunderland, with some of the ex-London buses running in Newcastle. Older double-deckers are mainly Alexander-bodied Atlanteans, but there are a small number of similarly-bodied Fleetlines, which are based in Sunderland. The oldest of the Alexander-bodied buses have nearside staircases, a typical Newcastle feature. There are 27 Leyland Lynxes in the fleet and these too are concentrated south of the Tyne in Sunderland and South Shields.

Busways has a substantial fleet of Mercedes-Benz minibuses. Sixty were delivered in 1986-87, all Reeve Burgess conversions of 709D vans. There is also a batch of Alexander-bodied Renaults. For a period in the early '90s most minibuses carried Tyne & Wear fleetnames. The Tyne & Wear Omnibus Co was a post-deregulation thorn in Busways' side, running Bristol LHs on competing services. It was taken over by Go-Ahead Northern in 1989, then immediately re-sold to Busways and its LHs were then quickly phased out. Busways minibus operations were then rebranded with the Tyne & Wear name. However that is being phased out and almost all minibuses now carry Busways livery. The competing minibus operation started in 1991 by Welcome was taken over by Busways in 1993 and closed down in 1994. It had operated 38 new buses, mainly Renault S75s and Optare MetroRiders. The former Welcome S75s have now been transferred to the Stagecoach Darlington fleet, while the MetroRiders are with Newcastle Busways.

Top **Busways has a sizeable fleet of Alexander R-type double-deckers. Most are Leyland Olympians, but there are also 10 Scania N113s which entered service in 1990. Stagecoach is adding more R-types to the operation – but of lowheight construction and on Volvo Olympian chassis.** Tony Wilson

Centre **When the Bexleybus operation of London Buses lost most of its contracts in 1991 a fleet of 28 three-year-old Olympians was suddenly up for sale. Twenty-one of the vehicles were bought by Busways. The buses have Greater Manchester-style Northern Counties bodies and are divided between the Newcastle and Sunderland fleets.** Mike Harris

Right **The blue in the South Shields Busways livery is a reminder of South Shields Corporation Transport, which was absorbed by the Tyneside PTE 25 years ago. This is a 1978 Atlantean in the town centre. The individual town identities are being abandoned as buses receive Stagecoach colours, with the fleet running simply as Stagecoach Busways.** Russell Upcraft

Blue Bus Services is another Busways operation. It runs ECW-bodied Bristol REs which have come from a number of operators and which wear their age well. The youngest are 1975 P-registered buses from Thamesdown. Modernity struck at Blue Bus in 1991 with the introduction to the operation of Busways' first two Darts. These have Plaxton Pointer bodies and were initially the only new buses in a fleet made up of elderly Leopards and REs. More Pointers have since joined the Blue Bus operation. There are 60 vehicles in the Blue Bus operation, including almost 20 Atlanteans. Blue Bus services run mainly to the North West and reach out to the city's rural hinterland. The Blue Bus name was adopted as part of Busways post-deregulation strategy. Newcastle's municipal buses were dark blue until around 1950.

Between Sunderland and South Shields services are operated by Busways using vehicles in Economic livery. These are Leyland Atlanteans, Olympians and Lynxes and five Dennis Darts. Economic was a small operator running between the two towns until 1975, when it was bought by the Tyne & Wear PTE. The name was revived by Busways in 1986 and is currently carried on over 20 buses.

Favourite is another revival of an old independent company's name and is used primarily for operations in County Durham. Favourite was started by Busways in 1987 to compete with Trimdon Motor Services in response to Trimdon's incursion into Newcastle with its Tyne & Wear Omnibus fleet. The first buses were ex-Greater Manchester Leopards and the livery they carried was adopted for the Favourite operation. Since then Atlanteans and Fleetlines have been transferred into the fleet from the main Busways operation, and three Plaxton-bodied Dennis Darts have been allocated to it. Favourite runs 25 vehicles and its operations embrace Sunderland. Busways also has a coaching subsidiary, Armstrong Galley.

Top **Blue Bus Services has all the trappings of an independent business, with its distinctive livery and unusual fleet. ECW-bodied Bristol REs are still used on all-day service. This Leyland-engined example was new to Colchester Corporation in 1972. It wears its age well.** Steve Warburton

Centre **Economic's main operation is between South Shields and Sunderland. This 1978 Atlantean is one of two-dozen buses in Economic colours.** Steve Warburton

Left **Favourite run services in County Durham and through to Sunderland. The most modern buses in Favourite livery are two Dennis Darts with Plaxton Pointer bodies delivered in 1994. There are 23 Plaxton Pointers in the Busways fleet.** Roy Marshall

The two other major operators in the Tyne & Wear area are both former NBC subsidiaries, Northumbria and the Go-Ahead Group. Northumbria was bought by its management in 1987 and a holding company, Proudmutual, was set up. Proudmutual subsequently bought Kentish Bus in the south, and then local operator Moor-Dale Coaches. In 1994 Proudmutual was purchased by British Bus. Following the takeover a large order was placed for new vehicles. These are Optare MetroRiders and Scanias with both single-deck and double-deck East Lancs bodies, including the first example of East Lancs' new Cityzen design. The fleet retains the distinctive red, grey and white livery which was adopted in 1986, when Northumbria was created out of the northern operations of United Auto, whose territory in the early 1980s (and for many years before) stretched from Berwick in the north to Scarborough in the south.

Berwick remains the northernmost town in Northumbria territory and here the company is the major operator following cutbacks by Lowland Omnibuses. The River Tweed marks the northern limit of the company's operations, while the Tyne effectively marks its southern boundary. During the Proudmutual period a lot of the group's investment in new vehicles was directed towards the considerable expansion of Kentish Bus operations into London. Northumbria consequently has not received many new buses in recent years. The newest double-deckers are eight Volvo Olympians with Northern Counties Palatine II bodies, the first examples of the type in the North East. These striking vehicles have coach seats and are used on the Hexham to Newcastle service. They were delivered in 1994. Other modern types are Optare Deltas, of which there are 17, Optare MetroRiders (which include ex-Lancaster vehicles) and, going back to 1988, Alexander-bodied long-wheelbase Leyland Olympians which marked the first break from established NBC vehicle types.

Most of the remainder of Northumbria's fleet dates back to NBC days with the usual mixture of Nationals, VRTs and Olympians. However, many of the Nationals have in fact been post-privatisation purchases from other former NBC operators with a good number having been transferred north from Kentish Bus. Similarly many of the Olympians were new to other NBC subsidiaries and they include unusual ECW-bodied double-deck coaches which were developed for London area commuter and Green Line services in the mid-1980s. One of these has had its body destroyed by a fire and was rebodied in 1992 by Northern Counties with an extra-long version of that company's standard double-deck body. Other non-standard double-deckers in the fleet are a few ex-Busways Atlanteans and Fleetlines and some former GM Buses Fleetlines. Older minibuses are Freight Rover Sherpas and MCW Metroriders delivered in 1986-87.

Top Striking new additions to the Northumbria fleet in 1994 were eight Volvo Olympians with Northern Counties Palatine II bodies. They have high-backed seats and operate the Newcastle to Hexham service. Mike Harris

Centre Northumbria runs 17 DAF SB220s with Optare Delta bodywork. These are finished to a high specification with 48 high-backed seats, tinted glazing and electronic destination displays. This one was new in 1990. Mike Harris

Right Older types in the Northumbria fleet include Bristol VRTs and Leyland Olympians, most of which were delivered to United Auto in NBC days. This 1982 Olympian with ECW body is among the oldest examples of its type. Russell Upcraft

Moor-Dale was acquired by Proudmutual in 1989 and initially retained its independence from the much larger Northumbria operation. However following the British Bus takeover the Moor-Dale coaching interests were sold to former directors of Northumbria, while the bus services were absorbed into the Hunters operation. This is a continuation by Northumbria of the operations of Hunters of Seaton Delaval, an old-established operator whose services were taken over by British Bus in July 1994.

While still independent Moor-Dale bought two Leyland Lynxes, and these are still in the fleet, now in Hunters colours. Under Proudmutual control three Dennis Darts were added in 1993. These have Plaxton Pointer bodies and are operated in Cramlington, again with Hunters names. Rochester & Marshall of Hexham, a Moor-Dale subsidiary, was also acquired by Proudmutual in 1989. It was closed down in 1994 and its operations absorbed by Northumbria.

Hunters main area of operation is around North Shields and Cramlington. When it was bought by British Bus the 15-strong fleet comprised a variety of second-hand types including ex-Greater Manchester Atlanteans and former NBC Leopards with ECW B51 dual-purpose bodywork. Under British Bus control some of these have been replaced by buses transferred in from Northumbria.

Small operators in Northumberland are few and far between. North Rider of Cramlington was founded in 1991. It operates a minibus service from the Metro station at Four Lane Ends using ex-GM Buses Iveco Fords but in 1995 bought some unusual big buses – Badgerline's last three Bristol REs. Hexham-based Tyne Valley operates to nearby towns running Leopards. These typically have Plaxton Elite Express bodies, a legacy of the influence New Bus Grant had on coaches in the 1970s. By specifying power-operated doors and using the vehicles on regular bus services, coach operators were able to claim capital grants which were aimed at helping bus operators buy new buses to speed fleet replacement and encourage the extension of one-man-operation. At Haltwhistle, Wright Bros of Nenthead operate south to Alston using Bedford coaches. A once-daily link is made by Wright Bros from Newcastle's cavernous Eldon Square bus station to Alston via Hexham, with a summertime extension through to Penrith.

To the north, a Bedlington town service is operated by Raisbeck using the only Volvo B7M in operation in Britain. It has a mid-mounted vertical 7-litre engine and an East Lancs 53-seat body. Two mid-1970s Bedford YLQ coaches make up the remainder of the Raisbeck fleet and cover the route when the B7M is off for maintenance. All three vehicles owned by Raisbeck were bought new. The B7M, purchased in 1985, was Volvo's first look at a light-weight bus for the UK, a role now filled by the rather different B6.

Top The Hunters of Seaton Delaval operation is now part of Northumbria, having been taken over in 1994. This 1987 Lynx was originally operated by Moor-Dale and was repainted in Hunters colours in 1995. Malcolm King

Centre Moor-Dale Coaches has been absorbed by Northumbria but has been retained as a trading name by the Hunters subsidiary. This Dennis Dart is one of three delivered to Moor-Dale in 1993. It has Plaxton bodywork. Richard Godfrey

Left Few buses are truly unique, but Raisbeck run one which is, a Volvo B7M with 53-seat East Lancs body. The mid-engined B7M was being evaluated by Volvo as a possible light-weight alternative to the Bedfords and Fords being run by a number of British operators.

The Go-Ahead Group has expanded considerably since it started off as a management buy-out from NBC of what was then Northern General. That was in 1987. Now it has shaken off the old Northern image, and since 1992 the bulk of the company's operations in the North East have been in the hands of five key subsidiary companies. Each has a distinctive livery, although all of the fleets share a common fleet numbering system.

In Gateshead, until 1995 the group's headquarters, Go-Ahead Gateshead is the trading name of the rather ponderous but geographically precise Gateshead & District Omnibus Co, the town's main operator. The Go-Ahead Group has maintained a healthy fleet replacement programme, and has been a major buyer of Dennis's popular Dart. Its initial orders had bodywork by Wright of Ballymena, and Wright-bodied Darts are among the more modern buses in the Go-Ahead Gateshead operation. These were followed by Dennis Lances with Optare Sigma bodies, 14 of which entered service in 1994 and made Go-Ahead Gateshead the first major user of Sigmas. Both Optare and Wright use a similar method of body construction, based on aluminium extrusions developed by Alusuisse.

Go-Ahead Gateshead's double-deckers include standard NBC Olympians, MCW Metrobuses, and Alexander-bodied Olympians. The Metrobuses are from three batches totalling almost 100 bought by Northern General in the early and mid-1980s, a rare example of an NBC company ordering double-deckers from a supplier other than Leyland. Go-Ahead Gateshead has just over 50. The Alexander-bodied Olympians were bought in 1989. There are five, and they are the only new double-deckers purchased by the privatised Go-Ahead Group for its North East operations. They have Cummins L10 engines, a type for which Northern General was an early buyer. Most of the company's B- and C-registered Olympians are L10-powered, at a time when Gardner's 6LXB was the normal NBC choice. Go-Ahead Gateshead's minibuses are mainly Optare MetroRiders and the company also runs full-size Optare Deltas.

North of the Tyne, the Go-Ahead Group's main operation is the Tynemouth & District Omnibus Co, trading as Coastline. This company made the headlines in 1994 with the introduction of five Dennis Lance SLFs to a service in North Shields and Whitley Bay. The SLF (Super Low Floor) allows access for pushchairs and wheelchairs, providing a service which is accessible to most people. The Coastline buses have bodywork by Wright, to a considerably more stylish design than that found on Coastline's Wright-bodied Darts. This is primarily a double-deck fleet, however, with both Atlanteans and Olympians. The Atlanteans include 10 Alexander-bodied buses dating from 1981. These were new to the Tyne & Wear PTE and were purchased by Northern General when they were just a few months old.

Top **Go-Ahead has a large number of ECW-bodied Olympians which are part of the group's NBC legacy. Those delivered in 1985 are unusual in having Cummins L10 engines at a time when the Gardner 6LXB was the NBC standard.** Russell Upcraft

Centre **The Go-Ahead group lived up to its name by being the first operator outside London to order a batch of low-floor Dennis Lance SLFs. Five with Wright Endurance bodywork are operated by Coastline.** Russell Upcraft

Right **Among the oldest double-deckers operated by the Go-Ahead group are a batch of Roe-bodied Leyland Atlanteans which were new in 1980. VFM Buses runs 13.** Mike Harris

Metro Taxis fleetnames are carried by some 10 buses run by the Go-Ahead Group as a low-cost operating unit under the control of Coastline. These are all elderly Atlanteans used primarily on tendered services and contracts in the North Shields area.

VFM Buses – the initials stand for Value For Money – is the catchy identity of the Tyneside Omnibus Co, based on the south bank of the Tyne. It runs a similar mix of vehicles, Atlanteans, Olympians and Darts, on services in South Shields and down to Sunderland. The Atlanteans which were inherited from NBC days have ECW and Roe bodies, both to standard NBC specifications.

In and around Sunderland services are provided by the Sunderland & District Omnibus Co, trading as Wear Buses. It has most of the Group's Leyland Nationals (all of which are Mark 2s), and all 12 of its Lynxes, bought in 1989 and among the company's first purchases after privatisation. Wear Buses' double-deckers are Atlanteans, Metrobuses and Olympians, the newest dating from 1986. Services stretch north to Gateshead and Newcastle and south as far as Hartlepool. Wear Buses' Darts include 17 with Marshall bodywork. The Go-Ahead Group has 120 similar buses on order for 1995 delivery, although most will be for its operations in the south.

The last of the major parts of what was the old the Northern General Transport company has retained that name and provides services in County Durham from depots at Chester-le-Street and Stanley. Chester-le-Street is where the original NGT company started running buses in 1914. Unique to the present-day Northern fleet are the only VRTs operated by the Group in the North East. There are fewer than 10 left and they have relatively uncommon full-height (14ft 6in) ECW bodies. Most NBC VRTs had 13ft 8in high bodywork which took full advantage of the VRT's low frame. Northern also has Atlanteans, Metrobuses and Olympians, and the Group's original batch of 14 Optare Deltas, delivered in 1989. It has the biggest Dart fleet, with 36, including six Plaxton-bodied examples which were originally part of the Shaws fleet. Northern services operate east to Sunderland and north to Newcastle.

An interesting feature of the Go-Ahead Group has been the way in which it has purchased small operators and – outwardly at least – left them to their own devices. By retaining the individual identities of small businesses the group is able to capitalise on any customer goodwill, something which is lost when a small company's identity is erased by a new, big, owner. However the takeover of OK Travel in 1995 has seen some rationalisation among the operations of the group's smaller businesses.

Top **New for Wear Buses in 1994 were 17 Dennis Darts with 40-seat Marshall bodies. The Marshall body is a direct descendant of the original Duple body developed for the Dart in 1988.** Michael Fowler

Centre **Metro Taxis runs elderly Atlanteans, including a number with ECW bodywork. Metro Taxis was set up as a low-cost unit within the Go-Ahead group.** Russell Upcraft

Right **Not all NBC subsidiaries happily accepted Leyland's Olympian when there were alternatives coming on to the market. Northern General was one, and its orders in the early 1980s included Metrobuses. Ten Mark IIs delivered in 1983 are now running for Northern.** Mike Harris

The first small operator taken over by the Go-Ahead Group was Gypsy Queen, which operates between Durham and Langley Park. Gypsy Queen was purchased in 1989 but still has the air of a family firm with a fleet which includes a Carlyle-bodied Dennis Dart, the first Duple 300-series bus to be built (on a Volvo B10M chassis) and a Mercedes mini transferred from the main fleet. There are seven vehicles in the Gypsy Queen fleet, which is now controlled by OK.

Two more small firms were acquired in 1992, Low Fell Coaches and Shaws of Craghead. Low Fell Coaches came to prominence in the early 1980s when it won a protracted battle for a licence to operate a cross-Tyne service from Gateshead to Newcastle. This was at a time when service licences were tightly controlled and the Tyne & Wear PTE's planners were trying to encourage cross-river travellers to use the expensive new Metro. Low Fell succeeded, and the service still runs. The Low Fell fleet is made up mainly of vehicles owned at the time of the take-over, including a Leyland Tiger and a Dennis Javelin with rare Duple 300-series bus bodies. A later addition, in 1993, was a Dennis Lance with Alexander PS-type body, a relatively unusual combination – most Lances bodied by Alexander have Strider bodies. This started life in SMT livery as an exhibit at the Coach & Bus 91 show and was in fact the first Lance with an Alexander body. Control of Low Fell passed to OK in 1995 and one of the first signs of the changes was the replacement of older vehicles in the fleet by two Alexander-bodied Volvo B10Bs transferred from OK.

Shaws was a coach operator which took advantage of deregulation to introduce bus services, starting with a route between Stanley and Chester-le-Street. Services are still operated in that area, and were also run into Gateshead and Newcastle for a time, principally with Leyland Nationals transferred from other parts of the Go-Ahead Group's North East based fleet. When Shaws services were cut back in 1995 to serve just the Stanley area the six most modern buses, M-registered Plaxton-bodied Darts, were transferred to Northern.

The Go-Ahead Group made three acquisitions in 1995. The smallest was J H Hammel of Stanley, which trades as Diamond. Hammel owned 10 vehicles, all bought new. The oldest buses in the fleet were Bedford Y-series with Duple Dominant bus bodies. When Bedford ceased bus building, Hammel switched to Dennis, first with three Javelin buses and more recently with a Dart. Two of the Javelins have Duple 300-series bus bodies. The third Javelin and the Dart were bodied by Plaxton. The appearance of Shaws vehicles on Diamond routes is becoming increasingly commonplace.

Top **The first Dennis Dart for the Go-Ahead group was delivered in 1991 to Gypsy Queen. It has Carlyle bodywork and is seen on its regular route between Durham and Langley Park.** Malcolm King

Upper centre **Shaws of Craghead were taken over by the Go-Ahead group in 1992 and the name is still retained for some operations around Stanley, as illustrated by a National 2.** P Chancellor

Lower centre **The takeover of Diamond of Stanley in 1995 consolidated the Go-Ahead group's position in the area. Among the vehicles acquired was this Plaxton-bodied Dart which was Diamond's newest bus. The operation continues outwardly unchanged.** P Chancellor

Right **The acquisition of OK by the Go-Ahead group in 1995 saw some changes to the way its smaller subsidiaries were run, including the transfer of control of Low Fell Coaches to OK. One fruit of this was the appearance of this 12-month-old Volvo B10B in Low Fell colours, applied in an OK-style layout.** Malcolm King

OK Travel operates some three dozen Atlanteans, including seven long-wheelbase models with 86-seat Metro-Cammell bodies which were new to the Tyne & Wear PTE in 1979. Gavin Booth

Five former London Transport Bristol LHs are run by OK. They have 39-seat ECW bodies and were new in 1977. Gavin Booth

Built as a demonstrator for operation in Bangkok, this rear-engined Leyland Tiger has an ECW body which had full-depth sliding windows and coach seats, before being rebuilt for local bus operation by OK. It is seen in Sunderland. Malcolm King

The second Go-Ahead Group acquisition in the North East in 1995 was of an altogether different character. This was the biggest privately-owned bus company in the region: OK Travel. OK's history can be traced back to just before World War I, but its most rapid growth has occurred since deregulation. In 1985 it operated some 70 buses and coaches. When the company sold out to the Go-Ahead Group it was running over 200. Indeed, in 1994 it bought more new vehicles – 47 – than in any other year in its long history. These comprised 33 Volvo B6s, 21 with Alexander Dash bodies and 11 Plaxton Pointers, five Volvo B10Bs, also bodied by Alexander, and nine Mercedes minibuses.

The most interesting addition to the fleet in 1994 was none of these, however, but was instead a unique rear-engined Tiger with ECW bodywork. It had been built by Leyland in the mid-1980s when the company was pursuing an order for 4,000 buses for operation in Bangkok – an order which never materialised. The Leyland story would have been a very different one if it had. The mid-engined Tiger was unsuitable for the extreme conditions in Thailand, as was the then new low-frame Lynx. Leyland's answer was to install a TL11 engine in the rear of a modified Tiger chassis and to have this bodied by ECW. The demonstrator never got any further east than Lowestoft, and in 1991 it was bought by the Leyland DAF football club for use as a team coach. OK Travel acquired it in 1993, at which stage it had two doors, coach seats, and full-depth sliding windows. It has been extensively modified to make it suitable for use as a bus.

The remainder of the OK fleet is not without interest. All of its double-deckers are Leylands, mainly Atlanteans. Most are second-hand, with a fair number having come from South Yorkshire Transport. These have Alexander bodies. There are also Atlanteans which have been transferred in from other Go-Ahead Group companies. OK Travel does not use fleet numbers, identifying vehicles by the number in the registration mark. To avoid duplication with existing buses in the fleet a number of the ex-SYT Atlanteans have been re-registered, as have some ex-Greater Manchester Atlanteans. The newest double-deckers in the fleet are five Northern Counties-bodied Olympians.

The single-deck fleet is dominated by Leyland Leopards. There are over 70, the biggest fleet of the type in the North East and, indeed, the biggest fleet south of the border. A number are in fact ex-SBG vehicles with Alexander Y-type bodies. There are T-type Leopards too, although some of these were new to Eastern Counties and have come north from East Anglia, rather than south from Scotland. Much of OK's post-deregulation expansion has been on the strength of judicious buying of Leopards. Other examples of the trusty Leyland model came from Inter Valley Link in South Wales, and have East Lancs bodies. There are also Leopards in the fleet which were bought new.

Until the arrival of the B6s and B10Bs, the only rear-engined single-deck buses in the fleet were Optare-bodied DAF SB220s. OK also runs mid-engined DAFs with Duple 320 coach bodies and these are used on service. Small buses play but a small part in the OK operation. Most are new Mercedes or older Iveco Fords. The company's depots are at Bishop Auckland, Peterlee and Team Valley and it serves major centres in County Durham, Tyne & Wear and Cleveland and has routes running to Gateshead, Newcastle, Sunderland, Stockton, Middlesbrough and Darlington, plus some operations reaching into North Yorkshire.

The Go-Ahead Group's third acquisition in 1995 was Armstrongs of Ebchester, just north of Consett, which operates local services using either Leopard coaches, a Mercedes minibus, or a high-capacity (60-seat) Leopard with Plaxton Derwent body. A later generation of Derwent body is carried on the company's newest bus, a Scania K93.

Bishop Auckland was for many years an island of independent operation surrounded by Tilling, BET and, later, NBC buses. Small fleets still serve the town. Bond Bros operate from Willington with second-hand Atlanteans, Fleetlines and a Leopard. The Eden of West Auckland for many years has run a predominantly Leopard fleet, and still uses both bus- and coach-bodied Leopards on its services, which run as far south as Richmond in North Yorkshire. The company also operates infrequently to Sunderland. The newest buses in the fleet are three MCW Metroriders purchased in 1988, and in 1994 it finally succumbed to the attraction of second-hand Leyland Nationals which have replaced some of the older Leopards.

Weardale Motor Services is another old-established company which operates from Stanhope to Bishop Auckland and to Newcastle. There are three double-deckers in the fleet – an Atlantean bought new in 1970, plus two second-hand examples – but the company's services are operated primarily by Leyland Leopards with Plaxton coach bodies. One Leopard was rebodied in 1993 by East Lancs. Three older coaches – two Volvo B58s and a Leopard – were built with two-plus-three seating in their Plaxton bodies, raising the seating capacity to an impressive 68.

Gardiner's of Spennymoor is a small operator serving Bishop Auckland, as well as Chester-le-Street and Durham. Coaches are often used on service work, but there are Leyland Swift buses in the fleet which have Reeve Burgess bodies and were purchased from Green of Kirkintilloch in 1991 when they were two years old. There are also a couple of Mercedes minibuses, one with Optare StarRider body, and some MCW Metroriders.

Top **Bond Bros of Willington is one of the declining number of established County Durham independents which remains independent. Its current fleet includes this 1980 Leyland Leopard with Willowbrook body which started life with United Auto.** Steve Warburton

Centre **The Eden operates five Leyland Nationals, acquired in 1993. All have been fitted with Volvo engines and have Ulster registration marks which hide their age and origin. This bus was new to London Transport in 1979 as a two-door 36-seater. It now has 42 high-backed coach seats.** Mike Harris

Below **Gardiners of Spennymoor operate two MCW Metrorider minibuses. New in 1987, they moved north from the Welwyn Hatfield Line fleet in 1994.** Steve Warburton

Right **Leyland's Leopard has a reputation as a straightforward, reliable chassis. Weardale bought this one in 1974 and in 1993 decided to extend its life by removing the original Plaxton body and having a new East Lancs EL2000 bus body fitted.** Tony Wilson

Despite the Go-Ahead Group's take-overs, there are still a substantial number of small operators in its territory. In its Gateshead heartland and in Derwentside Classic Coaches of Annfield Plain operate services with a variety of second-hand types. Atlanteans and Leyland Nationals predominate. Classic Coaches underlines its independence by carrying the lettering "Not part of the Northern group" on the front of most of its buses. The company's first new buses, Dennis Darts, were delivered in 1995. Other Dennises added to the fleet have been two East Lancs-bodied Dominators from Maidstone & District.

Classicliner or Superliner? The most consistent competition for the Go-Ahead group comes from Classic Coaches of Annfield Plain. Classic's fleet is made up mainly of Nationals, but includes four Atlanteans, the oldest of which is an ECW-bodied bus which was new to East Kent in 1976. Note the lettering below the windscreen which reads "Not part of the Northern group". The similar-looking Superliner is operated by Northern and is a 1986 Metrobus II.
P Chancellor, Russell Upcraft

Whitley Bay, served by Coastline, has a local minibus service provided by the 10-bus Amberline operation. All are second-hand; the most interesting is an ex-London Buses RH-class Iveco Ford which formed part of the short-lived Orpington Buses operation. Amberline's service runs into Newcastle.

Across the Tyne in South Shields, VFM Buses shares operations in the town not just with South Shields Busways, but with Catch A Bus, the name adopted in 1986 by Hylton Castle Motors for its expanding bus operation. Catch A Bus is based in East Boldon, and also serves Sunderland to the south. Its fleet is a varied one. Its newest buses are Dennis Darts with Plaxton Pointer bodies. Before these were delivered, the company went to Plaxton to have six Leopards rebodied with Derwent bus bodies. That was in 1991-92. It also runs Leopards with Duple Dominant bus bodies and a couple of Nottingham's Lilac Leopards of the mid-1970s, which had Dominant E bodies with bus seats in a coach shell. The most interesting buses in the fleet are two Atlanteans with East Lancs Sprint single-deck bodies. They are 1974 long-wheelbase AN68/2s and were rebodied in 1992 before entering service with Catch A Bus. Both came from Yorkshire Rider and have lost their original SUG-M registrations in favour of Ulster HIL marks. East Lancs Atlantean Sprints are few and far between with the only other users being Southampton Citybus (which took the first), South Notts and Sheffield Omnibus.

In Wear Buses country, St George Travel of Washington operates Mercedes minibuses on two services to Chester-le-Street. George Bell of New Silksworth on the outskirts of Sunderland runs a service into the town centre. An Iveco Ford mini shares this with an unusual Leyland Cub which was the first of that type to be bodied by Reeve Burgess and the only one built by the Derbyshire coachbuilder for psv rather than welfare use. Jolly of South Hylton ran into Sunderland for over 70 years but the Duple-bodied Bedfords which operated the route for the last 15 years came to the end of the road in mid-1995 when Mr Jolly retired and his service was taken over by Busways with Dennis Darts in Favourite livery replacing the Jolly Bedfords.

Top **Amberline of Whitley Bay run minibuses. One of the more interesting is this Robin Hood-bodied Iveco which was new to London Buses in 1985. They were bought for the Orpington Buses operation.** Mike Harris

Centre **When Darlington Transport closed in 1994, Catch A Bus bought seven of its vehicles – Plaxton-bodied Leopards which had been new to Lancashire United in 1976. One is seen in South Shields.** Mike Harris

Right **The idea of rebodying Atlanteans as single-deckers never really caught on, although a few were treated – mainly by East Lancs in the early 1990s. Catch A Bus has two which have 1992 bodies on 1974 long-wheelbase AN68/2 chassis. The chassis came from Yorkshire Rider. In their new guise the Atlanteans are 46-seaters.** Stewart J Brown

An entrant to Sunderland at deregulation was Michael Franks, serving Easington Lane, some 10 miles to the south-west of the town. Franks operates six Leyland Leopard coaches. A number of Sunderland local services are provided by Redby Travel, with a mixed fleet, including the company's first new buses, two Alexander-bodied Volvo B6s which entered service in August 1995. Most interesting are four Dennis Lancets with Alexander's angular P-type body. These were new in 1984 to Northern Scottish, which was looking for a replacement for its large fleet of Fords. The most common type is the Leyland National, re-powered with 10-litre Volvo engines. Modern second-hand additions to the fleet have included a pair of J-registered Lynx IIs which were new to Whitelaw of Stonehouse.

At Tantobie, Hunter's (not to be confused with the Seaton Delaval based company) operates locally with Duple-bodied Bedford Y-series and a Mercedes 609D minibus. Bob Smith Travel of Langley Park provides services in and around Durham. The regular bus on the Langley Park to Durham route is a 1980 Leopard with a 1990 Willowbrook Warrior bus body. The chassis was new to Midland Red and originally carried a Willowbrook coach body. The company also has Leopard coaches, and operates minibuses locally in Durham. Scarlet Band of West Cornforth run into Durham, normally with ex-SBG Alexander-bodied Leopards.

Top **The first new bus for Redby Travel entered service in the summer of 1995. It was a Volvo B6 with Alexander Dash body. The combination of the old-style Dash windscreen and an N-prefix registration point to it having been a stock vehicle built earlier in the year.** Steve Warburton

Centre **Bob Smith Travel serves Durham, usually with a minibus. The newest is a 1992 Iveco Ford with Carlyle body which was originally operated by Robson of Thornaby-on-Tees.** Mike Harris

Right **The Scarlet Band bus fleet is made up of second-hand Leopards and minibuses. The latter include an Alexander-bodied Dodge S56 acquired from United Auto.** Steve Warburton

Darlington is a town which has seen remarkable changes in its bus services. In a much-publicised battle at the end of 1994 Stagecoach launched new routes in the town, forcing the closure of Darlington Transport, the municipally-owned fleet which had been put up for sale by the district council. Darlington Transport has vanished without trace, its place taken by Stagecoach Darlington, running a smart fleet in corporate white-and-stripes livery. Stagecoach Darlington is a trading name for Cleveland Transit, although the operation was initially under the wing of Busways.

The biggest buses are ex-Busways Atlanteans with panoramic-windowed Alexander bodies and ex-Cleveland Fleetlines, but these are in a minority. Smaller buses play a big part in the Stagecoach Darlington operation, with Alexander-bodied Dennis Darts, Volvo B6s and Mercedes 709Ds sharing the bulk of the work with Plaxton-bodied Renault S75s transferred south from the erstwhile Welcome operation in Newcastle.

The other key operator in the town is United, since November 1994 part of the West Midlands Travel group. The head-on competition with Darlington Transport which characterised the arrival of Stagecoach has vanished. Instead the town's two main operators have a joint map and timetable leaflet, such is the spirit of co-operation which now prevails. United's headquarters are in Darlington (although no longer in the grand United House, which has been demolished and replaced by a Safeway supermarket car park) and its area of influence extends north to Newcastle and south to Ripon. It runs 250 vehicles. All of this is a far cry from the company's heyday when it had over 1,000 buses and coaches serving most of the North East.

United shrunk in 1986, when its northern portion became Northumbria Motor Services and its southern operations were transferred to East Yorkshire as a prelude to deregulation and privatisation. It was sold to Caldaire in 1987 and when the Yorkshire-based Caldaire group split in 1992, United became part of the new Westcourt group set up by former Caldaire directors. Caldaire/Westcourt also ran TMS and Tees & District, and these too are now subsidiaries of West Midlands Travel.

Top **Stagecoach Darlington operates a mixed fleet which includes buses drafted in from other Stagecoach subsidiaries in the North East. This 1977 Alexander-bodied Fleetline came from Busways.** Stewart J Brown

Centre **United's newest double-deckers are five 1993 Leyland Olympians with Cummins engines and Alexander R-type bodies. One leaves Darlington for Newcastle.** Mike Harris

Right **United's minibus fleet includes Mercedes, Optare and Dodge models, the last-named being 1987 S56s with Alexander bodies. They operate under the Roadranger name.** Mike Harris

A small number of Teesside buses retain the old dark blue livery, as shown by a former Bristol Omnibus LH in Middlesbrough. Tony Wilson

Tees & District was formed by Caldaire in 1990 to take over United's Cleveland operations, and it covers an area stretching from Stockton down to Scarborough. TMS – Teesside Motor Services – was a post-deregulation offshoot of Trimdon Motor Services, and both TMS and Trimdon were purchased by Caldaire in 1990. The old-established Trimdon business was quickly absorbed into the United fleet, and some of its Leopard and Tiger buses are still in use. However TMS has continued to provide services in and around Stockton and Middlesbrough. All three fleets are numbered in a common series.

The change of ownership hasn't led to any change in vehicle policy as yet. United still run ex-NBC VRTs and Olympians. There are just over 80 Bristol LHs in the Tees & District and TMS fleets making it easily the biggest anywhere, although many are now delicensed. There is also a substantial fleet of second-hand Tigers for uses on inter-urban services operated by both United and Tees & District. The majority have Plaxton Paramount bodies, but of more interest are seven ex-West Riding vehicles with Alexander TE-type bodywork. Second-hand National 2s are also a feature of both the United and the Tees & District operations. Most were new to Ribble but were acquired from Shearings in 1991. Four are ex-Blackpool Transport. More recently around 20 Leyland Nationals from the West Midlands fleet were transferred to TMS to replace LHs.

More modern additions to the fleet under Caldaire/Westcourt ownership have been Optares. First came Deltas, and then Vectas. There are 43 MAN-based Vectas running for the three associated businesses, giving the area the biggest concentration of MAN buses in the UK. The newest buses – running in Middlesbrough and Redcar for the Tees & District fleet – are Optare's latest model, the Prisma. The Prisma is built on a Mercedes-Benz O405 chassis and incorporates a standard Mercedes front end which lacks the styling flair of Optare's own designs. There are 25 Prismas being delivered in 1995.

Unusual buses in the United fleet at Darlington are two Leyland Tigers with Alexander (Belfast) Q-type bodies, bought for evaluation in 1990 as part of United's quest for a low-cost bus to succeed the LH.

United's minibuses fall into three main types. The oldest, a relic of NBC's buying policy, are Alexander-bodied Renaults and Reeve Burgess-converted Mercedes L608Ds. Some retain old-style Roadranger livery but most are now in cream and red fleet colours, although still with Roadranger names. The newest are altogether more attractive Optare MetroRiders which are based at Richmond. The last purchases before the company was sold to WM Travel were 10 Olympians from Atlas Bus in London, following the loss of a London Transport contract by Atlas. Nine have Northern Counties bodies while the tenth is bodied by Leyland. These buses are divided between the United and Tees & District fleets.

Centre and left **The first Optare Prismas entered service in 1995, based on Mercedes-Benz O405 underframes. Five were delivered to Tees & District in the summer of 1995. More are to follow. However the fleet has also been modernised with some selective second-hand buses, including Northern Counties-bodied Leyland Olympians from Atlas Bus in London, rendered redundant through a change in tendered service contracts.** Mike Harris

Change affected United, TMS and Tees & District in the latter part of 1995. In North Yorkshire United closed its bases at Northallerton and Thirsk following the loss of tendered services to smaller operators, and Tees & District withdrew from Hartlepool in exchange for some operations elsewhere in Cleveland Transit territory.

Cleveland Transit is the main operator in Cleveland. The name was adopted in 1974 as being rather more catchy than the Langbaurgh, Middlesbrough and Stockton joint board – which is what it was. It succeeded Teesside Municipal Transport which had itself only been created in 1968 as an amalgamation of three municipal fleets – Stockton, Middlesbrough and the Teesside Railless Traction Board. Cleveland Transit was privatised in a management-led employee buy-out in 1991 and two years later bought the Kingston-upon-Hull City Transport business, jointly with KHCT's employees. In 1994 it sold out to Stagecoach. Cleveland Transit is for the time being retaining its attractive green, yellow and white livery.

Cleveland Transit was among the last buyers of Daimler Fleetlines – by then being built at Leyland of course – and although it didn't get the last chassis to be built (it went to South Notts), it did get the last Fleetlines to enter service. These are eight FE30AGR models which took to the road in 1983 and are the only Fleetlines with Y-suffix registrations. The Fleetlines were followed by Dennis Dominators although some of these have now been sold, with a number heading south to have their roofs removed to join the London Pride sightseeing fleet. New Volvo Olympians with Northern Counties bodies joined the fleet in 1995.

Since 1989 Cleveland has bought mainly single-deckers. Initially it standardised on the Leyland Lynx, of which there are 30 in operation, including one ex-demonstrator. With the demise of the Lynx the company switched to Volvo B10Bs with Plaxton Verde bodies, and B6s – its first midis – which were also bodied by Plaxton. At the time of the Stagecoach takeover there were 12 B10Bs and eight B6s in the fleet. B10Ms have now been added by Stagecoach, and these have Northern Counties Paladin bodies. Minibuses are Renault S56s with Northern Counties bodies.

Cleveland Coaches, the coaching arm of Cleveland Transit, was sold to Delta Coaches in 1995. This was part of a deal which saw an end to bus service competition from Delta. Delta had been running Bristol REs in Stockton and Middlesbrough. Its routes – but not the REs – were taken over by Cleveland Transit. Five REs have been retained by Delta for contract work. There is competition from Robson of Thornaby-on-Tees, running Stockton local services with Leyland Nationals and assorted minibuses. Leven Valley operate in the Eston area. The company is actually based in North Yorkshire, at Great Ayton, and also operates south to Northallerton. Most of its buses are Mercedes 709Ds with coachbuilt bodies by Alexander, Dormobile and TBP.

Top **When Stagecoach took over Cleveland Transit there were still 36 Northern Counties-bodied Fleetlines in operation. Some have since been moved to Darlington, being replaced by new Volvo Olympians. These have Northern Counties bodies which look little different from those on the 15-year-old buses they are replacing.** Mike Harris

Centre **While still independent Cleveland Transit was buying Plaxton-bodied Volvo B6s and B10Bs. This is a B6, one of eight delivered in 1993-94.** Tony Wilson

Right **Stagecoach has introduced Volvo B10Ms with Northern Counties bodies to the Cleveland Transit operation. There are 10, delivered in Cleveland rather than Stagecoach colours.** Mike Harris

To the north of Cleveland county lies Hartlepool. It is served by Hartlepool Transport. This former local authority fleet was privatised in a buy-out in 1993, but after 18 months was sold to Stagecoach at the end of 1994. The 68-strong fleet was unusual in having more Bristol REs in it than any other type, which helped to push its average age up. More modern buses – the term modern is relative – were Mark 1 Nationals, some of which had come from Brighton & Hove, and Dennis Falcons with bodies by Wadham Stringer and Northern Counties.

Here the livery is not being retained, and the fleet is now part way through a process of changing from traditional maroon and cream to Stagecoach white with stripes. None of the REs have been repainted, and they are in the process of being replaced by new Northern Counties-bodied B10Ms, similar to those running for Cleveland Transit, but in Stagecoach colours. They are the first new buses for the fleet for 10 years – the last were B-registered Falcons. Some of the Falcons have received Stagecoach livery. Hartlepool's services run primarily within the town. There are also a few second-hand coaches in the fleet.

The withdrawal of Tees & District from Hartlepool leaves Hartlepool Transport with a virtual monopoly of the town's services, although United does work in from the north. Hartlepool Transport is controlled by sister Stagecoach subsidiary Cleveland Transit.

Top **The most modern 'big bus' operated by Robson is a 1984 National 2 which was bought from British Airways in 1993. When new it was a three-door standee bus. It is now a conventional 49-seater.** Mike Harris

Upper centre **The Leven Valley fleet is made up mainly of Mercedes minibuses bought new. Two delivered in 1994 have unusual TBP bodywork. TBP of Birmingham is perhaps best known as the manufacturer of the Pullman three-axle minibus.** Stewart J Brown

Lower centre **Ten B10Ms have also entered service with Hartlepool Transport, where they are the first new buses for 10 years. Here the municipal livery is giving way to corporate Stagecoach white with stripes. The Volvos are replacing 20-year-old Bristol REs.** Tony Wilson

Left **Among the odd buses to appear in Stagecoach colours during 1995 have been some of what were Hartlepool's newest buses, six Dennis Falcons with dual-door Northern Counties bodies.** Tony Wilson

YORKSHIRE

Top **The newest double-deckers in the Keighley & District fleet are four Alexander-bodied Leyland Olympians which are allocated to the Keighley-Leeds-Wetherby service. Blazefield Holdings, the owners of Keighley & District, are strong believers in route branding to promote ridership.** Malcolm King

Above **Extensive rebuilding of the front end, and in particular the high front skirt, radically alter the appearance of this Mark I National operated by Black Prince. It was new to United Auto.** Tony Wilson

There are 56 Alexander Dash midibuses in the Yorkshire Rider fleet. Fifty are on Dennis Dart chassis but the first six, one of which is seen here in central Leeds, are on Volvo B6s. L M Whitehead

The delivery to Yorkshire Rider in 1995 of 48 Dennis Lances with Plaxton Verde bodies is a sign of the Badgerline influence. The Lance/Verde was Badgerline's standard single-deck bus. Malcolm King

Superbus livery is worn by a batch of Alexander-bodied Scania N113s delivered to Yorkshire Rider in 1994. They were ordered for operation on a guided busway which came into operation in Leeds in October 1995. L M Whitehead

The main centres of population in what can broadly be described as Yorkshire are to be found in the two former metropolitan counties – West Yorkshire centred on Leeds and South Yorkshire on Sheffield. Both cities and their substantial satellite towns are served by privatised former PTE bus operations, along with a number of ex-NBC companies and some new-generation post-deregulation independents.

In Leeds and its environs, the big operator is Yorkshire Rider. This was the first PTE bus operation to be sold, being bought by its management and employees in 1988. Yorkshire Rider quickly consolidated its position as West Yorkshire's major transport operator by buying up parts of what had been NBC's West Yorkshire Road Car business from its new owners, the AJS group. This involved taking over West Yorkshire's Bradford area operations in 1989, followed in 1990 by those in York which were mainly being run by a newly-formed York City & District company – the nucleus of what is now Rider York. Yorkshire Rider was already the established operator in Halifax, Huddersfield and Bradford. Its services provide comprehensive coverage of most of West Yorkshire north of Huddersfield, and it also runs across the Pennines to Lancashire, with routes from Halifax to Rochdale, Oldham and Burnley.

Rider Holdings controlled both Yorkshire Rider and Rider York and also owned the small Quickstep Travel business, set up independently in 1992 and taken over by Rider in 1993. In the spring of 1994 it was bought by Badgerline. Consequently it is now part of the FirstBus organisation, created by the merger in June 1995 of Badgerline and GRT Bus Group.

New buses have been flowing in to the Yorkshire Rider fleet. In 1994 it received 25 Volvo Olympian double-deckers with Northern Counties bodies – but most new vehicles have been single-decked. The double-deckers were accompanied by 50 Alexander Striders – 30 Volvo B10Bs and 20 Scania N113s – and half-a-dozen B6s with Alexander Dash bodies. Yorkshire Rider was the first customer for the Strider body and its name is in recognition of this. Read it as St Rider if you wish. These were the last major orders placed by the old regime.

They were followed in 1995 by a major influx of Dennises, reflecting Badgerline's acquisition of the company. These comprised 48 Lances and 68 Darts, Badgerline's standard single-deck types, and they were accompanied by 63 Mercedes 709Ds. Fifty of the Darts have Alexander Dash bodies with a new design of front end which does away with the V-shaped dip in the windscreen, while all the other new Dennises and the 709Ds were bodied by Plaxton which has been the Badgerline group's preferred body supplier. Most of the Lances and a good number of the Darts are allocated to Huddersfield giving that town one of the most modern bus fleets in Britain. The 1995 deliveries introduced a new livery using two shades of green and cream and with a new fleetname which dispensed with the word Yorkshire, keeping Rider and the local town identity. However this has only been applied to one repaint – a Scania double-decker. Other repaints have been in the previous livery. Badgers had also been appearing on Yorkshire Rider's buses – but the badger's fate under FirstBus is clear: it is an endangered species. Most Yorkshire Rider buses which carried badgers have had them removed.

The 1994 Scanias wear Superbus livery, being used by Yorkshire Rider in the run-up to the introduction of a guided busway in Leeds, which was opened in October 1995.

As part of a policy of raising service standards, selected routes in Halifax and Huddersfield operate under the Flagship banner and to promote them a small number of buses have been painted in a predominantly white livery. Vehicles in Flagship colours include some of the 1994 Olympians with low-height Northern Counties bodies, a new Dart and a new Lance.

The arrival of so many new buses has been matched by the departure of old ones, with late 1970s Atlanteans and Fleetlines being withdrawn. There are a good number of Atlanteans still in use, but all of Yorkshire Rider's Fleetlines have been taken out of service. Most of the Atlanteans have bodies built in the Leeds suburb of Crossgates by Charles H Roe, the major supplier to the fleet in PTE days although its successor, Optare, has not fared as well in the supply of buses to its local major operator. There are still a few NBC-style Bristol VRTs in use on school contracts, and these are the most visible outward sign of Yorkshire Rider's take-over of parts of the West Yorkshire Road Car Company's operations.

When Fleetline and Atlantean production ended, the West Yorkshire PTE divided its double-deck orders between Leyland and MCW, and both Olympians and Metrobuses are to be found in the Yorkshire Rider fleet. There are around 80 of the latter and all but two are Mark II models with MCW's simplified body structure. The odd two are unusual in having Alexander R-type bodies and are the survivors of a batch of 10 delivered in 1982. The only other buyers of Alexander-bodied Metrobuses were the Merseyside PTE, the Scottish Bus Group and Leicester City Transport. All of the Metrobuses are based in Leeds.

Most of the company's early Olympians have Roe bodies and Gardner engines, although there are a few ECW-bodied buses which came from West Yorkshire Road Car. There are 15 C- and D-registered Olympians with Optare bodies built to Roe designs which are virtually indistinguishable from genuine Roe-built buses. More recent Olympians have had Cummins L10 engines and bodies by Northern Counties and Alexander. The 25 newest examples delivered in 1994 include 20 with Volvo engines – the fleet's first Volvo-powered double-deckers. There are 226 Olympians in service, making Yorkshire Rider the UK's second-biggest operator of the type (after Lothian).

Yorkshire Rider's other modern double-deckers are Scania N113s. There are 42, and they are based in Leeds. Delivered in 1990-91, all have Alexander R-type bodies except for five which were bodied by Northern Counties.

Top **Yorkshire Rider still runs a sizeable fleet of Roe-bodied Leyland Atlanteans with over 200 in use. Most were bought new and have bodies to a design developed for the West Yorkshire PTE. There are however a small number of NBC-style buses which were new to London Country and were bought by Yorkshire Rider from Sovereign Bus & Coach in 1989.** Stewart J Brown

Centre **The last of a long line of Roe bodies supplied to the West Yorkshire PTE and its predecessors were delivered in 1984, shortly before the Roe factory at Crossgates, to the east of Leeds, closed. They were 30 B-registered buses on Leyland Olympian chassis, all of which remain in service with Yorkshire Rider.** Malcolm King

Right **There are 25 Volvo Olympians with Northern Counties bodies in the Yorkshire Rider fleet built to two different chassis and body specifications. Most have Volvo engines but five are powered by Cummins L10s, and the bodies are to both lowheight and normal height designs. A normal height Volvo-engined bus, new in 1994, approaches Bradford Interchange.** Russell Upcraft

Until recently single-deckers played a relatively small part in Yorkshire Rider's operations, although the large numbers delivered since 1993 have changed that. Older single-deckers include Leyland Nationals, some bought new in PTE days and others acquired subsequently by Yorkshire Rider; Leyland Tigers with Duple Dominant bus bodies, and a few Leopard and Tiger coaches which are used on some of the inter-town operations which play a major part in West Yorkshire's transport. The distinctive short Leopard buses which for 20 years were part of the Halifax bus scene have finally gone.

First-generation minibuses have virtually disappeared from the Yorkshire Rider fleet too, thanks to the large numbers of new Mercedes delivered in 1994-95. A small number of MCW Metroriders are still in use, along with four Optare StarRiders on Mercedes 811D chassis. Ex-West Yorkshire Iveco Fords survive in Bradford.

The Quickstep operation was started in 1992 as a competitor in Leeds and had a fleet of second-hand Nationals. After 18 months independence it was taken over by Yorkshire Rider, but it has retained its own identity. The fleet is still made up mainly of Nationals, but there are five Ikarus-bodied DAF SB220s, three of which were new to Quickstep (and are the only new buses in the fleet) and two of which came from Yorkshire Travel of Dewsbury in 1994 when that company's short-lived bus operations were taken over by Caldaire. The first double-decker for Quickstep entered service in the summer of 1995. It is a Roe-bodied Atlantean transferred from the main Yorkshire Rider fleet. Quickstep run north from Leeds to Yeadon and Otley.

Another independent running in Leeds was Rhodes Coaches of Yeadon. This company's bus operations were taken over by Rider Holdings at the start of 1994 and added to the Quickstep business. Three of Quickstep's buses are ex-Rhodes vehicles: two Plaxton Derwent-bodied Tigers which were new to Loch Lomond Bus Service and a Volvo B10M which Rhodes had rebodied by East Lancs in 1993. A Volvo with Duple Dominant bus body which was in the Rhodes fleet has been transferred to Rider York. Two other modern Rhodes buses – a Lynx and the unique (in Britain) Van Hool A600 integral – were quickly transferred to Brewers in South Wales, which was also part of the Badgerline group.

Despite the demise of Rhodes and the acquisition of Quickstep, there are still small operators competing with Yorkshire Rider in Leeds and its other main centres of activity. In addition companies in the Caldaire group, which is based in Wakefield, have substantial networks of services in the area south of Leeds.

Top **A number of Yorkshire Rider routes form part of the company's Flagship operation on which higher standards of service are provided. To promote the concept a few vehicles run in Flagship livery. These range from a 12-year-old Olympian to this brand new Dennis Dart which is operating in Huddersfield. It has a Plaxton body.** Malcolm King

Centre **The bus operations of Rhodes of Yeadon were taken over by Yorkshire Rider and a few of the Rhodes vehicles were retained, including an East Lancs-bodied Scania K92 which was previously operated by Jones of Login.** Malcolm King

Left **Quickstep Travel started running in Leeds in 1992 and was taken over by Yorkshire Rider in 1993. Its new owners introduced new buses to the fleet - three DAF SB220s with Ikarus bodies.** Tony Wilson

The best-known of the smaller businesses is Black Prince of Morley which with a 60-strong fleet has grown to be quite a substantial operation. Its main routes run from Morley, south of Leeds, to the city centre, and from Leeds to Pudsey and Bradford. It is England's biggest operator of Ailsas, with 30 in stock. All bar one have Alexander bodies. The odd vehicle is a rare survivor from the batch of 62 Ailsas which were bodied in Eire by Van Hool-McArdle for the South Yorkshire PTE. It is a most distinctively styled bus which wears its 19 years lightly and is currently in a green livery to mark the 25th year of Black Prince's existence in 1994. The other Ailsas were new to A1, Central Scottish, London Buses, Tayside, West Midlands and Western Scottish.

There is also one Volvo Citybus in the fleet (it is a former London Buses trial vehicle), a Routemaster, a PD3 Titan and a couple of Atlanteans. The single-deck fleet is interesting too. There are standard Nationals, National Greenways and an Alexander-bodied Scania N113 single-decker which operated for London Buses for two years. The company's first new buses were delivered in 1995 – four Optare Vectas on MAN 11.190 chassis. The fleet is a smart one, illustrating the high standards which many small businesses with enthusiastic owners aim for but do not always achieve.

Top **Black Prince is the biggest user of Ailsas in England. Most have Alexander bodies and came from Scottish operators. This bus was new to Central SMT in 1979 and came to Black Prince from Kelvin Central in 1991.** Malcolm King

Centre **Van Hool-bodied buses are uncommon in Britain. This Black Prince Volvo B10M was one of a pair delivered to Hutchison of Overtown in 1984.** Tony Wilson

Below **For new vehicles in 1995 Black Prince supported local industry, buying four Optare Vectas. The 41-seat Vectas have MAN 11.190 underframes.** Tony Wilson

After Black Prince, the other small operators in Leeds seem quite pedestrian. AJC Coaches has 10 Mark 1 Nationals. Taylors, taken over by K Line in September 1994, has changed from an operation using second-hand double-deckers to one running new single-deckers. Nine new DAF SB220s were taken into stock after the K Line take-over. These have Ikarus bodies and joined two similar buses already in the K Line fleet. There are also three Nationals and an ex-Wright of Wrexham Optare Delta. Miramare operate from Morley with just two buses, a one-time West Midlands Fleetline and a former Eastern National Leyland National.

Outside Leeds, Yorkshire Rider faces comparatively little competition from smaller operators. In Huddersfield, Blue Bus of Horwich started running local services in August 1994. It operates Dennis Darts and second-hand Leopards which have been transferred from its Lancashire operation. K Line also runs locally in Huddersfield with DAF SB220s and second-hand Nationals.

Services in and around York are provided by a separate Rider Holdings subsidiary, Rider York. This was formed in 1990 when Rider Holdings took over the city's main operators. It bought York City & District and the associated Target Travel operation from AJS, and at the same time purchased the independent Reynard Buses business. York City & District had been created in 1988 out of the York operations of West Yorkshire Road Car, the former NBC subsidiary which had been purchased by AJS in 1987.

Rider York operates 85 buses, many dating from the 1990 take-overs. These include Renault minibuses with Reeve Burgess bodies, new in 1989, and Leyland Nationals which were part of the West Yorkshire Road Car fleet. The only double-deckers are ex-West Yorkshire ECW-bodied Olympians. The single-deck fleet includes Leyland Tigers with Duple Dominant bus bodies and Leopards which were rebodied as buses by Plaxton in 1990. The Leopards were previously owned by Reynard Buses.

New vehicles for the York fleet have been eight Ikarus-bodied DAF SB220s in 1992 and five Scania L113s with Alexander bodies in 1994. The SB220s were joined in 1995 by the six Optare-bodied examples from the main Yorkshire Rider fleet, thus bringing most of the Rider group's DAFs together at one location. The Scania L113s were the first to enter service with a British operator. The L113 differs from the N113s as operated in Leeds by virtue of having an in-line rather than a transverse engine. A major upgrade of the city's park-and-ride services is in hand and for this Rider York has ordered 20 new Scania L113s with Wright bodies.

Taylors of Morley were taken over by K Line in 1994 and nine new DAF SB220s with Ikarus bodies replaced Taylors second-hand double-deckers. Mike Harris

Blue Bus of Horwich in Lancashire has crossed the Pennines to set up an operation in Huddersfield. Most of the vehicles used are Leopards which are just a bit older than this East Lancs-bodied Dart with its distinctive BLU registration. Tony Wilson

Rider York operates all of the Optare Deltas owned by what was the Rider Group. There are six. This one was new in 1989. Russell Upcraft

Other operators serving the city include East Yorkshire with routes from Pocklington and Bridlington, United Auto running from Ripon, and Harrogate & District coming, of course, from Harrogate. Leopard coaches are used on service by Glenn Coaches from Wiggington and by Stephensons from Helmsley and Easingwold. Sykes of Appleton Roebuck run into York usually with the company's only double-decker, a one-time Eastern Counties Bristol VRT. City tours are operated by Viking Tours with a varied collection of open-top double-deckers. Four are Bristol VRTs, but a Lodekka is also owned, and a couple of Atlanteans. Other operators running open-top tours include Guide Friday and Lothian Region Transport. LRT started its York operation as a response to Guide Friday launching tours in Edinburgh, where LRT had previously been the only city tour operator. York Pullman, since 1993 a subsidiary of Durham Travel Services, runs tours with open-top Atlanteans and a VRT, and also has ex-Hull Atlanteans which operate contracts and a Pocklington service. The Hull Atlanteans give a clue to the company's ownership by Kingston-upon-Hull City Transport from 1990 to 1993 when KHCT – at that time still owned by the local authority – was going through an expansionist phase and had subsidiary companies in York, France and Holland.

When Rider Holdings took over the AJS operations in York, a small part was retained by AJS and reformed as Yorkshire Coastliner. Based at Malton, that survives as part of the Blazefield Holdings business and operates trunk services from Leeds to York, Malton, Scarborough and Whitby, generally using high-specification coach-seated double-deckers. Yorkshire Coastliner was the first customer for the Alexander Royale which was unveiled in the autumn of 1993. It now runs six, all on Volvo Olympian chassis. These join three Northern Counties-bodied Leyland Olympians and four Cummins-engined Leyland Tiger coaches. The company also operates local bus services in Whitby, using Reeve Burgess-bodied Mercedes transferred north from Blazefield's Welwyn-Hatfield Line operation, and in Malton using either coaches or a rare Wadham Stringer-bodied Leyland Swift which was new to Lucketts of Watford.

Blazefield's other northern centres of operation are in Harrogate and Keighley, both once served by West Yorkshire, and both taken over by Blazefield from AJS. Harrogate & District provides bus services in the area described in its title. A trunk route extends south to Leeds and north to Ripon and on this the company runs a dedicated fleet of Volvo B10Bs with Alexander Strider bodies. These were delivered in the spring of 1995 and replaced Leyland Lynxes. Local routes in Harrogate are mainly operated by 14 Volvo B6s with Alexander Dash bodies. Blazefield is a staunch supporter of both Volvo and Alexander for anything bigger than a midibus and in 1994-95 added no fewer than 32 Alexander-bodied Volvos to its Yorkshire fleets.

Top **There are nine double-deckers in the Yorkshire Coastliner fleet, all fitted with coach seats for use on services from Leeds to York and the coast. The oldest are 1992 Leyland Olympians with Northern Counties bodies, of which there are three. Subsequent deliveries have been Volvo Olympians with Alexander bodywork.** Tony Wilson

Centre **The only midibus operated by Yorkshire Coastliner is a Leyland Swift with Wadham Stringer bodywork.** Malcolm King

Right **Harrogate & District has 14 Volvo B6s with Alexander Dash bodies. The newest were among the first to feature Alexander's revised front end with a neater windscreen arrangement and a dummy grille between the headlights.** Malcolm King

Harrogate Independent, started in 1987 by a group of ex-West Yorkshire employees, was taken over by AJS in 1989 and finally integrated into the Harrogate & District business in 1994. The legacy of this is a fleet of six Wadham Stringer-bodied Leyland Swifts which include the first to be delivered to an English operator, E-registered buses new in 1987. The Harrogate fleet includes a few National 2s and five ECW-bodied Olympians (its only double-deckers) all of which were new to West Yorkshire. Harrogate & District runs 53 buses and coaches, 19 of which are less than two years old. WM Travel's United Auto operation also serves Harrogate with buses running in from Ripon and Boroughbridge.

Blazefield's Keighley & District fleet is quite different in its composition from that in Harrogate. Here there are many more double-deckers – almost 60 Olympians out of a total fleet of 107 vehicles – and proportionately fewer new buses. Recent deliveries have included a trio of B6s in 1994 and four Olympians in 1993, all bodied by Alexander. The Olympians are used on the 760 service to Leeds and Wetherby. There are also Northern Counties-bodied Olympians, with six bought new in 1990 and three K-registered buses transferred from Yorkshire Coastliner in 1995. The remaining Olympians are former NBC buses most of which have ECW bodies, although there are a few bodied by Roe. Some have been moved up from Blazefield's Sovereign company in Hertfordshire and are to London Country specification with Park Royal-style windscreens which were specified to provide commonality with London Country's sizeable fleet of Park Royal-bodied Atlanteans. The NBC standard at the time was the BET-style screen. The single-deck fleet comprises Lynxes and Nationals, while minibuses are mainly Plaxton-bodied Mercedes.

Keighley is a substantial town and in fact had its own municipal transport system which operated trams, buses and trolleybuses. It ceased in 1932. Keighley & District is the main operator but Yorkshire Rider also serves the town – and nearby Otley and Ilkley – as a result of its acquisition of part of the West Yorkshire Road Car business.

Keighley & District has gone through a few changes of identity. It inherited West Yorkshire's dark red, and in 1989 replaced this with an unusual grey called chinchilla, which is presumably the colour of what Collins dictionary describes as "a small gregarious rodent". So perhaps it is just as well that since 1993 this has been gradually phased out in favour of a much brighter white livery with blue and red relief. Keighley & District has a depot at Skipton, which is the focus of Pennine Motor Services' operations. Skipton also marks the north western limit of Yorkshire Rider operations, with an hourly service from Leeds.

Top **The oldest buses in the Harrogate & District fleet are five 1981 Leyland National 2s which are the company's only buses with year suffix rather than year prefix registrations. They were new to West Yorkshire Road Car.** Tony Wilson

Centre **Keighley & District has gone through a few changes of livery before arriving at its present bright white-based scheme. There are almost 40 ECW-bodied Olympians in the fleet. All started life with West Yorkshire Road Car, although some spent time with other companies in the AJS/Blazefield group before ending up in Keighley.** Mike Harris

Left **A number of Blazefield subsidiaries run Plaxton-bodied Mercedes-Benz minibuses. Keighley & District has 13. This is a 711D with 25-seat Beaver body.** Mark Bailey

Pennine is based in Gargrave, a few miles to the north of Skipton, and has a history which can be traced back to 1925. In recent years the fleet has been 100 per cent Leyland Leopard/Plaxton, generally bought new but supplemented by good second-hand examples. Then in 1994 came a complete change of policy with the purchase of the company's first rear-engined bus, a one-time London Country Leyland National which came from Northumbria. It proved to be the first of many, and there are now nine Nationals in the fleet. Most have Ulster registrations which obscure both their age and their origin. And, it has to be said, all are Mark 1s and are in fact no newer than the Leopards they are replacing. However the integrity of the National structure is legendary, and no doubt short-distance passengers appreciate the wide entrance and low steps, even if the Leopard/Plaxton seems an altogether more genteel means of transport. With the arrival of the Nationals Pennine has introduced fleet numbers for the first time in its 70-year history. Pennine's services run north to Settle and across the Lancashire border to Barnoldswick.

In Settle Blazefield's subsidiary is Ingfield Northern Rose, running Leopard coaches and Ford Transit and Iveco Ford minibuses. It is a small fleet with just 13 vehicles, all second-hand, and was set up in 1992 when Blazefield took over Ingfield of Settle.

Some of the northern routes operated by Blazefield companies run into areas served by the southern part of WM Travel's United Auto operation, while to the east lie the operations of East Yorkshire Motor Services, one of the few former NBC subsidiaries which has not yet been bought by one of the big groups. EYMS is based in Kingston-upon-Hull, in what is now Humberside but was Yorkshire prior to the 1974 reorganisation of local government. The main urban operator in Hull is owned by Stagecoach.

There are in fact two very different Stagecoaches in Hull, with nary a sign of a white bus with red, orange and blue stripes. First there is Humber Stagecoach, which has nothing to do with the Scottish multi-national – or with anything much else come to that. Humber Stagecoach was taken over by Pride of the Road in 1993, but its name lives on on the side of at least one Mark 1 Leyland National still in service with Pride of the Road. Other vehicles in the Pride of the Road fleet, most in a white and orange livery, are more elderly Nationals (there are 21 all told) and six new Ikarus-bodied DAF SB220s.

Top **A major change in direction took place at Pennine Motor Services in 1994 with the arrival of Leyland Nationals in a fleet made up entirely of Leopard coaches. This bus, seen in Skipton, is a 1977 model which came from Northumbria. It has a Volvo engine.** Michael Fowler

Centre **Pride of the Road is one of a number of operators in the region to have added Ikarus-bodied DAFs to its fleet. Hughes DAF, the supplying dealer, is conveniently located just off the M62 in West Yorkshire. Six new SB220s joined Pride of the Road's Hull operation in 1995. The company already operated two second-hand examples.** Stewart J Brown

Right **Humber Stagecoach was taken over by Pride of the Road in 1993, but the name lives on as seen on this one-time Maidstone & District Leyland National.** Tony Wilson

More significant is Kingston-upon-Hull City Transport, trading as KHCT. It is owned by the real Stagecoach, having been acquired in 1994 along with the business of Cleveland Transit. Cleveland Transit bought the KHCT business in 1993 and promptly adopted an attractive blue, white and yellow livery which was derived from Cleveland Transit's green, white and yellow. The fleet has in fact been repainted in the Transit-style livery with remarkable speed, and the colours are being retained by Stagecoach. Few KHCT buses are still in the previous dark blue and white. An interesting detail is the legal ownership address on the side of what to many in Hull must still be the Corporation's buses. It is Church Street, Stockton, the head office of Cleveland Transit 75 miles away.

Stagecoach has invested heavily in Hull, and 12 smart Northern Counties-bodied Volvo B10Bs joined the KHCT fleet in the spring of 1995, replacing double-deckers. However the operation remains a predominantly double-decked one, with Dennis Dominators, MCW Metrobuses and Scania N113s. Most of the Dominators and all of the Scanias have East Lancs bodies. Three Northern Counties-bodied Volvo Olympians delivered in 1995 were the first new double-deckers since 1990. The new KHCT Volvos are among the very few buses built for a Stagecoach company in 1995 not to be in corporate colours.

Hull was among the pioneers in the provision of bus services for disabled travellers and its Handyrider fleet includes a National 2 – the only National bought by KHCT – which offers access for wheelchairs by way of a lift. A lift-equipped Dennis Lancet, ex-Leicester Citybus, is also operated. KHCT's minibuses are Robin Hood-bodied Ivecos which originally ran under the Royale banner but are now being repainted in fleet colours. There are a couple of coaches in Stagecoach colours for use on an express service to Meadowhall. One is an unusual Plaxton-bodied Dennis Dorchester which was new to Leicester City Transport.

Top **Dennis Dominators are the majority type in KHCT's double-deck fleet. Most have East Lancs bodies to Alexander's R-type design. This blue, white and yellow livery was adopted after KHCT was taken over by Cleveland Transit and is being retained at present by Stagecoach.** Stewart J Brown

Left **A dozen new Northern Counties-bodied Volvo B10Ms were the first sign of Stagecoach's ownership of KHCT. The Hull operation has long been predominantly double-decked. These were KHCT's first new buses for five years. They come from a batch of 40 vehicles ordered by Stagecoach for its subsidiaries on the North East coast.** Malcolm King

East Yorkshire is the city's other major operator. It runs one of the country's biggest fleets of Bristol VRTs with around 125 in use – the only company with more VRTs is Eastern Counties. Many are second-hand, but all originated with NBC fleets. EYMS was an NBC subsidiary until 1987 when it was bought by its management in association with Alan Stephenson of AJS Group fame. It is still management owned, making it the largest of the ex-NBC companies to survive independently of the fast-expanding groups.

Its VRTs include relatively rare highbridge ECW-bodied examples which were new to London Country Bus Services. Other buses which were new to London Country but can now be seen in EYMS service are four long-wheelbase Olympians with ECW dual-purpose bodywork, built in 1985 for Green Line operation. They moved north quite early in their lives and have now been running in Yorkshire for longer than they ran in London.

Older double-deck types are Atlanteans, including ex-Cleveland Transit PDR1s which have mid-1980s Northern Counties bodies on 1970 chassis. Ulster NIJ registration marks have replaced their original H-suffix numbers and effectively disguise the age of the chassis. EYMS had from 1988 been running Routemasters in Hull, painted in the company's traditional dark blue colours. These were taken out of service in 1995 bringing to an end one of the longest-established provincial RM operations.

More recently EYMS has been buying Olympians. It inherited NBC-style ECW-bodied examples, but from 1990 standardised on Northern Counties-bodied Olympians. A solitary Optare Spectra has the distinction of being the northernmost example of the type. Of 20 Olympians ordered for 1995, sixteen were bodied by Alexander.

Top **East Yorkshire runs one of the biggest fleets of Bristol VRTs with around 125, two-thirds of which came from other operators. These include Western National, which supplied three with ECW highbridge bodies in 1993. They were part of a batch of 15 which were new to London Country in 1977.** Stewart J Brown

Centre **This 21-year-old Atlantean wears its age well thanks to extensive refurbishment which included retrimming the interior and fitting an Alexander-style front panel to its Park Royal body. It has been owned by the company twice – first when it was new in 1974, then again from 1992 when it was taken over with the operations of Metro of Hull.** Malcolm King

After just three years on Green Line operation four extended-wheelbase Olympian coaches were sold by London Country North East to East Yorkshire. New in 1985, they have been running for East Yorkshire since 1988. The striking 69-seat bodywork with fixed windows and forced-air ventilation was built by ECW. Stewart J Brown

Single-deckers in the EYMS fleet are mainly Leopard coaches and Nationals. There is only one midibus, a Volvo B6 with Northern Counties body which is based in Hull. The Nationals include East Lancs Greenway rebuilds which operate in Scarborough and which, like the ex-Cleveland PDR1 rebodies, have been given Ulster registrations to hide their ages. In the Leopard fleet are three with East Lancs EL2000 bodies and these too can be seen in the Scarborough area. Most of the town services in Scarborough are operated by Mercedes minibuses with Reeve Burgess Beaver bodies. These carry Scarborough & District and Skipper fleetnames. Routes are also operated up the coast to Whitby, and inland to Pickering and Helmsley. An unusual open-top Bristol RE provides a summer sea front service in Scarborough in competition with Shoreline Suncruisers and Appleby, both running Fleetlines.

A small number of vehicles operating around Scarborough and Filey carry Primrose Valley Coaches names, including a few double-deckers. Primrose Valley Coaches was taken over by East Yorkshire in 1990. Part of what is now Scarborough & District was taken into the EYMS business in 1987 soon after its privatisation when it purchased the Hardwicks services operated by Wallace Arnold. There are still five ex-Hardwicks Plaxton-bodied Leopards in the fleet.

Full-size EYMS buses, including most of those run under the Scarborough & District and Primrose Valley Coaches names, carry a deep red and grey livery which was adopted after privatisation to replace NBC poppy red. This itself is now being phased out and since the spring of 1995 a smart combination of crimson and cream has been applied to vehicles as they become due for repaint. Olympians and VRTs in the new livery can be seen in Hull. The Scarborough & District minibuses and East Lancs Greenways are grey with red and blue relief.

In Scarborough EYMS faces year-round competition from Appleby, generally running Leopard coaches on local services. These include two with Willowbrook bodywork which were new to West Yorkshire. Possibly of more interest are an ex-Preston Northern Counties-bodied Dodge minibus and a former West Midlands Fleetline. These both perform on the company's service to Eastfield, site of the Plaxton coach-building factory. Appleby's main operations are in fact in Lincolnshire and its Scarborough area bus services represent post-deregulation expansion. Elsewhere in East Yorkshire territory there are few small operators. In Bridlington, a service is operated to Frodingham by Frodingham Coaches. A Mercedes 811D with Whittaker bodywork, bought new in 1991, is the regular bus. A second-hand Iveco acts as a spare.

Top **The first buses to be delivered in East Yorkshire's new livery are two batches of Volvo Olympians with bodywork by Alexander and, as shown here in Hull, Northern Counties.** Tony Wilson

Centre **Scarborough & District operate inland to Pickering, generally using Leopards. This 12m-long PSU5 started life in 1981 as a Wallace Arnold coach and was taken over in 1988 with the Hardwicks services in Scarborough. The East Lancs body was fitted in 1991.** Tony Wilson

Left **Local services in Scarborough are operated by Mercedes minibuses and East Lancs Greenways, all using the Scarborough Skipper name. Six Greenways are operated and all have Ulster registrations to hide their original identities. This was originally a T-registered bus in the East Yorkshire fleet. East Lancs reworked it in 1992.** Tony Wilson

Caldaire Holdings takes its name from a combination of two Yorkshire rivers, the Calder and the Aire which, with a bit of poetic licence, can be seen as marking the northern and southern boundaries of the company's operations. Caldaire was formed by the NBC management buy-out team which purchased West Riding of Wakefield in 1987. Part of the West Riding operation around Dewsbury traded as Yorkshire Woollen and that is now a separate company within the Caldaire group using the Yorkshire Buses name. Yorkshire Buses is the dominant operator in Dewsbury but there is one long-established small operator worthy of note, Longstaff of Mirfield running an ex-London MCW Metrobus II from the fleet which operated the Harrow Buses network from 1988 to 1991. Longstaff also owns a Volvo B58 with Duple Dominant bus body, bought new in 1979.

Caldaire's Selby operations were set up as an autonomous Selby & District company in 1988. The final piece of the Caldaire jigsaw is South Yorkshire Road Transport of Pontefract which was purchased in July 1994. South Yorkshire was an old-established business with an 18-strong fleet and it continues as a separate operating unit under its new owners. Caldaire lost its independence in the spring of 1995, selling out to British Bus.

West Riding in the 1960s was one of the last of the big independents. It sold out to the state-owned Transport Holding Company in 1967 and thus became part of the new NBC organisation two years later. Yorkshire Woollen had been a BET company in the days before NBC. Under NBC ownership the two companies were gradually united under a common management structure. After the management buy-out in 1987, Caldaire took over United Automobile Services and established Caldaire North East – that became the Westcourt group and is now owned by WM Travel.

Caldaire's operations cover much of the southern part of West Yorkshire around Dewsbury, Wakefield and Castleford, with routes in to Leeds, Huddersfield, Halifax, Barnsley and south to Sheffield. South Yorkshire serves Pontefract and runs from Doncaster to Leeds. Selby & District serves – well, Selby and district. It also has a trunk route from Leeds via Selby to York. Thornes Motor Services run from Selby to Bubwith using a smart ex-Tayside Fleetline. This is a service which pre-dates deregulation. Similarly Jaronda Travel's operations to Cawood and York were running before deregulation, being taken over in 1983 from their previous operator, Majestic of Cawood. They are now operated by Dennis Darts or Bristol LHs. There are three Darts, all bought new, with bodies by Duple, Carlyle and Plaxton. The Jaronda name comes from the first names of owners Janet and Ron Barwick.

Top **The Caldaire group standardised on the Leyland Lynx and runs 131, including 46 of the less common Mark II variety, identifiable by its protruding front end, designed to accommodate the intercooler on Volvo-engined buses. The upswept band of colour has been abandoned in favour of a straightforward half-and-half colour split on recent repaints.** Mark Bailey

Centre **Caldaire bought 30 Dennis Lances, 18 of which are in the Yorkshire Woollen fleet. They have 47-seat Alexander Strider bodies and entered service in 1993. A Yorkshire Woollen Lance pulls out of Halifax bus station.** Tony Wilson

Right **Nine Volvo B10Bs were purchased in 1993, five with Alexander bodies for the Selby operation, and four with Wright bodies for West Riding. They are the only Wright-bodied buses in the fleet.** Tony Wilson

Caldaire has bought nothing but single-deckers and minibuses since its privatisation. Its double-deckers are all Leyland Olympians – there are around 90 built between 1982 and 1985 and all with standard NBC-style ECW bodies. These are divided between each of the Caldaire companies, including South Yorkshire which has had some transferred in to allow the withdrawal of its last Fleetlines. South Yorkshire's standard bus from 1982 was the Northern Counties-bodied Olympian. It had eight when it sold out to Caldaire.

Caldaire's oldest single-deckers are National 2s. There are 15 bought new in NBC days and a further 25 second-hand examples including late C-registered buses which were new to Provincial of Fareham and were among the last Nationals supplied to an NBC subsidiary. Many have Gardner engines. There are no Nationals in the Selby fleet, but each of the other Caldaire operations has a number. The company established a policy of maintaining a high level of investment in new vehicles and selected the Leyland Lynx as its standard bus. It built up a fleet of 131 before the collapse of the UK bus market forced Volvo to close the Leyland Bus factory at Workington, bringing an end to Lynx production. Caldaire's Lynxes include an early C-registered ex-demonstration model, four G-registered ex-demonstrators and three former Merthyr Tydfil buses. It is the only operator running C-registered examples of both the National and its Lynx replacement.

The demise of the Lynx forced a rethink on vehicle policy which saw the company turn first to Dennis, taking 30 Lances with Alexander Strider bodies, and then to Volvo, which has supplied 33 B10Bs. Most of these have Alexander Strider bodies which have double-glazing, a rare luxury on an urban bus in Britain. There are four B10Bs with Wright Endeavour bodies.

Small buses are mainly Optare MetroRiders, of which there are 45 in the West Riding fleet, and Plaxton-bodied Mercedes, eight of which are in Yorkshire Buses' colours. A few Alexander-bodied Dodge S56s are owned, some of which have been transferred to the South Yorkshire fleet. There are no midibuses in the Caldaire group fleets. South Yorkshire's newest buses at the time of the take-over were three new Dennis Darts, which were quickly sold to Yorkshire Traction and replaced by Optare MetroRiders.

Top **West Riding's double-deckers are all Olympians and most are standard NBC-specification buses with Gardner engines and ECW bodies. The oldest are 1982 buses, one of which is seen in Pontefract.** Stewart J Brown

Centre **A recently repainted Optare MetroRider in the Selby & District fleet illustrates the simplified livery being adopted by the former Caldaire companies under British Bus ownership. This uses a straight colour split, doing away with the upsweep at the front.** Michael Fowler

Left **The Caldaire companies run 40 National 2s, 25 of which are second-hand. Two were new to SBG companies, in this case Central Scottish. This example is seen running for South Yorkshire Transport, which was taken over by Caldaire in 1994.** Stewart J Brown

Based in Barnsley, Yorkshire Traction is another former NBC subsidiary which was bought by its management and has remained independent of the new wave of big bus groups. Indeed YTC has itself expanded. It owns Strathtay Scottish, the only SBG company sold directly to an English buyer, and Lincolnshire Road Car. It has also bought Lincoln City Transport's operations, and more recently has been expanding in Sheffield, by taking over four of the independents which have been competing with Mainline – Andrews, South Riding, Sheffield Omnibus and Yorkshire Terrier. Between them they operate some 230 vehicles in and around Sheffield and Rotherham.

Yorkshire Traction's services cover much of South Yorkshire and extend into West Yorkshire too. Its routes reach Huddersfield and Leeds, but the heart of its operations is in the area around Barnsley and east towards Mexborough and Doncaster. Southwards it has a strong presence in Rotherham (made even stronger through ownership of Andrews and Yorkshire Terrier) and has services through to the busy Meadowhall shopping centre alongside the M1 motorway, and in to central Sheffield.

This is another company which has moved away from double-deckers since it was privatised in 1987. In round numbers it has 100 (out of a total fleet of 365), of which just over 70 are standard NBC-specification Olympians with Gardner engines and ECW bodies. These date from the 1981-85 period. In 1986, while still owned by NBC, Yorkshire Traction took 16 Metrobuses with MCW bodywork built to a slightly lower height than normal. Since privatisation the only double-decked additions to the fleet have been five ex-West Midlands Metrobuses and four East Lancs-bodied Volvo Citybuses which were transferred from the Lincoln City Transport fleet. These have coach seats and are used principally on the company's express services between Barnsley, Doncaster, Sheffield, Leeds and Bradford.

The single-deck fleet has just over 50 National 2s, an NBC legacy. There are also eight Leyland Lynxes which were operated for a short time in Barnsley by Shearings before that company decided to give up its operations in the town. Since 1991 Yorkshire Traction has adopted a three-strand buying policy, ordering Scanias where it needs full-size buses, Darts for midibus operations and Renaults and Mercedes for its minibus operations which run under the Townlink name.

There's considerable variety in the Scanias. The first five, in 1991, were N113s with Alexander PS-type bodies. Then came two batches of the cheaper K93 with Wright Endurance bodywork. There are 10 in all, delivered in 1992-93. The most recent deliveries have been of the new L113. There are five bodied by Northern Counties and five with East Lancs bodies. The Dart story is more straightforward. Of the 29 in the fleet, 20 have Wright Handybus bodies while the remainder are Plaxton Pointers, including the three ex-South Yorkshire Transport buses which were just a few months old and barely run-in when they were snapped up by Yorkshire Traction in 1994.

The company's oldest minibuses are MCW Metroriders, including 10 ex-SUT examples, but more recently it has been buying Mercedes 811Ds and Renault S75s. Ten S75s bought new in 1991 were followed in 1994 by 13 acquired from London Buses where they formed part of the RB-class. YTC in fact purchased all 33 of London's RBs, the other 20 being allocated to Strathtay and Lincolnshire Road Car.

Barnsley & District is a YTC offshoot which revives the original name of its parent company. The original company disappeared in 1928; the new one was formed in 1990 to take over the local bus operations being run by Tom Jowitt, who was running in competition with YTC. As well as serving Barnsley, it has routes running south to Sheffield. Most of Barnsley & District's 40 buses are ex-Yorkshire Traction Nationals, but there are four former West Midlands Fleetlines, transferred from the Andrews fleet (and B&D's only double-deckers), and a few Mercedes and MCW minibuses. Local operator Globe Coaches competes in Barnsley with Leyland Nationals, a Cub and elderly coaches.

Top Since privatisation all new full-size buses for Yorkshire Traction have been Scanias. It now has 25, including 10 K93s with Wright Endurance bodies. These are regular performers on the Huddersfield to Leeds service. Tony Wilson

Centre Most of the double-deckers in the Yorkshire Traction fleet are Leyland Olympians with ECW bodies, delivered in the early 1980s when the company was part of NBC. There are 73 broadly similar buses in operation. Richard Godfrey

Right The Barnsley & District company runs more Nationals than any other type. New in 1976, this Mark I came from Go-Ahead Northern in 1992. It is seen in Barnsley. Richard Godfrey

Sheffield was once a hot-bed of competition with severe traffic congestion in the city centre and a multiplicity of operators running a variety of second-hand buses. It's still a colourful place, but one by one most of the new breed of small companies have sold out to established operators. However most of the small operators' liveries have been retained by their new owners – so while some of the competition has eased, Sheffield still has a plentiful supply of multi-coloured buses. Its bus operators also have competition from the South Yorkshire Supertram which started running in 1994 and has a fleet of 25 German-built double-articulated trams.

The main operator in Sheffield is the Mainline Group. The Mainline name first appeared in 1989 when it was adopted by South Yorkshire Transport to create a new image for selected services where SYT faced or expected competition from new operators. First came Sheffield Mainline in yellow and red, to be followed in 1990 by Rotherham Mainline in yellow and blue and Doncaster Mainline in grey and red, which was perhaps the least successful of the new colour schemes.

The decision to adopt Mainline as the trading name for the entire fleet was taken in 1992, and the bright yellow and red Sheffield livery was modified for fleet-wide use with the addition of blue and silver relief. But there are still buses around in the first generation Mainline liveries – and even a very few Dennis Dominators in the previous SYT red and biege. Mainline was privatised in a management/employee buy-out at the end of 1993. In 1994 Stagecoach acquired a 20 per cent share in the company, but was instructed by the Department of Trade and Industry to divest itself of this interest which was viewed as being anti-competitive. In the summer of 1995 FirstBus took over Stagecoach's interest in Mainline.

In Sheffield Dominators dominate, most with Alexander R-type bodies. But there are also significant numbers of MCW Metrobuses and even a few Leyland Atlanteans, some with rare Marshall double-deck bodies. Cambridge-based Marshall made a brief foray into the double-deck bus business between 1978 and 1983 and the South Yorkshire PTE was its biggest customer, taking 30. The only other buyers of Marshall double-deck bodies were Bournemouth, Derby, Leicester, Newport and Strathclyde.

Top **A small number of Mainline buses are still running in the old South Yorkshire Transport colours. They include this 1983 Dennis Dominator with Alexander bodywork seen in Sheffield's impressive Interchange. Mainline is Britain's biggest Dominator operator.** Stewart J Brown

Centre **Mainline operates 72 MCW Metrobuses. The oldest are Mark I models with asymmetric windscreens. They were delivered to South Yorkshire Transport in 1981.** Stewart J Brown

Right **Being delivered at the same time as the Metrobuses were Leyland Atlanteans with Voith gearboxes and Marshall bodies. Marshall double-deck bodies were never particularly common. Around a dozen survive in Mainline service.** Stewart J Brown

In recent years Mainline has standardised on single-deckers which means that the most modern double-deckers in operation are D-registered Dominators. The single-deckers are mainly Volvo B10Ms with Alexander's PS-type bodywork – there are 140 in service – although in 1995 these were joined by 30 Plaxton-bodied Volvo B6s. The B6s were purchased after comparative trials of a B6/Plaxton and a Dart/Northern Counties, both of which are still in the fleet.

Unusual vehicles operated by Mainline are 13 Leyland-DAB articulated buses, some of which can be found running between Sheffield and Meadowhall. Mainline also runs the first Volvo B10L low-floor bus in Britain, a Swedish-built prototype with Saffle bodywork. It is on extended loan from Volvo. Minibuses are mainly Renaults with Reeve Burgess Beaver bodies, a few of which retain the yellow, red and blue Eager Beaver livery introduced in 1989 to give a bright new image to SYT's small buses. Most are now in fleet colours. Some of the Renaults – and four Reeve Burgess-bodied Ivecos – were purchased second-hand from Lincoln City Transport in 1989 following the failure of an attempt by LCT to run services in Scunthorpe.

Top Before adopting Mainline as a fleet-wide identity, each of the main towns in South Yorkshire had its own Mainline livery. Doncaster Mainline was perhaps the least successful. It is seen here on a 1990 Volvo B10M with Alexander PS-type body. A few buses are still running in this colour scheme. Malcolm King

Centre Rotherham Mainline is also disappearing. The use of blue in the livery was a throwback to the days of municipal buses in the town. A Volvo B10M - one of 140 in the Mainline fleet - loads in Rotherham town centre. Stewart J Brown

Left Articulated buses have so far failed to make much impression on British operators. Mainline is the only significant user of the type with 13 Danish-built Leyland DABs. New in 1985, this three-door bus is a 60-seater. Stewart J Brown

SYT took over a number of small operators in the late 1980s (incurring the wrath of the Monopolies & Mergers Commission in doing so). These were SUT, Sheaf Line, Caldaire's Sheffield & District operation and Groves Coaches. They were ultimately combined in SYT's Sheaf Line subsidiary, which built up a fleet of around 100 Leyland Nationals. Sheaf Line has now been absorbed into the Mainline fleet, but a number of Nationals retain its red, white and blue livery although most are now in Mainline colours. The Nationals came from a variety of sources and most are 500-engined Mark 1s although there are some Mark 2s and two Greenway rebuilds, as well as a few Mark 1s which have been fitted with Gardner engines. Odd buses operated by Sheaf Line were two Neoplan N416 single-deckers which are now in Mainline colours. These were added to the SUT fleet when it was owned by ATL, whose main business was Carlton PSV, the Neoplan importer. Carlton had plans to assemble Neoplans at its workshops on the outskirts of Rotherham.

One small Mainline operation which retained its identity until the middle of 1995 was Don Valley Buses, running 17 second-hand minibuses. This operation was based on the Drabble's coach business which had been acquired by Skills of Nottingham. It was taken over by SYT in 1991 and runs in Sheffield with a varied fleet including seven Mercedes taken over from Skills, and Dodge S56s transferred from the Mainline fleet. However this operation is now losing its individuality and the fleet is being repainted in Mainline colours.

Top **The integration of Sheaf Line into the Mainline operation has seen some unusual types appearing in Mainline colours. These include a pair of East Lancs Greenways. The National on which this one is based came from West Riding.** Tony Wilson

Centre **Forty Volvo B6s with Plaxton Pointer bodies were delivered to Mainline in 1995, marking the first significant intake of midibuses. Previously there were only two – one B6 and one Dennis Dart.** Stewart J Brown

Below **Sheaf Line has not disappeared completely and its colours can still be seen on a number of the Mark 1 Nationals which were the mainstay of the fleet. This bus was new to Yorkshire Woollen in 1977.** Stewart J Brown

Two of Mainline's erstwhile competitors lost their independence in the early part of 1995 but their operations continue with little outward change. The first to fall was Sheffield Omnibus. This dated back to January 1991 and its livery – cream and blue – was that carried by its first buses, seven ex-Preston Atlanteans. It was bought by Yorkshire Traction in March 1995, by which time the fleet strength was 95 with a mixture of new and second-hand buses. The latter are primarily Atlanteans, but there are three Bristol VRTs with Alexander bodies which were new to Northampton Transport and came via Sheffield Omnibus's ill-fated Nottingham Omnibus venture. There are also nine Leyland National 2s. Single-deck oddities are two Atlanteans rebodied with East Lancs Sprint bodies. Both had their chassis lengthened to accommodate 47-seat bodywork and entered Sheffield Omnibus service in 1992 and 1993. How long will they last?

Recent new additions to the Sheffield Omnibus fleet have all been Alexander-bodied and have included five Leyland Olympians (among some of the last to be built), three Volvo B10Ms which are generally similar to Mainline's standard bus and, bought shortly before the company's take-over, 14 Volvo B6s. Among the B6 fleet are some of the early Austrian-built chassis which were bodied by Alexander and operated for a short time by Stagecoach's Cumberland subsidiary. Volvo had originally intended to import the B6 chassis to Britain from its Steyr factory, before deciding to start production at its Irvine truck plant on the Ayrshire coast. While much of the Sheffield Omnibus operation is centred on the city, it does run north to Barnsley.

No sooner was the ink dry on the Sheffield Omnibus take-over contract than Yorkshire Traction had its cheque book out again, buying Yorkshire Terrier in May. Yorkshire Terrier had started operating in 1988 with a fleet of seven Leyland Nationals. The 76-strong fleet in 1995 is still made up mainly of Mark 1 Nationals from a variety of sources, but also includes a small number of new buses. These are Dennis Darts with Plaxton Pointer bodies and Alexander-bodied Volvo B6s. If you like jokey registrations watch out for the Pointer registered K9YTB – canine, Yorkshire Terrier Buses. Unusual second-hand purchases were six 1987 Scanias which came from British Airways. Their East Lancs bodies originally had large luggage lockers which were removed by Willowbrook. One body has since been substantially rebuilt using Leyland National window pans. Yorkshire Terrier took over Kingsman of Matlock in 1992 and Kingsman remains a separate company which is also owned by YTC. The Kingsman name is carried on a few Nationals and some coaches.

Top **Sheffield Omnibus started up in 1991 running ex-Preston Atlanteans and then adopted the Preston livery for subsequent additions to the fleet, as illustrated by an ECW-bodied AN68 which coincidentally came from the other major Preston-based bus company, Ribble. It is one of seven similar buses acquired in 1994.**
Stewart J Brown

Left **Most of Yorkshire Terrier's buses are Leyland Nationals. This example seen in Sheffield centre came from Wilts & Dorset.**
Stewart J Brown

Above **South Riding had a short existence as an independent. It started in 1992 and sold out to Yorkshire Traction in 1994. Its fleet is made up entirely of Leyland Nationals.** Stewart J Brown

Right **Andrews was a double-deck operation until it was taken over by Yorkshire Traction. Its new owners have been replacing elderly Fleetlines with marginally younger Leyland Nationals. This bus was transferred from Yorkshire Traction in 1994.** Tony Wilson

Below right **The first signs of rationalisation among Yorkshire Traction's subsidiaries in Sheffield came in the summer of 1995 with the appearance of a combined Andrews Sheffield Omnibus name and livery using Andrews blue and Sheffield Omnibus cream. An early repaint was this ex-demonstration Volvo B6.** Tony Wilson

Sheffield Omnibus and Yorkshire Terrier considerably strengthen YTC's presence in Sheffield. It already owned two other operations – Andrews and South Riding. Andrews ran a predominantly double-deck fleet and while these are still much in evidence, under YTC ownership almost half of the 50-plus fleet has been replaced by Leyland Nationals. There are now 26 former YTC Nationals in service. The double-deck fleet is still made up largely of Daimler Fleetlines, smartly turned out despite their age. All were at the very least second-hand when acquired by Andrews. They include a DMS look-alike which was new to SYT, and two former Cleveland low-height examples with old-fashioned five-bay Northern Counties bodywork. The oldest are N-registered ECW-bodied buses which were new to the South Yorkshire PTE. The newest is a W-registered bus from the GM Buses fleet. All of Andrews' vehicles are named. No doubt if you stood in central Sheffield long enough it would be possible to see Robin Hood being pursued by the Sheriff of Nottingham, or Sheffield Wednesday facing up to Sheffield United. The first sign of rationalisation by YTC was the adoption of a new cream and blue livery and the use of the Andrews Sheffield Omnibus name on repainted buses acquired from both operators.

South Riding was short-lived as an independent operator. It started in the summer of 1992, and was bought by YTC in the autumn of 1994. Its 40-vehicle fleet is made up solely of Leyland Nationals and one of its main routes is to Crystal Peaks, where it competes with Mainline running new B10Ms. All of YTC's Sheffield-based subsidiaries provide local services in and around the city, although Yorkshire Terrier has a route to Rotherham, trading under the Kingsman name and running Leyland Nationals.

Above **Northern Bus is one of the main supporters of the Bristol RE and runs most variants of what was the most successful of Britain's first-generation rear-engined single-deck chassis. This 1973 RELH6L, photographed at Dinnington, came to the operator from Trent in 1990.** Mike Harris

Left **The REs, because of their relative rarity, tend to overshadow the other Bristols in the Northern Bus fleet. These are mainly Series 3 Bristol VRTs, the newest of which are V-registered buses. This one came from Crosville Wales.** Tony Wilson

Below left **Thompson Travel run two of these Alexander-bodied Leopards. They look like typical ex-SBG vehicles but were in fact new to Lothian Region Transport.** Malcolm King

The rapid absorption Sheffield's small operators leaves just one significant truly independent operator in the city, Northern Bus. This operation, based at North Anston, has achieved fame through its fondness for Bristols, and both REs and VRTs can be seen on services in Sheffield city centre and at Meadowhall. Some of the VRTs wear a Tilling-style green livery and operate under the Bradfield Bus banner. The REs have ECW bus and Plaxton coach bodies. Recent additions to the fleet have been Leopard coaches including some from Crosville Wales still running in their previous owner's colours. The company's two midibuses, stylish Bedford JJLs which were truly ahead of their time, are still owned but out of use. Northern Bus routes are largely to the east and south of Sheffield.

Thompson Travel runs south from Sheffield to Dronfield using Leopard coaches with bodywork by Alexander, Duple and Plaxton. The Alexander-bodied Leopards started life with Lothian Region Transport. Another operator serving the area south of Sheffield is Aston Express, running to Eckington and Crystal Peaks in competition with Mainline. Aston owns nine vehicles, five of which are second-hand minibuses. Its full-size vehicles include a former Green Line RB-class AEC Reliance which is used on the service. Stagecoach livery can be seen in Sheffield on East Midland buses running in from Mansfield and Doncaster.

The eastern centre of Mainline operation is Doncaster, where a number of Alexander-bodied B10Ms and Dominators still carry the grey-based Doncaster Mainline colours, although most buses are now in the current standard Mainline yellow. Here there are also a few Atlanteans, some of the new B6s, and minibuses – some still in Eager Beaver colours. The minibuses include ex-Lincoln vehicles.

Doncaster, unusually for a town of its size, boasts two bus stations. Both are 1960s edifices located under multistorey car parks. The North bus station is located alongside the East Coast Main Line near the railway station and is served by Mainline, Yorkshire Traction, Yorkshire Rider (from Wakefield), East Midland, West Riding and Wilfreda Beehive. The last named runs Leyland Nationals and Dennis Darts on local services. There are 17 Nationals, including one East Lancs Greenway rebuild with a wheelchair lift, and eight Darts, all with Plaxton's popular Pointer body.

The South bus station is also served by Mainline and East Midland, as well as by the sole survivor of the original generation of Doncaster area independent operators, Leon of Finningley. Leon's fleet includes Daimler Fleetlines (two of which were bought new), Optare MetroRiders (its newest buses), and two Optare-bodied Leyland Cubs from the batch of 15 bought by the West Yorkshire PTE in 1986, but soon sold on to other operators. Leon's routes run east to Finningley and points beyond. Retford & District, the Chesterfield Transport subsidiary, serves both the north and the south bus stations with infrequent services from Askern and Sykehouse.

Meadowhall is among some of Britain's busiest bus stations, with up to 1,800 departures a day. Situated between the giant shopping centre and the new Supertram terminal, it is served by virtually every operator in Yorkshire and by some from further afield too. It can appear deceptively quiet because it is not a terminal for most of the services using it. This means that most buses are only in the station for as long as it takes to drop off and pick up passengers. It has a comprehensive passenger information system in the main concourse, as does the recently renovated bus station in Sheffield city centre. Work is in hand on upgrading Rotherham bus station to similar high standards.

Wilfreda Beehive operate Nationals and Darts in Doncaster. There are eight Darts, all with Plaxton Pointer bodies. Stewart J Brown

Leon operates a varied fleet which ranges from minibuses to double-deckers. It includes a pair of Leyland Cubs from a batch of 15 bodied by Optare for the West Yorkshire PTE. They had short lives with their original owner, entering service in 1986 and being sold in 1987 – which is when Leon acquired this bus. Stewart J Brown

Rotherham is also Mainline territory and a few vehicles, mainly Alexander-bodied B10Ms, are still in the yellow and blue Rotherham Mainline colours. Many of the Volvo B6s delivered to Mainline in the spring of 1995 are in the Rotherham area. Smaller operators in the town are Globe Coaches of Barnsley, running a fleet of down-at-heel Dodge minibuses with Reeve Burgess bodies. Some of these were new to SYT. Gordons Coaches run a few out-of-town routes, using in the main Plaxton-bodied coaches which have been demoted from front-line coaching duties.

Pontefract is still South Yorkshire Transport territory, although ownership of the company has passed via Caldaire to British Bus. Among the smaller operators serving Pontefract is Ross Travel, with MCW Metroriders operating to Featherstone, the company's home town. Of more interest are five ex-Lothian Leyland Cubs, which are also used on service. They have Duple Dominant bus bodies. Stringers, a local coach operator, also serve the town. Two former Bristol Cityline VRTs are operated, along with Leopard and Bedford coaches. The VRTs started life as two-door buses but were later converted to single-door. The centrally-located stairs give the game away to those in the know. Coach operator Clarksons of South Elmsall run into the town and in 1995 bought its first new service buses, two Ikarus-bodied DAF SB220s which entered service in white. These joined four Leyland Nationals in the company's blue and white fleet livery.

Top **Another unusual batch of Cubs was supplied to Lothian Region Transport, which took 18 in 1981 with Duple bodies. They lasted with their first owner until 1993, when Ross Travel bought five. The Cub is front-engined and was built at Leyland's Bathgate truck plant.** Phillip Stephenson

Right **Stringers of Pontefract operate two Bristol VRTs which were new to Bristol Omnibus. They have been in the Stringers fleet since 1993.** Stewart J Brown

Below **The first new buses for Clarksons of South Elmsall took to the road in 1994. They are two DAF SB220s with Ikarus bodies.** Michael Fowler

Below right **Globe Coaches of Barnsley operate anonymous minibuses in Rotherham. They include three Reeve Burgess-bodied Dodge S56s which were new to South Yorkshire Transport in 1986 but came to Globe via other operators, including Moffat & Williamson in Fife.** Stewart J Brown

THE MIDLANDS

Top **The bus fleet operated by Ludlows of Halesowen is made up mainly of Mark 1 Leyland Nationals.
This 1974 bus was new to London Country and came to Ludlows in 1992 by way of Southend Transport.** Mark Bailey

Above **An odd vehicle operated by Cave of Shirley is this short Bedford YRQ. It was new in 1974 to Cleveland Transit who cut off both body and chassis aft of the
rear wheels in the early 1980s when they needed a small vehicle to replace a midibus. Its Duple body originally seated 47. It now has 36 seats.** Malcolm Keeley

Britain's biggest bus operator is West Midlands Travel, with a fleet nudging the 1,900 mark. In 1994 it adopted WM Buses as its trading name, followed by a local identity for each of the company's main garages. WM Buses is the inheritor of the former West Midlands PTE operation. Despite its size at a time when the Government was preaching that small was beautiful (or at least more conducive to competition), it was privatised as a single company in 1991 in a management-led employee buy-out. Some deft work by the company's management and local politicians helped achieve this – which is in stark contrast to what happened in Manchester where the whole privatisation process was handled less ably and the former PTE operation was forced by the Government to split in two before being sold.

The bulk of the WM Buses fleet is double-decked. It is the biggest operator of the locally-built MCW Metrobus with a fleet of almost 1,100. These were produced at Washwood Heath to the north-east of the city between 1979 and 1990. London Buses was of course the biggest buyer of Metrobuses, but its fleet (which totalled 1,471) is now divided between the privatised former London Buses subsidiaries. WM Buses also runs the biggest fleet of Fleetlines, with just over 150 remaining. Most of these have bodywork by MCW or Park Royal to designs evolved by the PTE, but whose history can be traced back to the last days of Birmingham City Transport. The company's only other double-deck buses are 40 Alexander-bodied Scanias delivered in 1990. These are numbered from 3201 but because of WM's desire to match fleet and registration numbers and the DVLA's policy of retaining those numbers which they believe may be saleable, the highest numbered Scania is in fact 3247. All of WM Buses' double-deck types can be seen in and around central Birmingham. Most are in the current silver, blue and red livery, but a small number of double-deckers survive in the previous colour scheme in which a grey-like silver predominated.

Single-deck types in Birmingham are mainly Leyland Lynxes, from the record 250-bus order delivered in 1989. This makes WM Buses far and away the world's biggest Lynx user. There are also Leyland Nationals, including some taken over with the Metrowest business in 1993 and now repainted in WM Buses colours, following Metrowest's absorption into the main fleet in 1994. These can be identified by their 16xx and 17xx fleet numbers and by having registrations issued in places other than Birmingham. With over 100 in the fleet, WM Buses is now also the country's biggest Leyland National operator.

WM Buses' minibuses are few and far between in the city centre. Those that do run in to the central area are Mercedes 709Ds from a batch of 20 delivered in 1990 and bodied locally by the now defunct Carlyle company, or earlier MCW Metroriders of which there are around 80 in the fleet.

Top **West Midlands Travel has the country's biggest fleet of MCW Metrobuses. A 1981 Mark 1 heads through Solihull.** Stewart J Brown

Centre **West Midlands Travel also has Britain's biggest surviving Fleetline fleet, with around 150 still in use. Park Royal bodywork is fitted to this example.** Stewart J Brown

Left **The oldest buses in regular West Midlands Travel service are 1974 Leyland Nationals. There are around 50. Local fleetnames – Wolverhampton on this bus – were introduced in 1994.** Stewart J Brown

In 1994 WM Buses bought a controlling interest in the Your Bus operation run by Smiths of Shennington. Your Bus had been a strong competitor for a number of years on trunk routes south of the city. WM Buses' vehicles are generally turned out to a high standard, although the same cannot be said of the Your Bus operation where standards of vehicle presentation are varied. Most carry WM Buses logos on their Greater Manchester-inspired brown, orange and white livery. The Your Bus fleet is a fairly modern one, and varied too. There are 19 buses with Plaxton Derwent bodies (another WM Buses record) on a mix of Leyland Tiger and Volvo B10M chassis. Then there are 21 DAF SB220s, five with Optare Delta bodywork and the remainder with Hungarian-built Ikarus bodies. These are all dealer-registered which obscures the fact that six of the Ikarus-bodied buses are second-hand. Indeed there are three with consecutive registrations which came from three different sources. Recent additions to the Your Bus fleet have been Leyland Nationals which came to WM Buses with the Metrowest business. These have ousted the last double-deckers from regular service.

Midland Red West runs into Birmingham, primarily with Dennis Lances, while Midland Red North operates a variety of types including Olympians, Volvo Citybuses (ex-London & Country) and Tigers. Sister British Bus subsidiary Stevensons of Uttoxeter operates in from Lichfield and Burton. There is little visible sign as yet of Stagecoach in central Birmingham, but the group is represented by Midland Red South running in from Stratford with Olympians which at present retain the Stratford Blue colours used for buses serving the town. The appearance of corporate Stagecoach colours is simply a matter of time.

There are a number of small operators serving the city, most of whom use the ubiquitous Leyland National. There is some irony in a bus which was shunned by small operators when it was new – largely because of its cost and complexity – being snapped up by a new generation of small operators as it nears the end of its design life.

The biggest National fleet serving the city – apart from WM Buses – is that run by the Birmingham Coach Company. It has just over 50, drawn from a wide range of operators country-wide. Services are operated in Halesowen, West Bromwich and Wolverhampton. The company was formed in 1984 and moved into local bus operation in 1986. Falcon Travel operate south to Maypole – a route over which WM Buses and Your Bus fought – and their seven-vehicle fleet is made up solely of Nationals. Rest and Ride of Smethwick run a National-operated service in an unexciting white livery.

Top **Your Bus has retained its Manchester-inspired colour scheme under its new ownership, but most vehicles carry a WM prefix to the Your Bus fleetname. This is a DAF SB220 with Ikarus body.** Stewart J Brown

Centre **The Birmingham Coach Company is a major user of Leyland Nationals, with a fleet of just over 50. These have come from a number of operators, including Merseyside Transport.** Mike Harris

Right **Falcon Travel's fleet consists solely of Leyland Nationals. There are seven, operating between Birmingham city centre and Maypole. This smart example came from Wilts & Dorset in 1993, the year in which Falcon Travel started.** Stewart J Brown

Serveverse started running to Chelmsley Wood in 1992 and have a seven-strong fleet comprising five Nationals and two minibuses. Chelmsley Wood is also the destination for a service run by Claribels, using Leyland Leopard coaches, most of which have Duple Dominant bodies. One National operator to have vanished – possibly temporarily – is City Buslines of Hockley. City Buslines was formed in 1993 by ex-WM Travel employees. The company built up a fleet of 13 Nationals which turned out to be an unlucky number when most were put off the road by the traffic commissioner in the summer of 1995. The reason was a common National failing: excessive exhaust smoke. Hi-Ride of Handsworth runs a suburban service from Bearwood in the west to Witton in the north which by-passes Birmingham city centre. The fleet is made up of elderly Leopards.

The only regular double-deck operation by a small operator is the North Birmingham Busways route north from the city to Sutton Coldfield. This started in 1994 and is run by five ex-Blackpool Transport Atlanteans, still in Blackpool colours. There are a few minibus operators in the city too. Little Red Bus of Smethwick – no prizes for guessing the fleet livery – run around a dozen Dodge S56s which were new to Ribble, GM Buses, Go-Ahead Northern and Merseyside. Bodywork is by Dormobile (rare on an S56), Northern Counties and Alexander. Pete's Travel run Reeve Burgess-bodied Dodge S56s and a PMT-bodied Sherpa.

Solihull is solid WM Buses territory, but Cave of Shirley run locally, normally with Leyland Nationals. More interesting vehicles in the fleet are the only two bought new, a Carlyle-bodied Dennis Dart and a Willowbrook-bodied ACE Cougar. The Cougar is one of two built in 1991 by West Yorkshire-based Alternative Chassis Engineering; the other runs for People's Provincial. Cave also has Duple bus-bodied Bedfords. Lionspeed also run into Solihull and nearby Shirley, as well as having operations on the other side of the city at Sutton Coldfield. The Lionspeed fleet is made up of rather less dramatic vehicles than the name might imply – seven second-hand Sherpas.

The biggest shopping centre in the West Midlands is at Merry Hill. Services to the centre are provided by a number of operators including Merry Hill Minibus, started in 1988 with the aim of running a 100-strong fleet. The recession put an end to that, but it does run just under 50 buses, most of which are Carlyle-bodied Sherpas. WM Buses, Ludlows and Midland Red West run to Merry Hill, and added transport interest is provided by a monorail service on the site.

Top **Some Serveverse vehicles confusingly carry Serverse as a fleetname, including this B-series Leyland National seen in Tamworth.** Tony Wilson

Centre **North Birmingham Busways started operating between Birmingham and Sutton Coldfield with five ex-Blackpool Transport Atlanteans. These retain Blackpool's livery – which has now been applied to subsequent additions to the fleet. The ex-Blackpool buses are long-wheelbase AN68/2s with 86-seat East Lancs bodies. This one was new in 1978.** Malcolm Keeley

Left **Pete's Travel run between Walsall and West Bromwich, mainly using Dodge S56s. A recent addition to the fleet is this example with Northern Counties body. It was new to Merseyside Transport.** Mark Bailey

In Coventry, standard WM Buses predominate – Metrobuses, Lynxes and Fleetlines. But there is also a strong Stagecoach presence, albeit in a variety of guises. The modern corporate look is represented mainly by Midland Red South, with Alexander-bodied Mercedes minis, along with the occasional B6 and B10M. Midland Red South – which trades simply as Midland Red on corporate-liveried full-size buses – also runs under the Metro name, inherited with silver-liveried Ford Transits which came from the Gloucester Metro operations of Cheltenham & Gloucester and which are still in use. Many Midland Red South vehicles retain their previous poppy red, grey and white scheme, which can be seen on Olympians, Nationals, and Wright-bodied Mercedes minibuses. Buses in Stratford Blue colours also run in to Coventry. Midland Red South holds contracts from Centro (the West Midlands PTE's trading name) to provide Easyrider services for disabled travellers, using specially-liveried Nationals with wheelchair lifts, and for a park-and-ride service, operated by new green and cream liveried Mercedes 709Ds. One of the Midland Red South National 1s has been converted to run on LPG. It sounds much the same as any diesel-powered National 1, but does have a noticeably cleaner exhaust. Perhaps City Buslines should have given LPG a try.

Stagecoach also owns two smaller operations which came, like Midland Red South, with its acquisition of Western Travel at the end of 1993. G&G is based at Leamington Spa and shows little sign of its new status as a Stagecoach subsidiary. It is still running a mix of new and second-hand buses. The former are Leyland Lynxes; the latter include VRTs. Many look just a bit tired. The initials are those of the founding partners, two gentlemen by the name of Green and Griffin. Vanguard of Bedworth is an altogether smarter operation than G&G, running Nationals into Coventry. Some are in Stagecoach colours and some in Vanguard livery. The latter include a dual-door ex-London bus. Vanguard also operate ageing Leopards, some in the company's old colours (such as two East Lancs-bodied buses which were new to Rhymney Valley), and others in Stagecoach white-and-stripes. The Vanguard operation is entirely single-deck.

Small operators running in Coventry include A-Line of Bedworth with assorted second-hand Nationals. Most originally ran for NBC subsidiaries, but there is an ex-Northampton Transport bus. A-Line operate to Rugby and to Leamington Spa. Coach operator M J de Courcey has a Willowbrook-bodied Leopard, which appears on a local service. The front end of its Crusader coach body has been heavily rebuilt. The body was built in 1988 on a 1976 chassis.

Top **The growth of Stagecoach leads to some interesting vehicle transfers. Still in full Ribble livery, this Bristol VRT is now running for Midland Red South. At least it's red!** Stewart J Brown

Centre **The final Midland Red South livery prior to the Stagecoach takeover retained NBC poppy red, but with grey and white relief. A Mark 1 National is seen in Coventry.** Stewart J Brown

Right **The Stratford Blue name was used by Midland Red South for its operations in Shakespeare's birthplace, along with an appropriate livery which is now being superseded by corporate Stagecoach white. This 1985 ECW-bodied Leyland Olympian is one of a batch of three which were the most modern double-deckers in the Midland Red South fleet when Stagecoach took control.** Malcolm Keeley

Still looking for all the world like a small independent, Vanguard is part of the mighty Stagecoach group, having been acquired with Western Travel at the end of 1993. This National was originally part of London Transport's fleet. Stewart J Brown

A-Line of Bedworth operate Nationals between Coventry and Rugby including this bus which was one of a batch of 48 delivered to Midland Red in 1977. A sister vehicle still running with Midland Red South is shown on the previous page. Stewart J Brown

An Ulster registration mark hides the fact that the chassis of this Leyland Leopard in the de Courcey fleet was new in 1976 to Leicester City Transport. The Willowbrook Crusader body was fitted for de Courcey in 1988 and has subsequently been rebuilt with Plaxton Paramount windscreens. It is seen loading in Coventry's recently modernised bus station. Stewart J Brown

Wolverhampton has attracted a fair number of operators to challenge WM Buses. The WM Buses Wolverhampton fleet includes a few non-standard types among the Fleetlines, Metrobuses, Nationals and Lynxes. It has the company's Volvo single-deckers. There are six Alexander P-type Citybuses purchased in 1986 for evaluation against six Leyland Lynxes, a trial in which the Lynx won and which led to WM Buses having the world's biggest fleet of the type – 256. More recently, in 1994, WM Buses took six B10Bs with Alexander Strider bodies and these too can be seen in Wolverhampton. Some of the Plaxton-bodied Dennis Darts acquired with Your Bus have been repainted in WM Buses livery and are running in Wolverhampton. Among the double-deckers serving the town are the surviving East Lancs-bodied Fleetlines which are based in Walsall. A free city centre service is operated by dual-door National 2s in an odd livery which retains WM Buses colours on the front but with off-white sides.

The biggest of the smaller operators serving Wolverhampton and Walsall is Chase Bus Services, which has a fleet of almost 60 buses, most of which are Leyland Nationals. A good number of these have come from London Buses, but there are examples from all over the country – from Western Scottish in the north to Bristol Omnibus in the south. All are Mark 1s, a couple of which have been re-engined with Leyland 680s. These can be identified by their rebuilt rear ends, which have been modified to allow for the repositioning of the radiator – the 680 engine takes up more space than the standard 500-series unit. The only other buses in the Chase fleet are five Leopards with East Lancs bodies. Chase Bus Services is based in Chasetown and operates north to Lichfield and occasionally south to Birmingham. The Chase livery is a straight copy of that used by Greater Manchester Transport in the early 1980s – the company's first buses included a pair of ex-GMT Nationals.

Choice Travel, previously Midland Choice, also serves both Walsall and Wolverhampton with Leyland Nationals. It runs 10, and like those in the Chase fleet they have come from fleets spread around the country. Again, all are Mark 1s. The company's first new bus, delivered in 1995, was a Dennis Dart. Glenstuart is based in Wolverhampton and runs to Pendeford, with second-hand Nationals in a red and white livery which is not unlike that used by Red & White in South Wales. Of more interest are a pair of ex-Lancaster Leopards with Alexander Y-type bodywork and an 18-year-old Bedford Y-series with Willowbrook bus body, a rare type to find on an urban bus service in the mid 1990s.

Top **West Midlands Travel's newest buses are six Volvo B10Bs with Alexander Strider bodies. They are allocated to Wolverhampton. More B10Bs are on order, but with bodywork by Wright of Ballymena.** R Godfrey

Centre **Chase Bus Services is another West Midlands independent with a large fleet of Leyland Nationals. These include over two dozen which started life with London Transport.** Mark Bailey

Right **The first new bus for Midland Choice was this Dennis Dart, which entered service in 1995. It has Northern Counties bodywork and joined a fleet composed mainly of Leyland Nationals.** Mark Bailey

Operating minibuses in Wolverhampton is Banga Travel, with a mixture of Sherpas and Dodge S46s. The latter are Northern Counties-bodied buses which were new to Alder Valley and an Alexander-bodied bus originally owned by Central Scottish. Farestage Travel runs a Sherpa with PMT body. PMT tried to break away from the uninspiring designs used for most first-generation minibuses by adopting a distinctive sloping waistrail and angular windows.

A pre-deregulation operator is Green Bus Service. The 24-strong fleet is made up of 23 Leylands (none younger than 16 years old) and one Bedford OB. The single-deckers are all Leopards with bus bodies by Duple, East Lancs, Plaxton and Willowbrook. Its double-deckers are mainly Atlanteans, but one lowbridge PD3 survives. It was new in 1965 to Caerphilly Urban District Council. The Atlanteans include examples built for the South Yorkshire and Greater Manchester PTEs. The company is based in Great Wyrley and runs to Rugeley and Cannock, as well as in the Wolverhampton area. It uses traditional shaded numerals for its fleet numbers, redolent of a bygone age in public transport.

Walsall has much the same mix of WM Buses vehicles as can be seen in most other parts of the company's territory. WM Buses Walsall has, as mentioned above, the few surviving East Lancs-bodied Fleetlines which date from 1977-78. It also has the only midibuses bought new by the company, five Dennis Darts with Wright Handybus bodies which were registered in Ulster by the bodybuilder. Note that they have two different front end styles. Some have the standard single-piece flat glass screen while others have the split screen with the offside window recessed, as specified for later deliveries to London Buses. From Walsall services run as far north as Lichfield.

Competition for WM Buses in West Bromwich comes from Sandwell Travel running an odd mixture of buses, four of which have in common Wadham Stringer Vanguard bodywork. These are two Ford R-series, a Dennis Lancet and a Leyland Cub. There are also East Lancs-bodied Dodge S56s (another rare combination) which were new to Maidstone Boro'line.

Top **Banga Travel operate local services in Wolverhampton using second-hand minibuses. A recent arrival is this Alexander-bodied Dodge S56, one of a fleet purchased by Central Scottish for post-deregulation expansion in Glasgow.** Stewart J Brown

Centre **In the 1970s the Willowbrook-bodied Bedford Y-series was a favourite choice for many small operators, offering reliability and relatively low running costs. Few survive in the 1990s. Glenstuart Travel have one which is used on the company's Wolverhampton local service.** Keith Grimes

Left **Green Bus Service is well-known for its fleet of Leylands, of which make Leopards are the predominant type. The newest are V-registered buses, including this one-time Lancaster vehicle with Duple Dominant body. It is seen in Wolverhampton.** Stewart J Brown

To the north of Birmingham lies British Bus country, with Midland Red North and Stevensons of Uttoxeter. Midland Red North is based in Cannock. The company is in the throes of an identity change. The traditional all-over red livery and Midland fleetname which was adopted in 1993 was ousting the brighter 1988 yellow-based and white-based schemes which replaced NBC poppy red. Minibuses in the old scheme are yellow and dark red, while big buses are white and dark red. By contrast the new identity is at best sombre, even on a sunny day. Were Midland Red buses really this dull in the company's hey-day? A feature of the old livery was the use of local fleetnames alongside the Midland Red name – Cambrian, Chaserider, Hotspur, Mercian and Tellus. These can still be seen, but on a steadily decreasing number of buses. In 1995 the company reverted to a brighter red and yellow scheme.

This former NBC company was privatised in 1988, being sold to Drawlane, as British Bus was then known. Its operations cover much of Staffordshire and run west into Shropshire. Local services are provided in Tamworth, Lichfield, Stafford, Cannock, Telford and Shrewsbury, and the company also has a substantial network of inter-urban and rural routes. The company's Crewe operations were taken over from Crosville at the end of 1989 when Drawlane was busy re-drawing the boundaries of its growing number of subsidiaries – a process which has continued.

New buses in recent years have ranged from Mercedes minis through to low-floor Scania MaxCis, with a substantial number of Dennis Darts – 22 with East Lancs bodies were delivered in 1994 and can be seen in Telford, Stafford and Wolverhampton. These were the first new buses in the current red livery. The Scania MaxCis, with East Lancs bodies to Swedish designs, provide a park-and-ride service in historic Shrewsbury. For this they wear a blue and yellow livery. A distinctive feature of the Midland Red North fleet is its use of rebodied Leyland Tigers. There are 27 which were given new East Lancs bus bodies between 1989 and 1992. The chassis are mostly ex-London & Country, and were originally Green Line coaches. Other interesting Tigers are nine built as buses in 1984, with Duple Dominant bodies, and four with Alexander (Belfast) bodies which came from Timeline Travel in 1993.

Top **Midland Red North had a major intake of Dennis Darts in 1994, adding 22 to its fleet. All are 9m-long models with 33-seat East Lancs bodies.** Stewart J Brown

Centre **Low-floor Scania MaxCis with East Lancs bodies are used by Midland Red North on a park-and-ride service in Shrewsbury. The MaxCi, based on the N113, has a low front section which allows wheel-on access for pushchairs and shopping trolleys.** Tony Wilson

Right **Unusual buses in the Midland Red North fleet are Leyland Tigers with Alexander (Belfast) N-type bodies – a design more usually associated with operations in Ulster. They were new to Shearings and came to Midland Red North from Timeline Travel.** Stewart J Brown

The company's double-deckers are a mixed bag. Until 1995, the newest were six East Lancs-bodied Dennis Dominators, delivered in 1990 and based at Crewe. These followed four similarly-bodied Olympians which were new in 1989. Of a similar age are eight Northern Counties bodied double-deckers which came from Bee Line Buzz in 1993 and operate in the Tamworth area. Four are Olympians which were new to Kentish Bus while the other four are Volvo Citybuses which were new to London & Country. There are small numbers of older NBC-style Olympians and VRTs with ECW bodies. Five new Scania N113s entered service in the summer of 1995.

Apart from the Tigers, Midland Red North's full-size single-deckers include Dennis Falcons with East Lancs bodies, and Leyland Nationals – some delivered new in NBC days, others added more recently from sister British Bus companies. Minibuses are mainly Transits and Iveco Fords, although there are a few Sherpas, Dodges and Mercedes too. Most of the Dodges are Northern Counties-bodied buses which formed part of the original Bee Line Buzz fleet in Manchester. Alexander-bodied Mercedes are the company's newest buses.

Top **Transfers within British Bus have seen four Northern Counties-bodied Olympians move from Bee Line Buzz in Manchester to Midland Red North. They were new in 1989 to Kentish Bus, moved to Bee Line in 1992 and to their present owner in 1994.** Mike Harris

Left **A batch of East Lancs-bodied Scania N113s delivered to Midland Red North in the summer of 1995 saw a reversion from overall red to the previous, brighter, red and yellow livery. The first were put to work between Tamworth and Birmingham. They have high-backed seats and split-step entrances.** Tony Wilson

Below **North Western Road Car took 11 Dodge S56s with Northern Counties new-style bodywork in 1988. Ten of them have since 1991 been part of the Midland Red North fleet. The improved frontal styling disguised the S56's light truck origins.** Stewart J Brown

In Shrewsbury most of the local services are provided by Midland Red North. Midland Red West operate to the town from Ludlow. Minsterley Motors run in to Shrewsbury, either with a Bedford coach or a minibus, usually a Renault Master, a type seldom seen on service work. Williamsons, primarily a coach operator, have three Dennis Darts which are used on a park and ride service in Shrewsbury. The company also has a service to Telford. Worthen Travel link Shrewsbury with Montgomery, just across the Welsh border and for this generally use a Leopard/Plaxton coach. King Offa run to Welshpool and here, too, a Leopard coach is the standard choice of vehicle. Boultons of Shropshire, who are based at Church Stretton, have routes to Shrewsbury and Bridgnorth. A couple of Optare StarRiders are used, with Bedford coaches available too. Boultons also provide seasonal heritage services in the Ironbridge Gorge area using a magnificent Leyland Royal Tiger with Burlingham Seagull body.

There are a number of small operators running in the Telford area. Britannia provide a few tendered services using assorted 1980s coaches, as does Elcock Reisen. King Offa runs from Telford with a Dennis Dart and Timeline Travel of Leigh has an outpost in Shropshire, running single-deckers with Alexander Belfast bodies. Like the company's main operations in the North-West, those in Shropshire were taken over from Shearings in 1992.

Stevensons of Uttoxeter was a flourishing independent until 1994. Its fleet had grown from just over 50 in the early 1980s to 270 by 1994. The company had a firm hold on the area around Burton-on-Trent and had extended its sphere of influence south to the West Midlands, with the launch of local services in WM Travel territory. A bus war broke out in 1994 with WM Travel introducing services in Burton in May using its newly acquired interest in Your Bus to do so. In June Stevensons sold out to British Bus and the war was soon over. British Bus withdrew the Stevensons services in the West Midlands in August, while WM Travel pulled out of Burton in September.

However rationalisation by British Bus has seen Stevensons gain territory in the north. What had been the C-Line operation in Macclesfield with services running up to Manchester had been taken over by Midland Red North in 1993 and the green and cream C-Line livery gave way first to Midland Red North's white and dark red, with Midland Red C-Line fleetnames, and then very quickly to the new all-over red. But at the end of 1994 this operation was transferred from Midland Red to Stevensons, bringing yet another change of colour for bus users in the area.

Top **There are three Optare StarRiders in the fleet of Boulton of Church Stretton. The newest entered service in 1990. The chassis is the Mercedes-Benz 811D.** Malcolm King

Centre **Stevensons bought two Alexander-bodied Olympians in 1988. One is seen leaving Macclesfield for Manchester, illustrative of the company's northwards expansion under British Bus ownership.** Tony Wilson

Right **Under British Bus ownership the Stevensons fleet has retained an independent outlook on vehicle acquisitions, exemplified by this Willowbrook rebodied Leopard which joined the fleet in 1995.** Tony Wilson

Most Wadham Stringer-bodied Darts are in the south. Two of this uncommon type run for Stevensons. This one was new to Jim Stones of Glazebury in 1990 and was acquired by Stevensons in 1993.
Tony Wilson

Three Scania K93s are operated by Stevensons, two bought new, the third acquired from Capital Citybus. The ex-Capital Citybus vehicle has a Plaxton body. It was new in 1989 to Kettlewells of Retford. Mike Harris

The newest Stevensons double-deckers are two DAF DB250s with Optare Spectra bodies. One is seen in Derby on a school service. They are the only Spectras operating in the Midlands.
Stewart J Brown

Much of Stevensons' expansion has been with small buses, both new and second-hand. It has bought almost 100 Mercedes-Benz minibuses, mostly 709Ds and 811Ds with coachbuilt bodies by just about everyone you've ever heard of and a few you haven't – Alexander, Carlyle, Dormobile, LHE, Made-to-Measure, Phoenix, PMT, Reeve Burgess, Robin Hood, Scott, Whittaker, Wright. Not many on that list survive, a reflection of the volatility of the minibus market which grew rapidly and then collapsed just as quickly, bringing down a few bodybuilders with it.

For midibuses Stevensons favoured the Leyland Swift. It has 17 – the biggest fleet of the model in psv use – six of which were bought new. There is again variety in the body-work with the most unusual being four which are fitted with an adaptation of Wright's Handybus body, a com-bination unique to Stevensons. Another odd Swift carries G C Smith bodywork and was originally operated by Gloucestershire county council. There are ten Dennis Darts in the fleet. Six have Plaxton Pointer bodies while the other four are second-hand examples, one each bodied by Carlyle and Duple to the latter's Dartline design, and two with unusual Wadham Stringer Portsdown bodies.

The variety continues in the company's bigger buses, with at least one of most recent types. There's a MAN 11.190 with Optare Vecta body; a Mercedes OH1416 with Wright body; a Mercedes O405, also bodied by Wright; a pair of Scania K93s with Alexander PS-type bodies; two DAF SB220s with Optare Delta bodies (ex-Edinburgh Transport) and 12 Leyland Lynxes. Even the Lynxes are noteworthy. One came from Kelvin Central and was the only Lynx bought by the Scottish Bus Group. Two were new to Wrights of Wrexham, purchased when that company closed down at the start of 1994. And seven are to a unique specifi-cation with Alexander Belfast bodies. They were built in 1986 for operation by Citybus in Belfast. This was a time when Leyland's policy dictated that home market cus-tomers could only buy complete Leyland-bodied Lynxes but that export customers could have Lynx underframes bodied locally. Recognising that Citybus would want to support its local body manufacturer, Ulster was designated as export territory. In the end Citybus bought Tigers, and the non-standard Lynxes were sold to Stevensons in 1992. Four have Gardner engines while three are Leyland-powered. Leopard buses, once the mainstay of the fleet, have all but vanished.

There are some 40 double-deckers in use and while second-hand Metrobuses are the standard, there are a few other interesting types. The Metrobuses started life with a variety of operators including Greater Manchester, South Yorkshire, West Midlands and, with Alexander bodywork, Kelvin Scottish and West Yorkshire. There are also two ex-MCW demonstrators, an early S-registered bus and a late F-registered example. There are a pair of F-registered Alexander-bodied Olympians bought new, and a prototype Olympian with ECW body which was sold by Leyland as an untrimmed shell and fitted out by Stevensons. It has a VRT-style front panel – the body was completed before the Olympian body's frontal styling had been finalised. The bus was built in 1979 but did not enter service with Stevensons until 1985. The newest double-deckers are a pair of 1993 Optare Spectras, the only ones in the Midlands. In Burton-on-Trent services are operated by Metrobuses, Mercedes minibuses, Darts and Swifts. Tiger coaches operate north to Derby on a joint half-hourly express service with Trent and both operators' vehicles wear a distinctive X38 livery. School services are also operated in the Derby and Mickleover areas.

First Bus briefly had a small presence in this British Bus enclave through erstwhile Badgerline subsidiary Frontline Buses. However Frontline was sold to British Bus in the summer of 1995 and now comes under the control of the Stevensons business. Frontline's vehicles are all second hand and include Leopard coaches acquired when the business was set up in 1993. Buses had been drafted in from other Badgerline companies with Leyland Nationals coming from Eastern National and a VRT from Bristol City Line. One Routemaster is owned. Frontline operate from Tamworth to Birmingham. There is a school of thought which suggests that Frontline was set up by Badgerline to provide a base for expansion in British Bus country just in case British Bus harboured any expansionist ideas in Essex after it took control of the Colchester and Southend municipal fleets.

To the north of Midland Red North, the main operator is PMT. This NBC operation was bought by its management in 1986 and expanded northwards by taking over Crosville's operations in Chester and on the Wirral peninsula in 1990. Badgerline took control in 1994, which means that PMT is now a subsidiary of First Bus. The company's bright red and yellow livery introduced in 1985 when NBC's corporate image was crumbling is applied to most of the fleet, but buses in Crosville country carry either Crosville or Red Rider names. Red Rider was a title initially used for minibus operations in Merseyside. Crosville's legacy to PMT is its fleet numbering system, which uses a three letter vehicle classification producing such delights as DOGs (Double-deck, Olympian, Gardner) and SADs (Single-deck, DAF, DAF). Londoners with long memories might be surprised to find that an STL isn't a vintage AEC double-decker, but a relatively modern Tiger coach.

Frontline Buses was set up by Badgerline, was owned briefly by First Bus, and is now part of British Bus under the control of Stevensons. The fleet includes two Leyland Leopards with Willowbrook Warrior bodies, seen loading in Tamworth. *Stewart J Brown*

PMT's varied fleet of VRTs includes a couple with dual-door ECW bodies, transferred from Bristol City Line in 1994. They date from 1980. PMT also has VRTs delivered new, and a number acquired with the Crosville operations. Note the Crosville-style fleet number with a three letter prefix. *Stewart J Brown*

PMT's headquarters are in Stoke-on-Trent. The initials originally stood for Potteries Motor Traction, although the company's name is now PMT Ltd. The core of its operations is the built-up area which forms the Potteries towns, centred on Stoke and Newcastle-under-Lyme (it has depots in both towns), but services are also operated from a depot in Biddulph and there are routes south to Stafford. The company has a presence in Stockport, and owns Pennine Blue which is based in Hyde.

PMT's standard bus in the early 1990s was the Dennis Dart, generally with Plaxton Pointer bodywork, although there are a couple of Marshall-bodied buses too. The only new full-size addition to the fleet since 1990 has been a solitary Dennis Lance with Northern Counties body which is part of the Crosville operation. Prior to that PMT did buy a batch of Leyland Lynxes and a batch of Optare Deltas for comparative evaluation – but that was before it discovered the Dart. The 11 Lynxes bought new were joined in 1993 by a pair of ex-Westbus buses. The only other big buses added to the fleet since privatisation have been 10 Leyland-bodied Olympians, seven of which have coach seating and are branded for the Hanley to Crewe service.

Much of PMT's post-deregulation investment has been in small buses and it has a fleet of 300 minibuses which range from 16-seat Sherpas and Transits through to 33-seat 811Ds. In PMT's vehicle classification the 811Ds are coded as midibuses (I) where all other types are minibuses (M). The latter include Dodge S56s and Mercedes 709Ds with coachbuilt bodywork. For a time PMT was building its own minibus bodies, and even supplying them to other operators. The most stylish was the Ami, an Optare StarRider look-alike on Mercedes 811D. There are 38 in the PMT fleet. Most of the company's minibuses were bought new, but there are some inherited from Crosville and a few from other operators including Milton Keynes City Bus and Strathclyde Buses. A tri-axle Pullman is owned and runs in Merseyside as part of the Red Rider operation. The most recent delivery of small buses included three Optare MetroRiders.

The biggest body built by PMT was perhaps its least successful in terms of styling. This was the Knype on Leyland's midi-sized Swift. There are nine in service, all dating from 1988-89.

The company's NBC inheritance is a fleet of Bristol VRTs and Leyland Olympians with around 70 of the former and 50 of the latter. Most of the Olympians and many of the VRTs came with the Crosville operations. The only other double-deckers are two former West Yorkshire PTE Roe-bodied Olympians which were taken over with the business of Turners of Brown Edge in 1988. These are now in fleet colours, but the Turner name and livery have been applied to two Olympians which were new to PMT, as well as to one Dart and four Mercedes minibuses.

Small operators in PMT's Staffordshire territory include Bassetts of Tittensor which has been running coaches since 1950 and also operates a substantial haulage fleet. Services are run to Stafford and Stone, generally with a Leopard coach. Blue Buses of Bucknall operate in Hanley with a fleet of ex-National Welsh Sherpas, as does Moorland Rover. In Longton, Copeland Tours run three Dodge minibuses on local services. The entire Copeland fleet 21-strong – carries Ulster MIB registration marks. On the Dodges this disguises the fact that two came from Plymouth while the third was new to Greater Manchester Transport. In Newcastle-under-Lyme PMT faces competition from Matthews Motors running seven second-hand minibuses under the Handybus name. Transits predominate. Of more interest is Knotty, running to Hanley and Burslem with a remarkable collection of rare types. Knotty only started up in 1988 and runs 16 buses and coaches. Of these, 14 are AECs, including three rear-engined Swifts. The oldest is a 1971 bus which was new to St Helens and has dual-door Marshall bodywork. Then comes a 1972 example with Alexander W-type body, which was new to London Country as part of its SMA class. The youngest Swift is a former Blackpool bus, also bodied by Marshall, and now 21 years old. Most of the fleet's Reliances are coaches, but there are two buses – one with Park Royal body, the other bodied by Plaxton. The former is an ex-London Country RP. The two non-AEC vehicles are a Marshall-bodied Dennis Lancet which was new to Blackpool, and the only surviving Daimler Roadliner licensed as a psv. This was one of the 38 bought by Black & White Motorways.

Leek, on the edge of the Peak District National Park, is served by a long-established service from Hanley operated by Procters, generally with a Leopard coach. Also running in Leek are AEC Reliance coaches owned by Boydon of Winkhill, operating a service from the company's home base and surrounding villages. Boydon's Reliances – there are seven in all – range from 1973 to 1980 models. The oldest has a Duple body; the others are bodied by Plaxton. A Leek to Ashbourne service is provided by Warringtons of Ilam, using either a coach or a Mercedes minibus.

Moorland Buses of Werrington operate Freight Rover Sherpas. This Carlyle-bodied bus was originally part of the fleet of 175 used to launch the Bee Line Buzz operations in Greater Manchester. Moorland also run Sherpas with Dormobile bodies. *Stewart J Brown*

AEC Swifts are few and far between. Knotty operate four in the Potteries, the oldest of which is a 1971 bus with Marshall body. It can probably claim to be the only bus still in revenue-earning service which started life with St Helens Corporation. *Stewart J Brown*

On the other side of the Peak District, Chesterfield Transport is the main operator in the town famed for its crooked church spire, a feature which has lent its name to the company's Spire Sprinter minibus operation. A stylised spire, which bears more than a passing resemblance to a shark's fin, is carried alongside the company's name on the sides of its buses. This was a municipally-owned operation until 1990 when it was sold to its employees, a fact recognised by the wording "100 per cent employee owned" carried under the fleetname on some vehicles. During 1994 and 1995 protracted negotiations went on with Mainline about a possible sale of the company. These came to naught, and in July 1995 the company was sold to Stagecoach which already owns East Midland Motor Services, the town's other main operator. The references to employee ownership can be expected to disappear pretty smartly.

At the time of the takeover by Stagecoach, Leyland Nationals dominated Chesterfield Transport's services, with both new and second-hand buses in the fleet. Double-deckers are Roe-bodied Fleetlines delivered in 1977-78 (and unusual in having two-door bodies) to which have been added various second-hand types. These are two ex-GM Buses Fleetlines, South Yorkshire PTE's only two Olympians (acquired in 1987 when they were still quite modern buses), and four Roe-bodied Atlanteans purchased from Yorkshire Rider which re-introduced Atlanteans to the Chesterfield fleet after an absence of eight years.

The newest big buses are Leyland Lynxes delivered in the late 1980s. Since then the only new purchases have been Mercedes minis, most with Alexander bodies which won't look out of place when they are repainted white with stripes. The Chesterfield livery was being altered prior to its sale to Stagecoach, with a change from blue roofs to white roofs on full-size buses, and the adoption of the big bus livery layout on minibuses in place of a diagonally-striped scheme.

A subsidiary Chesterfield Omnibus operation was established in 1993, initially running second-hand Sherpas and set up to face a threatened incursion into the town by Sheffield Omnibus. The threat disappeared, but Chesterfield Omnibus survives, now running Leyland Nationals. These serve Newbold, where the company faces competition from Omega running Sherpas, and Peakbus with a mixed fleet which ranges from a Dodge S56 to a slightly dog-eared one-time Brighton R-registered Atlantean. Peakbus also own a couple of Bristol LHs and what may be the only surviving Seddon Pennine IV:236 midi available for regular service, a former Edinburgh Corporation bus.

Top **Chesterfield Transport's oldest double-decker is a 1973 Daimler Fleetline CRL6 with two-door Roe body.** Mike Harris

Centre **Chesterfield Omnibus was set up by Chesterfield Transport in 1993 as a counter to competition which was expected from Sheffield Omnibus. The name and livery survive on a number of Leyland Nationals, including this ex-GM Buses vehicle.** Mike Harris

Left **Peakbus runs a varied fleet which includes this Seddon Pennine IV:236 which was new in 1973 to Edinburgh City Transport. It has Seddon bodywork. Few examples of Seddon's pioneering midibus survive.** Tony Wilson

Chesterfield's blue, yellow and white colours are carried on two subsidiary operations. Retford & District was set up in 1988 to operate tendered services which had previously been run by local operator Kettlewells. The Retford fleet is made up mainly of second-hand Leopards with Alexander-bodied buses from Western Scottish and Plaxton dual-purpose vehicles from Cleveland Transit. In 1993 Chesterfield took over the business of Whites of Calver, and that name is carried on a number of vehicles operating on services as far north as Buxton. Whites' buses are mainly Leopards, with ex-Trent examples fitted with Alexander T-type bodies, and some former Midland Red Marshall-bodied buses.

Back in Retford there are still services run by Kettlewells. Where double-deckers are needed, the operator has two ex-London Buses Ailsas, which were new to West Midlands, and an ex-West Midlands VRT, unusual in having MCW bodywork. Two East Lancs-bodied Dodge S56s are owned, both bought new. Services run as far south as Newark.

East Midland has since 1989 been part of the Stagecoach empire. It is a former NBC subsidiary which was bought by its management in 1988 before being sold to the expanding Scottish-based group. There are now no traces of East Midland's green and cream livery, although there are still a fair number of pre-Stagecoach buses in use. These include standard NBC VRTs, Olympians and National 2s (but no National 1s). Of more interest are some Leopard and Tiger buses which were unusual vehicles for an NBC fleet. There are seven Tigers with Alexander's uncompromisingly square P-type bodies. These were new in 1985 and at the same time an eighth P-type body was ordered for fitment to a 1979 Leopard chassis. The other Leopard buses are four which were rebodied by Duple in 1985. Here as elsewhere there has been steady investment in new buses by Stagecoach. These are Olympians with both Alexander and Northern Counties bodies, Volvo B6s and Mercedes 709Ds. There are also Plaxton-bodied B10Ms for use on longer-distance services. Older minibuses include Mercedes and Ivecos with Reeve Burgess bodies which were the only new buses ordered for the company during its short period in management ownership. They were delivered in 1989 after the Stagecoach takeover and have been in Stagecoach corporate colours since new.

East Midland has depots in Chesterfield, Mansfield and Worksop, and its services run north to Sheffield and Doncaster, east to Newark and south to Nottingham. A small operator running in Worksop is Unity of Retford, with a minibus route to Clumber Park.

Top **In 1993 Whites of Calver were taken over by Chesterfield Transport. The name was retained. Chesterfield bought two former London Transport Nationals from Haven Coaches of Newhaven in 1993 for the Whites fleet, one of which is seen here in Bakewell. Whites coach business was carried on too, but was closed down following the Stagecoach takeover in 1995.** Tony Wilson

Centre **An early sign of the Stagecoach takeover of Chesterfield Transport was the appearance of standard Stagecoach types on the company's routes, including this Volvo B10M which carries East Midland fleetnames. East Midland is taking control of the Chesterfield Transport business.** Tony Wilson

Right **The last NBC-style Olympians with ECW bodies for East Midland were delivered in 1986.** Russell Upcraft

In 1993 Stagecoach purchased local authority-owned Grimsby-Cleethorpes Transport and that is now administered as part of East Midland. This take-over, giving Stagecoach a base on the east coast on the edge of Lincolnshire Road Car country, brought with it a number of unusual types for the group.

The Grimsby-Cleethorpes double-deckers include two types which are not well represented in the Stagecoach fleet – Dennis Dominators and Daimler Fleetlines. There are 25 Fleetlines and seven Dominators, and examples of both types arc now in Stagecoach corporate colours rather than Grimsby-Cleethorpes orange and cream. There are also four ECW-bodied Olympians, two of which were unusual in being of dual-door layout. The Fleetlines are also two-door buses.

Grimsby-Cleethorpes' single-deckers include a number of unusual vehicles. There are four Dennis Falcons with Wadham Stringer bodies and four Alexander P-type Tigers – a type which by coincidence could already be found running for East Midland. However, where the East Midland buses have the standard Leyland TL11H engine, those bought by Grimsby-Cleethorpes are in unusual in that they have Gardner 6LXCT power units. Gardner-engined Tigers are rare outside Scotland. In course of delivery when Stagecoach took over were eight East Lancs-bodied Falcons. The first entered service in GCT livery but the final deliveries arrived from East Lancs in Stagecoach white. The only small buses operated are 10 Metroriders.

One small operator running into Grimsby is Emmersons of Immingham, with a Wadham Stringer-bodied Bedford from the Maidstone fleet. Ford and Bedford coaches are run on school contracts around Immingham. Applebys also operate into Grimsby.

Top **Grimsby-Cleethorpes was a Fleetline user and a small number survive. The newest are 1980 FE30AGR models with 74-seat Roe bodies.** Michael Fowler

Right **An unusual type to carry Stagecoach colours is this Dennis Falcon with Wadham Stringer body. It is one of four bought by Grimsby-Cleethorpes in 1983.** Tony Wilson

Below **The last buses to be ordered by Grimsby-Cleethorpes were five Dennis Lances with East Lancs bodies, which were in course of delivery when Stagecoach took over. Although some were delivered in Grimsby-Cleethorpes orange and cream, all are now in corporate Stagecoach colours.** Tony Wilson

The biggest operator in this part of England, from the Humber south to the Wash, is Lincolnshire Road Car. In NBC days it traded as Lincolnshire; now it trades as Road Car. The company was bought by Yorkshire Traction when it was sold by NBC in 1988. Its headquarters are in the city of Lincoln, and Yorkshire Traction bought the Lincoln City Transport operations in 1993, consolidating its position in the area. Lincoln City Transport had been privatised in 1991, being sold to its employees, with a major share being bought by Derby City Transport. Road Car has depots in Humberside at Grimsby and Scunthorpe (and has services running over the Humber Bridge to Hull), but the bulk of its fleet is in Lincolnshire with bases in Gainsborough, Grantham, Louth, Scunthorpe and Skegness as well as Lincoln. It also serves Nottinghamshire from its Newark depot. Its position in Newark was strengthened in 1989 when it took over W Gash & Sons, a company best known for its elderly Daimler double-deckers. A few ex-Gash buses survive, including a preserved 1948 Daimler.

Double-deckers play a comparatively small part in Road Car's operations. The newest are three ECW-bodied Olympians dating from 1985. The remainder are VRTs, including some ex-Yorkshire Traction buses, and assorted second-hand Atlanteans from GM Buses, Ipswich Buses, Lancaster City Transport and Gash. One of the ex-Gash buses is a V-registered AN68 with Roe bodywork which was bought new by the independent at a time when new double-deckers for small operators were comparatively rare. There are 70 VRTs in all, the most unusual of which are eight East Lancs-bodied buses bought by Lincoln City Transport in 1980-81, some of which are now in the Road Car rather than the Lincoln City fleet.

There is considerable variety in Road Car's single-deckers, with a fair number of basic specification coaches and dual-purpose vehicles to cater for the many relatively long distance services which criss-cross Lincolnshire, connecting the main towns. Here late-model Leyland Leopards and early Leyland Tigers rule the road, many transferred from Yorkshire Traction and Strathtay Scottish, but with a fair number bought second-hand or acquired with other businesses – Gash in 1989 and Barnard of Kirton-in-Lindsey in 1992. There are also a few bought new in NBC days, with Willowbrook and ECW bodies. Five Tigers have had new East Lancs EL2000 bodies fitted. Four are conventional 57-seaters but the fifth has three-plus-two seating for a remarkable 72 people, which has to be a record for a rigid single-decker in Britain. There are 35 Nationals, all but four of which have come from other operators including Yorkshire Traction, Cumberland and Barnard.

In fact, second-hand buses outnumber those bought new by a factor of something like two to one in the Road Car business, not counting those acquired with the Lincoln City Transport operation. Vehicles delivered new in recent times have been eight Wright-bodied Dennis Darts, eight Optare MetroRiders, three Optare bodied Mercs (with rare StarRider E bodies, using the standard Mercedes bonnet assembly) and three Wright-bodied Renault S75s. Yorkshire Traction and its subsidiaries were keen supporters of Renault's minibuses until the French builder decided to axe UK chassis production in 1993, bringing an end to the S75. Road Car's Renaults include four ex-London Buses RB-class buses and a former Renault demonstrator, among other selected used purchases. Older minibuses include 11 Dodge S56s with Reeve Burgess bodies from the Lincoln City fleet which were new to South Yorkshire.

Above **Road Car has a substantial fleet of Leyland Leopards. Most have Duple or Plaxton coach bodies, but there are also a number with Alexander Y-type bodies from sister company Strathtay Scottish.** Tony Wilson

Centre **Second-hand Tiger coaches have been bought by Road Car for rebodying by East Lancs as buses or dual-purpose vehicles. This 1992 rebody uses a 1984 Tiger 12m chassis which had originally carried a Duple Caribbean body for operation on National Express services by National Welsh.** Tony Wilson

Left **The last new Bristols bought by Road Car – or Lincolnshire as it then traded – were 10 ECW-bodied VRTs in 1981. All are still in use and the VRT remains the most numerous double-deck model in the fleet.** Tony Wilson

Another operator with a liking for Renaults is Hornsby, which runs two on a local service in Scunthorpe. However Hornsby's Renaults aren't yet more minibuses, but the only two French-style PR100 city buses in public service in Britain. The French built chassis have Northern Counties bodies to Renault's standard design for the model. Both date from 1989 when Renault made an ill-starred attempt to sell the PR100 in the UK. One was a demonstrator; the other was a trial vehicle for London Buses which reached Hornsby after a brief spell with Parfitts of Rhymney Bridge. Hornsby also runs Mercedes minis on local services and has double-deckers – two Atlanteans and three ex-London Fleetlines – which cover school journeys and a few regular services. Both of the Atlanteans are 1977 Roe-bodied buses, one bought new, the other ex-Yorkshire Rider. Tiger coaches, including a former Green Line vehicle, can also be seen in service.

The biggest traditional independent operator in Lincolnshire is Applebys, with a total fleet strength of 90, although that includes some vehicles based in Scarborough and the subsidiary Halcyon operation. Applebys' headquarters are near Louth, and services cover much of rural Lincolnshire, running as far west as Lincoln and as far north as Scunthorpe. Isle Coaches operate to Scunthorpe from Owston Ferry using ex-South Yorkshire National 2s. Daisy Bus Service link Scunthorpe and Brigg. The fleet is made up entirely of coaches, including an ex-Green Line Tiger which is used on service. Leopard coaches are used by Sweyne of Swinefleet on a service between Goole and Scunthorpe. Scunthorpe-based Trent Motors – not to be confused with Derby-based Trent Motor Traction – has a Leyland National running on a local tendered service.

Eagre, named after a tidal bore on the Trent, is based in Gainsborough and runs to Scunthorpe. The company is primarily a coach operator, but service buses include a 1978 Bedford YMT with a 1989 Willowbrook Warrior body, ex-GM Buses Atlanteans, Leyland Nationals, and the one and only low-height Ailsa, which was built for Derby. It has an Alexander body and was intended to be the forerunner of similar buses for SBG companies, but the compromises involved in its layout ensured that it remained unique.

In bracing Skegness, Road Car is the main operator. A number of smaller companies have appeared in recent years to compete and 5555 Taxis is one of the most recent, running Transits and Sherpas. Hunt's of Alford also serve Skegness with a Bristol LH which was new to Crosville. Hunt's have two double-deckers, both VRTs, and a Northern Counties-bodied Dodge minibus. The company has been operating bus services since the 1920s. Up the coast in Mablethorpe – the poor man's Skegness? – Grayscroft Bus Services run to Louth, generally with a Leopard. This is another company with a 70-year history of local bus operation.

Top **There are only two full-size Renaults on regular bus services in Britain and both run for Hornsby of Scunthorpe. They are Northern Counties-bodied PR100s and this one was originally operated by London Buses' East London subsidiary.** Michael Fowler

Centre **Eagre of Gainsborough operate the only low-height Ailsa. Built for Derby City Transport in 1975, it was planned as the forerunner of a series of lowheight Ailsas for Scottish Bus Group companies. Alexander built the body which is unusual in having deeper windows on the top deck than on the lower.** Michael Fowler

Right **Hunt's of Alford operate to Skegness and regularly use ECW-bodied LHs. This one was new to Crosville in 1975.** Tony Wilson

In south Lincolnshire the main town is Boston, and here Brylaine operate a number of services, generally using the Ford and Bedford coaches which make up the bulk of the 45-vehicle fleet. Many of the vehicles were acquired with the operations of Hogg of Boston in 1990. Two of the Fords have Alexander bodies and were new to Northern Scottish. Double-deckers are three former Bournemouth Fleetlines and three East Lancs-bodied VRTs which were new to Burnley & Pendle. Brylaine is an amalgam of Bryan and Elaine, the partners who run the business. A smaller operator serving Boston, with a route from Spalding, is Elseys. The company's buses are a Dennis Javelin with Duple 300-series bus body, a Leopard which was rebodied in 1989 by Willowbrook, and a new Iveco TurboCity with WS bodywork, bought to replace the Leopard. Kime's of Folkingham serve Boston, Spalding and Grantham. A varied collection of second-hand Fleetlines is owned, for use on both regular services and contracts. They range from a J-registered CRG6LXB 33ft-long bus which was new to Aberdeen Corporation, to a couple of T-registered Leyland-built FE30AGRs which started life with Cleveland Transit. There are also ex-London DMSs. The newest double-decker is a W-registered VRT ex-Red & White. Fowler's link Spalding with Kings Lynn, using Scania K93s with Plaxton Derwent bodies and an Alexander-bodied N113 double-decker. All four were bought new in 1989. They are currently the most modern service buses in the 20-strong fleet, although new Scania L113s are on order.

Top **The most modern bus operated by Elseys is a Dennis Javelin with Duple body. It was purchased new in 1989.** Malc McDonald

Centre **All of the double-deckers operated by Kime's of Folkingham are Fleetlines. An Ulster registration disguises the age of this Roe-bodied example – it dates from 1977 and was originally operated by Grimsby-Cleethorpes Transport.** Tony Wilson

Right **In 1989 Fowler's bought four Scanias – one Alexander-bodied N113 double-decker and a trio of K93 single-deckers with Plaxton Derwent bodies. One of these 57-seaters is seen in King's Lynn.** Malc McDonald

A small operator running regularly into Lincoln itself is Enterprise & Silver Dawn, generally with Bristol VRTs which are as likely as not in their previous owner's livery. The name is a revival of a major operator in the Scunthorpe and Gainsborough area which was absorbed by Lincolnshire Road Car in 1950. PC Coaches of Lincoln operate Mercedes minibuses to Saxilby.

In Newark the spirit of the Gash operation lives on in Marshalls of Sutton-on-Trent, who use a Gash-style fleet numbering system and own a preserved Gash Daimler CVG6. The company's service into Newark is normally run by an ex-PMT VRT. Wright's of Newark have been running bus services since before 1930, and generally use elderly coaches, although a couple of MCW Metropolitans are still in stock, mainly for schools work. Further south, Grantham is served by Reliance, whose fleet includes three Leopards with Duple Dominant bus bodies. Two were bought new, while the third was bought in 1986 for re-bodying and has an ex-National Travel coach chassis dating from 1976. Reliance also runs Metroriders bought new with two MCW-built buses and one from Optare. Modern bigger buses bought new are a Leyland Lynx and a Dennis Dart. There is an infrequent route between Grantham and Melton Mowbray run by Skinners, based in Saltby. An ex-Maidstone Boro'line Bedford YMT with Duple Dominant bus body is used.

One of England's best-known independents, The Delaine, has services to Grantham. The Bourne-based company also operates to Stamford, Peterborough and Market Deeping. The Delaine's fleet is among Britain's smartest and is made up mainly of Leylands. These range from two old-style Titans through to 1980s Tigers, three of which have Duple bus bodies. The company's first new double-deckers for over 20 years were delivered in 1994: two Volvo Olympians with East Lancs bodies.

From Newark, on the western edge of Road Car's territory, services through to Nottingham are provided by Pathfinder Shuttleco. The fleet comprises 18 minibuses, all bought new. Most are Mercedes with Dormobile bodies. The S1R display in the route number box is not a joke being played by the drivers – it is a genuine route number. There's also an S1S. There is some logic in it – the S1R reaches Nottingham via Radcliffe-on-Trent; the S1S via Southwell.

Top **Reliance of Great Gonerby has bought a variety of new buses over the years. Examples currently operated include Leyland Leopards, MCW Metroriders, a Leyland Lynx and the company's newest bus, a Dennis Dart with Plaxton body.** Colin Lloyd

Centre **The Delaine's newest buses are long-wheelbase Volvo Olympians with East Lancs bodies. The lengthened version of the East Lancs R-type look-alike is easily distinguished from that built by Alexander by the absence of the short centre bay used by Alexander. Note the discreet route branding on the top deck side panels.** Malcolm King

Left **Pathfinder of Newark runs a fleet made up entirely of minibuses bought new. Most are Mercedes-Benz, as seen here in Nottingham, but there are also a few Iveco Fords.** Stewart J Brown

In Nottingham the main operator is the local authority-owned Nottingham City Transport, which faces little local competition since it successfully saw off Nottingham Omnibus in 1994. For many years NCT bought double-deck buses to its own distinctive style. Although built with two doors they achieved the remarkably high seating capacity of 78 thanks in part to a single-width front entrance and an unusual seating layout at the front of the top deck with a longitudinal seat to squeeze in the maximum number of seats. Bodies to this design were built by East Lancs and Northern Counties and large numbers are still in use. The survivors are all on Atlantean chassis. One batch of Atlanteans has standard single-door Roe bodywork, although even in this NCT managed to fit 80 seats, which must be a record for a 9.5m rear-engined double-decker. The Roe bodies were purchased at a time when quick delivery was required.

NCT's search for high capacity saw it order mid-engined Volvo Citybuses, some of which have 85-seat dual-door East Lancs bodies. Leyland, anxious not to lose NCT's business, developed the Lion, which was built by in Denmark by DAB and features a mid-mounted TL11 horizontal engine. Nottingham operates 13 Lions – not many, perhaps, but still enough to count as the world's biggest fleet of the type. Some have coach-seated East Lancs bodies and introduced a Harrods-style green to the fleet which is now being used on other types of bus in place of the traditional darker green. There are 35 Scania double-deckers. Most were bought new, but some second-hand bargains have been snapped up including ex-demonstration buses, as well as examples bought from A1 Service, Kentish Bus and Harris of Grays. The Scanias range in age from a W-registered 1980 bus (the oldest in England?) through to a batch of L-registered vehicles delivered in 1994. Other modern 'deckers are seven long-wheelbase Volvo Olympians with East Lancs bodies. Odd double-deckers are two ex-London Titans purchased for evaluation in 1993, but obviously not deemed sufficiently cost-effective to justify any more.

Top **Nottingham's varied double-deck fleet includes 35 Scanias, most of which have Alexander R-type bodies. This is a 1990 example.** Mike Harris

Centre **The Leyland Lion is a rare beast, and was developed specifically to meet Nottingham's requirements for maximum capacity double-deckers. The East Lancs body on this bus has 88 seats. Nottingham runs 13 Lions.** Colin Lloyd

Right **The prototype two-door Plaxton Verde, built in 1990 as part of the company's body development programme, was bought by Nottingham City Transport in 1993 and converted to single-door in a rather unusual way with a solid centre panel. It is built on a Scania N113 chassis.** Richard Godfrey

The number of single-deckers operated by NCT has been rising. It has Nationals and Lynxes, and more recently has added Volvo B6s with Alexander Dash bodies. There are also Alexander-bodied Scanias and one Scania with a prototype Plaxton Verde body which was built to test the two-door Verde structure in 1991. It was purchased by NCT in 1993 and converted to single door in a most unusual way, with a solid unglazed panel. This means that midway along the nearside there's metal where you would expect to find a window. A number of B10Bs were added to the operation in 1995 with bodywork by Plaxton, Northern Counties, Alexander and Wright, along with five Alexander-bodied B10Ms, giving Nottingham a remarkable variety of modern single-deck types.

The minibus fleet is mixed. Older examples are generally Dodges; newer ones are mainly Mercedes with a few Optare MetroRiders. Bodies are principally by Reeve Burgess, Plaxton, Carlyle, Dormobile, Northern Counties and, on the newest buses, Alexander.

South Notts of Gotham was taken over by NCT in 1991 and continues outwardly as an independent operation, still running Northern Counties-bodied Fleetlines between Nottingham and Loughborough. The last two Fleetlines have ECW bodies and were the last Fleetline chassis built. At the time of the takeover South Notts' newest buses were two Northern Counties-bodied long-wheelbase Olympians delivered in 1989. Under NCT ownership two East Lancs-bodied Olympians were added in 1992 and a number of Mercedes minibuses and National 2s have been transferred from the NCT fleet. One of the most recent additions, in 1994, was a 1974 Atlantean rebodied by East Lancs as a Sprint single-decker. It is the only one owned by NCT.

There are not many places in England outside London where you can see more than one operator running Leyland Titans. NCT has two, while Kinch of Barrow-upon-Soar has around a dozen, purchased from London Buses between 1992 and 1994 and operating between Nottingham and Clifton. Kinch also runs three Leopards with Willowbrook Warrior bodies. The chassis were new in 1980; the bodies in 1991. Another operator serving Nottingham is newcomer Delta Arrowline which started operating to Hucknall in the spring of 1995 in competition with Trent. Most of the Delta Arrowline vehicles are green and red liveried minibuses bought new and second-hand, but one Marshall-bodied Dennis Dart and the first double-deckers have recently been added to the fleet.

Top **An alternative approach to single-deckers was tried by Nottingham in 1994 when a 1974 Atlantean was rebodied by East Lancs with a 45-seat Sprint body. On its return it was allocated to the South Notts fleet. It remains unique.** Stewart J Brown

Centre **Kinch operates local services in Nottingham and Loughborough using a variety of vehicles, ranging from ex-London Fleetlines to new Dennis Darts. There are also ex-London Titans, including this 1980 Park Royal-built bus.** Stewart J Brown

Left **Rapid expansion at Delta Arrowline has seen the introduction of double-deckers to augment the company's initial minibus operations. This Alexander-bodied Dennis Dominator in Mansfield started life with Central Scottish.** Richard Godfrey

In Derby, British Bus is the main operator through its ownership of Derby City Transport, which now trades as Blue Bus. It's an accurate description of the livery, if a bit ironic in that the original Blue Bus Services was a well-respected independent whose main route linked Derby with Burton-on-Trent. The real Blue Bus was taken over by Derby City Transport in 1973. Derby City Transport was privatised in 1989 in an employee buy-out with support from Luton & District. In the summer of 1994 British Bus bought Luton & District, which gave it a part-share in Derby, which was soon turned into total control of the former municipally-owned business.

There are a number of liveries on Derby's buses. The current style is a smart two tone blue with grey or cream relief. That was introduced in 1993 to replace a light and dark blue scheme which is still around but is fast disappearing. There are also a number of vehicles in cream and orange Camms colours (but with Camms names removed), and there are other former Camms-liveried buses where the orange has been overpainted blue, giving a blue and cream livery. Camms was an independent running in the town whose services were taken over by DCT in 1993. Initially the Camms name was retained, and some DCT buses were even repainted in Camms colours.

On certain services to Sinfin a yellow-based livery with City Rider branding was introduced in 1995. It is worn by a number of Volvo Citybuses and by the company's newest buses, East Lancs-bodied Scania N113s which were delivered in City Rider colours. Prior to the arrival of the Scanias Derby's most modern 'deckers were the Citybuses of which there are 28, delivered between 1983 and 1988. Before that, Derby was buying Ailsas and has 15 in operation. Most of the bodies are by Marshall and Northern Counties, although there are five Citybuses which were bodied by East Lancs. The older 'deckers in the fleet are Daimler Fleetlines with Northern Counties bodies, but there are a couple of ECW-bodied buses which were bought from Clydeside 2000 in 1983 for the Camms operation. At that time Clydeside 2000 was very indirectly linked to Derby by being another company in which Luton & District had a financial interest.

The only big single-deckers are seven Scanias which were among the first to be fitted with Alexander PS-style bodies. They entered service in 1988-89. The newest buses are midis – half-a-dozen Darts with East Lancs bodies delivered in 1994. The minibus fleet features attractive Optare CityPacers, and unattractive Dodge S56s with Reeve Burgess bodies and modified grilles. There are also S56s with Northern Counties bodies with the bodybuilder's own bonnet and windscreen assembly. All of the S56s are second-hand, with some having come from Cleveland Transit.

Top **Derby City Transport is now a subsidiary of British Bus. There are 15 Ailsas in the fleet, most of which have Northern Counties bodywork – not a common combination. They were new in 1982.** Malcolm King

Centre **Derby's only full-size single-deckers are seven Alexander-bodied Scanias – five K92s and two of the later K93. They were delivered in 1988-89.** Malcolm King

Right **Derby adopted a new City Rider name and livery for its services to Sinfin in 1995. Initially the livery was applied to existing Volvo Citybuses, but in the summer five new East Lancs-bodied Scanias were delivered in City Rider colours.** Tony Wilson

Trent is a former NBC subsidiary which has so far retained its independence from the major groups. It was privatised in a management buy-out in 1986, and expanded significantly in 1989 by taking over Barton Transport which at that time operated 210 vehicles, mostly Plaxton-bodied Leyland Leopards. In spite of the sterling service being given by the company's Leopards, Barton only operated one batch of Leyland Tigers and the newest vehicles when Trent took over were in fact Plaxton-bodied DAFs. In 1995 the typical Barton bus is still the Leopard/Plaxton combination, but there are also Optare Deltas and Leyland Nationals in the Barton fleet. The former were delivered new and were part of orders for 53 placed by Trent; the latter were transferred from the Trent fleet. Trent/Barton operate the country's biggest Delta fleet.

More recent purchases by Trent have all been single-deckers, but not on DAF chassis. In 1993-94 Trent took delivery of 38 Volvo B10Bs with Northern Counties Paladin bodies. However it also continued to buy Optare products, taking two Sigmas on Dennis Lance chassis, and 15 Vectas on MAN chassis. The Sigma, added to Optare's range in 1994, is still something of a rarity and the only others are running for Go-Ahead Gateshead and Ipswich Buses. Some of the Vectas are allocated to the Spondon Flyer in Derby (Trent's home town) and have a slightly modified livery. Others can be seen on services running south from Stockport. Unusual recent additions to the fleet are five B10Ms with Alexander Belfast Q-type bodies which run on the Trans-Peak service from Nottingham and Derby to Manchester. A number of Trent services are marketed as Rainbow Routes on which the company aims to provide a higher standard of service.

This influx of new buses to the Trent fleet has been matched by the withdrawal of older types. However there are still a substantial number of Mark 1 Leyland Nationals in use, a few of which retain the red and grey livery which was used until 1991 when the brighter red and cream layout was first adopted. Double-deckers are 24 ECW-bodied Olympians dating from NBC days, and 24 Volvo Citybuses with Alexander bodies which were the company's first post-privatisation purchases. Trent operates four minibuses on long-term hire from Nottingham City Transport and used on a city-centre service in Nottingham. They are in Trent colours, achieved by applying red paint over Nottingham's green. The buses involved are Dodge S56s with Reeve Burgess bodies. However during 1995 two batches of new small buses arrived – Optare MetroRiders and Wright-bodied Mercedes.

Barton faces competition in Long Eaton, west of Nottingham, from Annison, running two former PMT Leyland Nationals on a town service.

Top **Unusual vehicles in the Trent fleet are five Volvo B10Ms with ZF automatic gearboxes and Alexander (Belfast) Q-type bodies. They were bought for use on the Trans-Peak operation which links Nottingham and Derby with Manchester.** Tony Wilson

Centre **Trent has in recent years been buying a variety of single-deck types, including DAF SB220s, MAN 10.180s, Dennis Lances and, as seen here in Derby, Volvo B10Bs. The Volvos have 49-seat Northern Counties Paladin bodies.** Stewart J Brown

Left **A Barton Leyland National at Loughborough bus station.** Russell Upcraft

Felix run between Derby and Ilkeston with two modern single-deckers. One is an ex-demonstration Leyland Lynx, new in 1992, the other an Alexander-bodied Volvo B10B delivered in the spring of 1995. In Ilkeston itself Saxton Coaches run Sherpas on a local service. The Felix operation is an old-established one, dating back to the 1920s. By contrast, a recent operation is that run by Dunn-Line, operating ex-Nottingham Atlanteans on routes to Beeston and Ashbourne. GM Buses South has an infrequent service to Manchester on which it uses Tiger coaches. In the other direction Kinch operates between Derby and Leicester with modern Mercedes minis.

Kinch is the main operator in Loughborough, having gained ground in the town at the expense of Midland Fox. The quid pro quo was a cut-back by Kinch in Leicester. Services in Loughborough are operated by six Plaxton-bodied Dennis Darts, modern Mercedes minis – there are no fewer than 11 L-registered 709Ds bought new – and the occasional ex-London DMS. Loughborough is also served by South Notts and Barton Buses.

Leicester Citybus is part of the new FirstBus organisation, having been sold by the city council to GRT in 1993. The first thing GRT did was to get rid of the old-fashioned maroon livery which had been re-introduced in 1990 but really belonged to the 1940s. In its place came the standard GRT style with two shades of red on a cream base. A GRT-style fleetname was adopted too, with the characteristic thistle serving in place of a dot above the "i" in Citybus. The thistle is set to be a FirstBus casualty along with Badgerline's badger – perhaps because badgers have been known to eat thistles...

Prior to its sale to GRT, Leicester was a loyal Dennis customer and its double-deck fleet is made up mainly of Dominators. There are around 100 in operation, built between 1980 and 1989 and all but two with East Lancs bodies. The odd two are Marshall-bodied. To replace some of the oldest Dominators half-a-dozen MCW Metrobuses were transferred south from GRT's Midland Bluebird company. These have lowheight Alexander bodies. They joined four similar buses bought by Leicester in 1983 which were the only low-height Alexander-bodied Metrobuses supplied new to an English operator. The newest Dennises in the Leicester fleet are Falcons. There are 16, including some of the last to be built before the model was discontinued because its Gardner engine could not be adapted to meet tighter new European exhaust emission legislation. Bodies on the Falcons are by East Lancs (similar to vehicles supplied to British Bus) and, unique to Leicester, Northern Counties' current generation Paladin design.

Small buses in service are two dozen Iveco Fords with Carlyle bodies (more are held in reserve) and 15 Northern Counties-bodied Renault S56s. Under GRT ownership new buses were delivered in the summer of 1995. These were ten Optare-bodied Mercedes-Benz O405s. Leicester Citybus is primarily an urban operation.

One old-established independent in Leicester is Hylton & Dawson, with a service to Glenfield. The standard vehicle on the service is a Bedford YMT with Duple Dominant bus body, which was acquired from Maidstone Borough Transport in 1984, when it was six years old. Hylton & Dawson also run Bedford coaches. Other operators, generally running Leopards on tendered services, include Paul James Coaches and Fernie. Pam's Coaches of Enderby run from Leicester to Rugby using an ex-Metrobus of Orpington Mercedes with Reeve Burgess Beaver body.

Facing page top **Two modern single-deckers operate the Felix service between Ilkeston and Derby. The newer is a B10B with Alexander Strider body.** Tony Wilson

Facing page centre **A steadily decreasing number of Leicester buses are in the company's old livery, as shown on an East Lancs-bodied Dennis Dominator in the city centre.** G Mead

Facing page bottom **The GRT-style livery currently in use by Leicester Citybus is a vast improvement on the dark colour scheme which it replaces. This is a 1988 Dominator with a later style of East Lancs body.** Tony Wilson

Left **Leicester Citybus was among the last buyers of the Dennis Falcon, and is the only operator of Falcons with Northern Counties Paladin bodies. Seven were delivered in 1993. Note the representation of the city's clock tower alongside the fleetname.** Mike Harris

Centre **Leicester's latest buses are Mercedes-Benz O405s with Optare Prisma bodies, finished in GRT Advance livery, which uses a lighter base cream and less red relief.** Tony Wilson

Below left **Pam's Coaches operate between Leicester and Rugby. The only bus in the six-strong fleet is this ex-Metrobus of Orpington Mercedes-Benz with Reeve Burgess Beaver body. Early Beaver buses had a shallow destination display as on this 1988 vehicle. Later examples have a full-size destination box.** Tony Wilson

Below right **Hylton & Dawson run a long-established service between Leicester and Glenfield, generally using Y-series Bedfords. This is a 1979 YMT with Duple Dominant II body.** Colin Lloyd

Out of town services are run mainly by British Bus subsidiary Midland Fox. This was until 1984 known as Midland Red East, but while the three other Midland Red companies retained their geographic titles, this one went for something different. It was sold by NBC to its management in 1987, initially with involvement by Stevensons, passing to Drawlane (as British Bus was then known) in 1989.

Midland Fox was an early and enthusiastic user of minibuses and there are 150 in use. They run as Fox Cubs, an imaginative name chosen when other operators were coming up with Skippers, Hoppas and other such little gems. Some of the original 1985 Transit 16-seaters are still in use, confounding those fleet engineers who forecast a maximum five year life for the Transit in stop-start bus operation. Since then the Fox Cubs have grown, and the Transits were followed by 25-seat Ivecos and more recently 25-seat Alexander-bodied 709Ds. A fair number of the Fox Cubs are second-hand, including Ivecos from other British Bus subsidiaries, assorted Sherpas and even a few Dodge S56s from Stagecoach and South Yorkshire Transport.

Midland Fox has no midibuses and few single-deck service buses. There are 10 National Greenways and five standard Nationals. All other single-deckers are coaches – mostly Leopards and Tigers and mostly second-hand. They tend to be used on inter-urban routes. Double-deckers form the core of the big bus fleet, and until recently most of these were second-hand too. The newest 'deckers are 20 Scanias with East Lancs bodies, delivered in the second half of 1994 to replace late 1970s Fleetlines. But Fleetlines still abound, all either ex-London or ex-South Yorkshire. Many of the ex-London DMSs were re-powered with Iveco engines while still operating in the capital. The Scanias were not Midland Fox's first. They joined six 1989 N113s with Alexander bodies which were purchased from BTS of Borehamwood in 1993.

There's still more variety in the double-deck fleet. There are Metrobuses, both standard MCW-bodied examples from South Yorkshire Transport, and lowheight Alexander-bodied buses which were new to Midland Scottish in 1981-82 but reached Leicestershire by way of Merseyside, where they were operated for a short time by North Western. Even the Leyland Olympians are interesting. Yes, there are standard NBC-specification buses, some delivered new and some acquired from Crosville Wales. But there are five ex-Kentish Bus Olympians with Northern Counties bodies (bought in 1992 before Kentish Bus became part of British Bus), two ex-Reading Transport ECW-bodied coaches, two ECW-bodied buses transferred from the Colchester fleet and five similar vehicles from Merseyside Transport. There are also five Alexander-bodied Olympians bought new in 1989.

Top **Small buses in the Midland Fox fleet run as Fox Cubs. This 1992 Mercedes with Dormobile body came from Stevensons of Uttoxeter.** Colin Lloyd

Centre **East Lancs Greenway rebuilds of Leyland Nationals were added to the Midland Fox fleet during 1994. All have Ulster registrations; here the new number replaces the N-suffix mark which was originally carried by this ex-National Welsh bus.** Tony Wilson

Right **Rhymney Valley bought three long-wheelbase Olympian coaches in 1985. Two of these impressive vehicles are now with Badgerline while the third runs for Midland Fox.** Tony Wilson

Leicester is the heart of Midland Fox's territory but it also had depots in Coalville, Hinckley, Market Harborough and Melton Mowbray. Fairtax livery and fleetnames are carried on five ex-South Yorkshire Dodges operating in Melton Mowbray. Some coaches run as Foxhounds, including those operating services into Birmingham. Taxis – Fox Cabs – are operated in Leicester. Midland Fox's fleet numbering is a trifle confusing. Minibuses have an M prefixed number. Coaches occupy numbers below 999. Metrobuses and Fleetlines are numbered in the 2xxx series, and Olympians and Scanias in the 4xxx series. Nationals are numbered 3xxx – unless they're Greenways, in which case they carry 2xxx numbers. British Bus owns two of the former Midland Red companies, Midland Fox and Midland Red North.

United Counties, serving Northampton, Bedford, Kettering and the surrounding areas, was sold to Stagecoach in 1987, another of the Scottish group's purchases direct from NBC. The NBC inheritance is in the main Olympians and VRTs, although many of the latter are post-privatisation purchases from Devon General, acquired in 1991 when the Devon company was completing its programme of replacing big buses with little ones.

Stagecoach has added various examples of its Alexander-bodied standard buses, with Olympians, B6s and 709Ds joining the United Counties fleet. There are also 15 Olympians with Northern Counties bodies. United Counties operate long-distance services under the Coachlinks name, using in the main Leyland Tigers or new Volvo B10Ms with Plaxton Interurban bodies.

There is one former municipal bus operation in United Counties territory, Northampton Transport. This was acquired by GRT in 1993 and is now consequently part of FirstBus. GRT retained Northampton's basic colours – red and cream – but in different shades and applied in corporate GRT style. This means that buses in Northampton carry the same livery as those in Leicester, another GRT acquisition in middle England. The Northampton fleet has not seen any significant changes under its new owners, and still runs Olympians and VRTs alongside its recent standard purchase, the Volvo Citybus. The VRTs are unusual in having Alexander bodies; the only other operators to specify the Alexander/VRT combination were Cardiff, Lincoln and Tayside. Most of the Citybuses have Alexander R-type bodies (chosen long before any involvement by GRT) and the L-registered batch which entered service in 1993 are the last Citybuses built. Recent single-deckers have been Volvo B10Ms, while new vehicles in 1995 were three low-floor Volvo B10Ls with Alexander Ultra bodies. These were the first production Ultras.

Top **A number of British Bus subsidiaries have been buying East Lancs-bodied Scanias, including Midland Fox which has 20 N113 double-deckers.** Colin Lloyd

Centre **United Counties was one of the first Stagecoach subsidiaries to receive Northern Counties-bodied Volvo Olympians, back in 1993 before the type became more widespread in the group. There were 15 in the initial batch, one of which is seen in Northampton.** Stewart J Brown

Left **Northampton Transport's buses are now in GRT-style cream and two-tone red. The most modern double-deckers in the fleet are Alexander-bodied Volvo Citybuses.** Malcolm King

Midland Red West is part of First Bus, having been owned by Badgerline since 1988. This is a fleet which has seen some heavy investment. It started in 1990 with 50 Leyland Lynxes, one of the few substantial orders placed for the Lynx. Then in 1994 came 37 Dennis Lances with Plaxton Verde bodywork, with more following in 1995 to make the company one of the biggest users of both the Lance chassis and the Verde body. The 1995 buses have apt MRW registrations. As new buses have arrived, so older ones have gone, but Midland Red West still runs some 50 Mark 1 Nationals. These three types – National, Lynx and Lance – make up the entire big bus fleet. There are no double-deckers in the Midland Red West operation. Leopard and Tiger coaches operating under the Midland Express name are used for coaches on long-distance limited-stop services between the main towns in the company's area which covers much of Hereford and Worcester, and extends east into Birmingham and its suburbs. Unusual coaches are two Q-registered Leopards which were rebodied by Plaxton, and three with Y-registrations which were re-registered when they received new ECW B51 bodies in 1983. The chassis date from 1970.

The company operates a substantial fleet of minibuses with just over 150 Mercedes L608D 20-seat conversions dating from the mid-1980s. Most were bought new, but a few started life with other NBC subsidiaries including Bristol Omnibus and Southdown. The only more modern minis are seven Peugeot Talbot Pullmans which are in Centro's Quickstep livery and are used on tendered services.

Evesham is the location of the southernmost Midland Red West depot. It is the home of N N Cresswell running locally with a new Plaxton-bodied Mercedes 709D, a rare Bedford CF with Reeve Burgess's striking Reebur body which was perhaps a few years ahead of its time, and assorted Bedford coaches. All wear a distinctive blue and white livery. Spring of Evesham operate to Cheltenham using Leopard coaches. Most have Plaxton bodies but a recent addition has been a one-time NBC coach with Willowbrook 003 body. Across the M5, Worcester is served in the main by Midland Red West, although Astons Coaches run a service to Pershore. Further west, Bromyard Omnibus operates an interesting assortment of buses on rural routes. These include an Alexander-bodied Leopard which was new to Grampian Transport, an East Lancs-bodied Bristol RE which started life with Rossendale and a one-time Eastern Scottish Seddon Pennine VII.

Top **Midland Red West has a substantial fleet of Plaxton Verde-bodied Dennis Lances and the type can be seen in most parts of the company's operating area. This example is in central Birmingham.** Michael Fowler

Centre **The oldest single-deckers operated by Midland Red West are Leyland Nationals. All are Mark 1 models and most were inherited from the original Midland Red company when it was split up in 1981. A 1980 National loads in Hereford.** Malcolm King

Right **Bromyard Omnibus operates a small but interesting fleet. A recent addition is this smart Bedford Y-series with Plaxton Bustler body. It is seen in Hereford, operating the infrequent service south to Ross-on-Wye.** Malcolm King

Further north, Go-Whittle of Kidderminster, one of the region's most widely respected coach operators, runs local services in Kidderminster and Ludlow, and on certain days of the week also runs out from Ludlow to Bridgnorth and to Tenbury Wells. It has four Dennis Darts with Northern Counties bodies – two with the short-lived original style of Paladin midibus body and two delivered in 1995 with the improved post-1993 version. Bedford coaches are also used on rural services. Go-Whittle is an old-established business, with roots going back 70 years. A newcomer to bus operation in Kidderminster is Hollands, which runs Carlyle bodied Sherpas acquired from a variety of sources.

To the west, in Leominster, Lugg Valley Travel operate services to Hereford. This is real rural bus country and the routes are operated by 1970s Bedford coaches with Duple and Plaxton bodies, some of which were bought new. Lugg Valley owns 16 coaches. Leominster local services are run by Primrose Motors using two tri-axle Talbots bought new in 1988 and an ex-GM Buses Dodge S56.

Closer in towards Birmingham, Ludlows of Halesowen run local services with 18 Leyland Nationals and two Carlyle-bodied Dennis Darts. Ludlows also run services to the Merry Hill shopping centre. In nearby Bromsgrove, Blazefield Holdings have a small subsidiary, Associated Bus & Coach Investments – better known as Rover. Its fleet is made up mainly of coaches, but an ex-Harrogate VRT runs a local service.

A striking new bus in Hereford is the second Mercedes-Benz O405 to be delivered to a small operator in the UK. The operator is Sargeants of Kington, and the Mercedes with Optare Prisma body is running on the company's service between Kington and Hereford. It shares the service with a Bedford coach. The only other Prisma operators at present are Tees & District and Leicester Citybus. Sargeants also run an Optare StarRider and have a couple of ex-United Counties Bedford YRQs with Willowbrook bus bodies which are used on contracts. An old-established Hereford area operator is Yeomans Canyon Travel, with two Dennis Darts running a town service. One has a Carlyle body, the other an Alexander Dash. Four Bedford YMQ-S models with Lex Maxeta bodywork are owned, never a common combination. Out-of-town services are operated by bigger Bedfords, including some with Duple Dominant bus bodies. Ledbury, to the east of Hereford, is the home of Newbury Coaches which runs south to Gloucester using Plaxton-bodied Bedford coaches. Smiths of Ledbury also run to Gloucester, generally with a Duple-bodied Bedford Venturer. DRM Coaches run a service from Ledbury to Hereford with an early Volvo B58 coach, although a Leyland National is also owned.

Top **Go-Whittle has been a convert to Dennis, running Javelin coaches and Dart buses. There are four Darts, all with Northern Counties bodies. This is one of two delivered in 1994.** Stewart J Brown

Centre **A surprise addition to the fleet of Sargeants of Kington in 1995 was this Mercedes-Benz O405 with Optare body. Until its arrival Sargeants had used elderly second-hand vehicles on its bus operations. The Mercedes is used on the Kington to Hereford service.** Malcolm King

Left **Yeomans operate two Dennis Darts on its Hereford town service. The older of the two has Carlyle bodywork.** Malcolm King

EAST ANGLIA

Top **Whippet runs both new and second-hand double-deckers. The most recent additions to the fleet are two ex-London Buses Titans.
New in 1981, they moved to East Anglia in 1993.** Russell Upcraft

Above **There are 30 Dennis Darts in the Eastern National fleet, all with Plaxton Pointer bodies.
The early examples are 9m 34-seaters but those delivered in 1995 were 9.8m 39-seaters.** Russell Upcraft

East Anglia is FirstBus country. The amalgamation of GRT Bus Group and Badgerline in the summer of 1995 re-united under common ownership the region's two main operators, Eastern Counties and Eastern National. Both were former NBC subsidiaries (and Tilling group companies even earlier), and both had been privatised in management buy-outs in 1986-87. Eastern National was bought by Badgerline in 1990; Eastern Counties by GRT in July 1994. Out of Eastern National another significant operator was born – Thamesway. This was a Badgerline creation, set up in the summer of 1990 and taking over Eastern National's operations in south Essex and across to London. Thamesway is, of course, also part of the new FirstBus combine.

Eastern Counties runs just over 400 buses in an area stretching from Ipswich north to King's Lynn. It has depots in both towns. The company's headquarters are in Norwich, where it provides virtually all city services, and it also has depots in Bury St Edmunds, Great Yarmouth and Lowestoft. One of Eastern Counties' main claims to fame is its large fleet of Bristol VRTs. There are 143 in stock, making the company the largest user of Bristol double-deckers in Britain (or anywhere else, come to that). These range from late X-registered buses which include the last standard NBC-style ECW-bodied VRTs built, to five ex-Ribble J and K-registered flat-fronted Series 2 models which are rare survivors indeed.

During its seven years in management ownership Eastern Counties maintained a steady inflow of new buses, ranging from double-deckers to minis. The double-deckers are the only Olympians in the fleet, five delivered in 1989 with Northern Counties bodies, followed by five Leyland-bodied buses in 1991. These were to have had Northern Counties bodies but the order was switched to Leyland at a time when there were fears that Northern Counties might close down. Ironically Northern Counties is still with us, despite two changes of ownership, while Leyland is not.

For single-deckers Eastern Counties went to Dennis, a make last purchased new in 1941. In 1989-90 it took 15 Javelin buses, a relatively rare type. The first five had Duple bodies while the last ten were bodied by Plaxton. These were followed in 1992 by four Dennis Darts with Plaxton's ubiquitous Pointer bodywork for a park-and-ride service in Norwich, and in 1993 by five Lances which were among the first with Northern Counties' new Paladin body. More recent Dennis additions have been a further 10 Plaxton-bodied Darts which are fitted with lateral guide-wheels for use on Superoute 66 between Ipswich and Martlesham Heath on which there is a short section of guided busway – the first in the country since the short-lived experiment by West Midlands PTE in the mid-1980s.

Top **Eastern Counties runs the country's biggest fleet of Bristol VRTs, most bought new. This 1980 example wears the current GRT-style livery.** Richard Godfrey

Centre **Five Northern Counties-bodied Leyland Olympians delivered in 1989 were Eastern Counties' first new double-deckers since the last of the VRTs in 1982. Three were 75-seat buses but the last two were 65-seat coaches and were delivered in a mainly cream livery which provides an interesting comparison with the new GRT cream-based colour scheme.** Richard Godfrey.

Left **The first stretch of guided busway in Britain since bus deregulation in 1986 is used by Eastern Counties Superoute 66 in Ipswich. Plaxton-bodied Dennis Darts provide the service and they feature lateral guidewheels carried on yellow arms just ahead of the front wheels.** Geoff Mills

Eastern Counties also has 10 Plaxton-bodied Volvo B6s. They were bought by Mainline of Sheffield in 1994 for a planned new operation in Ipswich, which was intended to compete with Ipswich Buses. However when Stagecoach took a 20 per cent stake in Mainline in the summer of 1994 – around the same time as GRT bought Eastern Counties – it adopted a rather less aggressive stand and the 10 B6s were sold to GRT, repainted into Eastern Counties colours (some being done by Ipswich Buses) and added to the Eastern Counties fleet. Ipswich's was a bus war which never happened. New minibuses for Eastern Counties have been Mercedes 609D vans with conversions by Frank Guy of Chesterfield. There are 30, which entered service in 1993-94. Older minibuses are mainly Mercedes and Transits. The last of the Sherpas have been withdrawn. None of Eastern Counties' minibuses have more than 20 seats, so there are none of the bigger second generation models in the fleet.

Eastern Counties was, back in the early 1980s, one of the first operators to look at ways of improving the performance of its Nationals, going so far as to fit a Gardner engine in a Mark 1 model, which necessitated adding a short snout to the front to accommodate the radiator. This early willingness to experiment with up-rated Nationals makes the growing presence of East Lancs Greenway rebuilds in the present day fleet seem particularly apt. A number were delivered in 1995 as an alternative to buying new buses – a policy which stands in sharp contrast with GRT practice elsewhere.

Eastern Counties is having some of its older Leyland Nationals upgraded to Greenway specification by East Lancs, including the replacement of their original Leyland engines with Gardner power units. This 1977 bus was given the Greenway treatment in 1994; more recent rebuilds have been delivered from East Lancs in the new GRT-style livery. Geoff Mills

Rosemary Coaches of Terrington St Clement was taken over by Eastern Counties in 1993 and the name and livery survive on a few acquired vehicles. These include three ex-London Fleetlines. M G Doggett

Since GRT bought Eastern Counties a fair number of vehicles have been repainted in corporate GRT livery, with red stripes on a cream base. This is replacing the unusual cherry red which had been used by the company since privatisation. Eastern Counties has long used an alphanumeric fleet numbering system. This continues, with the first letter generally indicating the chassis type and the second letter the body maker. Whether it will survive under FirstBus control remains to be seen – elsewhere GRT/FirstBus has abandoned such schemes where they existed in acquired companies.

In 1993 Eastern Counties took over the business of Rosemary Coaches of Terrington St Clement and a few ex-Rosemary vehicles remain in stock including ex-London DMS-type Fleetlines.

There are a number of established independent operators scattered throughout the Eastern Counties operating area. The biggest family-owned coach businesses in Norfolk is Sanders of Holt with some 90 vehicles, most of which are Bedfords. Sanders operate a number of services in north Norfolk, including routes from Norwich to the coast at Cromer and Sheringham, and from Fakenham to King's Lynn. To the south west of Norwich, Semmence of Wymondham operates a large fleet of Bedford coaches, mainly on schools services. Simonds of Botesdale run south from Norwich to Diss and Stowmarket using Bedfords including an unusual high-capacity Venturer with 69-seat Plaxton Paramount body.

The GRT corporate style may prove to be short-lived as FirstBus examines its options on vehicle liveries. Its application on Eastern Counties single-deckers is shown in this view of a National 2. Geoff Mills

Most of Sanders services are operated by Bedford Y-series coaches, such as this 1977 YMT with Plaxton Venturer body. It has been in the fleet since 1985. Geoff Mills

There are two municipal operators in the Eastern Counties operating area, at Great Yarmouth and at Ipswich. Great Yarmouth's oldest buses are ECW-bodied AEC Swifts, new in 1973 and now the only Swifts in Britain still in regular use with their original owner. Nine survive. These are the only full-size single-deckers in the fleet. The company's other big buses are double-deckers, ten ECW-bodied VRTs and two Volvo Citybuses. Three ex-London Metrobuses were operated from 1991 but were sold in 1995. This leaves the bulk of the town's operations in the hands of midibuses and minibuses. The minibuses are MCW Metroriders – eight bought new plus four acquired from Blackburn Transport – and six Mercedes 811Ds. The midis are Dennis Darts, of which there are five, three with Duple bodies and two bodied by East Lancs. Great Yarmouth Transport operates 50 vehicles, including three Volvo B10M coaches which trade under the Yareside Coaches name.

Competition in the town comes from the unlikely-sounding Flying Banana which started in 1989 with a couple of Transits and is still going strong, now with 18 vehicles, the biggest of which is a new Mercedes-Benz 709D with Alexander Sprint body. All but one of the company's buses is second-hand. Neave of Catfield operates into Great Yarmouth (and also to Norwich), generally with Bedford coaches.

Ambassador Travel, based in Great Yarmouth, is primarily a coach company. It was created in 1984 to take over the coach operations of Eastern Counties and was privatised in a management buy-out from NBC at the end of 1987. It runs a small bus operation using ECW-bodied Leyland Leopards which have been downgraded from coach duties along with six Volvo B6s with Alexander Dash bodies, bought new in 1994 for park-and-ride services in Norwich.

Top Eight AEC Swifts are still in use with Great Yarmouth Transport. New in 1973 they have dual-door bodywork built in nearby Lowestoft by ECW. The cream-coloured window rubbers were briefly fashionable in the early 1970s. Geoff Mills

Right Small buses are playing a growing part in Great Yarmouth's operations, with both new and used vehicles joining the fleet. This is one of four Metroriders bought from Blackburn in 1994. Peter Newman

Below Flying Banana has been running in Great Yarmouth since 1989 and now has a fleet of 18 minibuses. The first to be bought new, in 1992, was this Leyland DAF 400 with unusual Minibus Options 20-seat body. Geoff Mills

Below right Ambassador Travel bought six Alexander-bodied Volvo B6s in 1994 for use on a park-and-ride contract in Norwich. They were the first new buses for this predominantly coach-based company. Geoff Mills

The other town in East Anglia with a local authority bus fleet is Ipswich, where Ipswich Buses runs the majority of local services. Its newest buses are three Volvo Olympians with East Lancs bodies, the first new 'deckers for the 85-strong fleet since 1988. Ipswich's only other double-deckers are two East Lancs-bodied Dennis Dominators and 21 Roe-bodied Leyland Atlanteans – plus a 1964 AEC Regent V. The town has a long history of running single-deckers on busy routes because of a low bridge near the railway station and most additions to the fleet over the last 10 years or so have been single-decked. In the 1980s the standard choice was the Dennis Falcon and there are 24 in use. Six have Northern Counties bodies while the remainder are East Lancs-bodied.

More unusual are 10 Leyland B21s with Alexander (Belfast) N-type bodies. Four were bought new in 1985; the other six came from Ulsterbus which had been evaluating them as a possible successor for the Bristol RE. The B21 was built in Leyland's Bristol plant and was designed to use Leyland National running units in a conventional chassis frame. The four bought new by Ipswich in 1984 were unsold stock chassis. Ipswich is the only British operator of the B21.

Ipswich runs five Optare Deltas and was the first operator to receive an Optare Sigma. The Deltas are based on DAF chassis; the Sigma on the Dennis Lance. An unusual feature of the Ipswich Deltas is the fitment of an exit door immediately behind the front wheel. Other operators of dual-door Deltas have the second door set in mid-wheelbase. At the same time as taking the Optare-bodied Lance, Ipswich took three with East Lancs bodies. Did someone say beauty and the beasts? Small buses in the Ipswich fleet are 16 Optare MetroRiders, including one ex-demonstrator and one which was new to Lancaster City Transport. Names – mainly of Thames barges – are carried by most of the Ipswich fleet. Ipswich, incidentally, was a latecomer to motorbus operation, only starting in 1950; it had previously run trolleybuses and trams.

Top **The oldest double-deckers in regular service with Ipswich Buses are 1976 Atlanteans with two-door Roe bodies.** Malcolm King

Centre **The only Leyland B21s delivered new to a British operator are to be found in Ipswich. There are four, with Alexander (Belfast) bodies. The B21 is a rear-engined chassis which Leyland developed for sale in export territories where the integral National was not an acceptable product.** Geoff Mills

Left **In recent years Ipswich Buses has bought a variety of single-deck types. The DAF-based Optare Delta is the most numerous - there are five. Ipswich has stayed loyal to two-door buses and specifies the exit immediately behind the front axle rather than in mid-wheelbase.** Malcolm King

A service from Ipswich to Stowmarket is operated by Galloway of Mendlesham using a new DAF SB220 with Ikarus body. In rural Suffolk Beestons of Hadleigh operate services in the Hadleigh and Sudbury areas. The company, and its associated Mulleys Motorways business based in Ixworth, is also a major provider of schools contracts. It's a big operation, with just over 90 vehicles. There are a few double-deckers, including an ex-London DMS and one unusual East Lancs-bodied Bristol VRT which was new to Rhymney Valley. But most regular service work is covered by seven Mark 1 Nationals acquired from a variety of sources. Most have been re-registered with dateless Ulster registrations which makes identification of their previous owners difficult. In Bury St Edmunds and Sudbury Felix run local services with modern Mercedes and Iveco minis. The services were taken over from Goldsmith of Sicklesmere. Rules of Boxford also serve both Sudbury and Bury St Edmunds. The company's eight-strong fleet is made up mainly of 1970s coaches but includes one full-size bus, a 1971 Ford R192 which was new to Midland Red.

Top **The only single-deck bus operated by Galloway of Mendlesham is a DAF SB220 with Ikarus body. It was delivered in 1995 for use on the Ipswich to Stowmarket service.** Geoff Mills

Centre **Jonckheere-bodied buses are rare in Britain. This Scania K92 in the Beestons fleet came from Your Bus of Alcester but was originally operated on a tendered service in London by Scancoaches. It was new in 1986.** Richard Godfrey

Right **Carlyle bodywork is fitted to this Iveco Ford 49.10 operated by Felix of Long Melford.** Richard Godfrey

In Colchester the bulk of local services are provided by Colchester Borough Transport, since November 1993 a part of British Bus. Here the fleet has undergone some dramatic changes. For example, all 14 of the fleet's Lynxes have been whisked away to Crosville Wales. A couple of its Olympians have gone to Southend Transport, while another pair are with Midland Fox. Replacements have been older types. There are six Leyland National 2s brought in from Midland Fox, and four former Ribble ECW-bodied Atlanteans have moved south from North Western, joining Colchester's existing fleet of the type. ECW-bodied Atlanteans were the standard fare at Colchester from 1975 to 1980. The changes mean that the only buses in the fleet which are now less than 15 years old are five Olympians bought between 1985 and 1991. The average age of the fleet has almost doubled to 18 years compared with 9.5 years when British Bus took over.

Colchester has long been a magnet for enthusiasts interested in small fleets, and despite the upheavals of deregulation the town is still served by a fair number of independents. One of the oldest-established is Osborne's, based in Tollesbury and running from there not only to Colchester but also to Witham and Maldon. The company's motor bus operations started shortly after the end of World War I. Osborne's run just over 30 vehicles including a number of modern coaches. Second-hand double-deckers are used on both regular services and on schools operations. The oldest are two N-registered long-wheelbase Fleetlines which were new to Tayside Transport in 1975 and moved south to Essex 10 years later. The others are an ex-London DMS, two VRTs with ECW bodies and an R-registered VRT with Alexander body which was bought from Tayside in 1980 when it was just three years old and Tayside had decided that rear-engined buses couldn't stand up to the punishing hilly routes of Dundee. Early 1980s coaches – mainly Leyland Leopards – are also used on service. There are now no single-deck service buses in the Osborne's fleet.

Top **Under British Bus ownership the Colchester Borough Transport fleet has been getting noticeably older. Leyland National 2s from Midland Fox have replaced younger Leyland Lynxes.** Keith Grimes

Centre **Colchester has acquired a number of Atlanteans from London & Country, including this 1976 bus which has a 1979 Roe body, fitted after the original (and generally similar) body was destroyed in an accident. It was new to Yorkshire Woollen. The Atlanteans have replaced Olympians.** Malcolm King

Left **The oldest buses in the Osborne's fleet are two 1975 Daimler Fleetlines with Alexander bodies. They came from Tayside in the mid-1980s. One is seen in central Colchester.** Keith Grimes

The biggest of the traditional independents running into Colchester is Hedingham Omnibuses, whose fleet has grown from 40 just prior to deregulation to 121 now. Part of that expansion has come by takeovers – Norfolk's of Nayland in 1991 and Partridge of Hadleigh in 1994. The company is based in Sible Hedingham, to the north of Braintree. The acquisition of the Partridge business strengthened the company's eastern operations with services to Ipswich and Bury St Edmunds. Over the years Hedingham has invested steadily in new buses and the company's oldest vehicles are mid-1970s Bedford Y-series, bought at a time when the government's new bus grant stimulated sales of new vehicles to many small companies. The most unusual of these is a 1973 YRT with Marshall Camair body. The last Bedfords bought new were two YMPs with Plaxton Derwent bodies in 1987. Since then, a variety of new types have been bought including a Leyland Lynx, a Swift, two Dennis Darts, two Volvo B6s and one Leyland Olympian, the only new 'decker in the company's history. Most of Hedingham's double-deckers are ex-NBC VRTs, but there are also five former Blackpool Atlanteans which came with the Norfolk's business. Other types include second-hand Lynxes and Nationals, and three ex-London DMSs acquired from Partridge. The Nationals are unusual in being former Crosville Mark 1s which have been repowered with Gardner engines. There are three, and they were previously operated by Norfolk's. The company's newest buses are two stylish Dennis Lance SLFs with Wright Pathfinder bodies, partially funded by Essex county council, and operated between Witham and Maldon.

Cedric Coaches of Wivenhoe run to Colchester, using ECW-bodied VRTs drawn from a variety of sources. Chambers of Bures also has a Colchester service and some interesting modern buses – three Alexander-bodied Olympians bought new in 1989, and a Leyland Lynx. Older Bedford buses remain in service as a reminder of how things used to be in the Chambers fleet.

Top and centre **Hedingham Omnibuses' biggest buses are five long-wheelbase Atlanteans with 86-seat East Lancs bodies. They were acquired by Hedingham with the operations of Norfolk's of Nayland in 1991. A number of new buses of different types have been purchased in the 1990s. Alexander Dash bodywork is fitted to three - two Volvo B6s and this Dennis Dart.** Keith Grimes, Malcolm King

Below **There are eight Bristol VRTs in operation with Cedric's of Wivenhoe. Two have high-backed seats and came from Badgerline.** Keith Grimes

Below right **Chambers of Bures operates three Bedfords with Duple bus bodies. The oldest, a 1984 YMT, pulls into Colchester bus station.** Colin Lloyd

Eastern National's headquarters are in Chelmsford but it has a depot in Colchester, adjacent to the bus station. Clacton-on-Sea marks the eastern extremity of its operations. Despite having ceded part of its operations to Thamesway, Eastern National remains a sizeable company with almost 240 buses. A substantial number – just over 100 – are Mercedes minibuses ranging from L608D van conversions bought in NBC days to new 709Ds with Plaxton Beaver bodies, the standard Badgerline group minibus. Bigger single-deckers are 30 Plaxton bodied Darts, 20 Nationals (an NBC legacy) and 14 1988 Leyland Lynxes from a batch of 30 bought by the company during its period under management ownership. The other 16 are with Thamesway. The double-deck fleet is rather older. The newest are 1986 Olympians (including some with ECW dual-purpose bodies) while the remainder are Bristol VRTs plus a pair of heritage KSW5G open-toppers. There are 49 double-deckers in the Eastern National fleet.

The Thamesway fleet is now larger than that run by Eastern National, thanks in part to the company's success in winning tendered services in London. Thamesway has almost 290 buses and coaches, and over 150 of these are Mercedes minis, most of which have Reeve Burgess Beaver bodies and were bought mainly for use in and around Southend. The company's newest buses are standard Badgerline group Plaxton-bodied Dennis Darts. Those delivered in 1994 introduced a new purple and yellow livery and this is now replacing the original maroon and yellow scheme on existing buses in the fleet as they become due for repaint. Full-size single-deckers are the 16 Lynxes already mentioned, plus some 40 Leyland Nationals which are now the company's oldest buses. There are only 15 double-deckers – 13 Olympians and two VRTs. Thamesway runs City Saver coach services to London, using an orange and yellow livery. This was started in 1993 with a fleet of second-hand Tigers. In 1995 the Tigers were replaced by 19 smart new Volvo B10Ms with Plaxton Interurban bodies.

Top and centre **Ownership by Badgerline of both Eastern National and Yorkshire Rider has seen a number of vehicles move south, including Leyland Tigers and Bristol VRTs. This Bristol in Colchester High Street came from Yorkshire Rider in 1995. The standard Badgerline group minibus is the Mercedes-Benz 709D with Plaxton Beaver body. Eastern National has 77 of the type, including some pre-Badgerline buses with Reeve Burgess-built bodies. This is a 1994 Plaxton-bodied 709D.** Malcolm King, Ivor Norman

Below **Thamesway is in the process of changing livery to the unusual combination of yellow and purple, seen on a Plaxton-bodied Dennis Dart in Romford. In 1991 Thamesway took delivery of 87 Mercedes 709Ds with Reeve Burgess bodies. Many of them are used on services in Southend.** Ivor Norman, Malcolm King

British Bus bought Southend Transport in June 1993, but here the change has been much less dramatic than in Colchester. The new owners quickly brought an end to Routemaster operation and withdrew a fair number of the second-hand Mark 1 Nationals which had been added to the fleet around 1990. But that apart, there's been little change in the fleet composition. The oldest double-deckers are 31 long-wheelbase Daimler Fleetlines. Five Q-registered examples have 1972 chassis which were rebodied by Northern Counties in 1984-85. More modern double-deckers are 15 Leyland Olympians, including four Leyland-bodied buses bought new. The remainder include examples from Crosville Wales (bought before the British Bus takeover), National Welsh and Southern Vectis, plus a pair transferred from Colchester Borough Transport by British Bus. The only other 'deckers are 15 ECW-bodied VRTs new to a variety of NBC operators. They include four highbridge buses which came from Ribble.

The single-deck bus fleet operated by Southend Transport comprises just two types – two quite different types. In the majority are Leyland Nationals, all Mark 1s and all second-hand. There are 19, including eight which were new to the Greater Glasgow PTE. The other single-deckers are four ultra-modern Dennis Lance SLFs with Wright Pathfinder bodies. These are used on an accessible bus service and are partly funded by Essex County Council. Similar buses, with similar council support, are operated by County Bus & Coach in Romford and by Hedingham Omnibuses. Southend also runs coach services to London and for this has a fleet of Leyland Tigers and Volvo B10Ms. Most are second-hand, although six 1984 Tigers with Duple Caribbean bodies were bought new.

Inland, small operators include District Bus of Wickford with nine minibuses, a mixture of new and second-hand Mercedes and Iveco 49.10s. The latter include two which ran briefly for Strathclyde Transport. District Bus was started in 1988 and at the end of 1994 was bought by British Bus. It changed hands yet again in mid-1995 when it was bought by FirstBus. It is now controlled by Thamesway. Another Wickford operator is NIBS – Nelson Independent Bus Services – which runs to Billericay. The NIBS bus fleet includes ex-Southern National Bristol REs, ex-London DMSs and a few Dodge minibuses. In the Grays area Harris Bus runs services which embrace the giant Lakeside shopping centre at Thurrock. The double-deck fleet was made up mainly of ex-Northampton Alexander-bodied VRTs. These are now being withdrawn. Single-deckers are four Volvo B10Ms with Plaxton Bustler bodies, bought new in 1986. Harris Bus also runs two Northern Counties-bodied Ailsas which started life with Greater Manchester Transport, two Scania double-deckers bought new in 1989 and a number of minibuses.

Top **Essex County Council helped fund 10 low-floor Dennis Lances which are in operation with three of the county's bus companies, including Southend Transport. They have stylish Wright Pathfinder bodies.** R Godfrey

Centre **Buses in the NIBS fleet are painted overall yellow or yellow and white. NIBS has four VRTs; this one came from Thamesway but was new to Eastern National in 1980. A number of NIBS vehicles carry BIL registrations – there are no prizes for guessing the owner's first name.** Geoff Mills

Right **Northern Counties-bodied Ailsas are relatively rare, having only been built for Cardiff, Derby and Greater Manchester Transport. Two of those which started life with GMT are now owned by Harris of Grays.** Mark Bailey

In the Cambridge area Cambus is the major operator. Cambus was created by NBC in 1984 to take over the western part of Eastern Counties operations. It was privatised in a management buy-out in 1986, and was purchased by Stagecoach at the end of 1995. Cambus has depots in Cambridge and Newmarket. Its northern operations, around Peterborough, were reformed as a new Viscount Bus & Coach company in 1989. Cambus operates 113 buses and coaches of which just under half – 49 – are Bristol VRTs. Most were inherited from Eastern Counties, although a few second-hand examples have also been purchased. The only other double-deckers in the Cambus fleet are 16 post-privatisation Leyland Olympians – the newest are three N-registered buses with Northern Counties bodies. The others are three Roe-bodied buses from the West Yorkshire PTE and two with Optare bodies (to Roe designs) bought new in 1988. The Optare/Olympian combination is a relatively rare one. There are also six 1989 Olympians with Northern Counties bodies and two ECW-bodied buses from Eastern National.

Optare figure prominently in the minibus fleet, with nine CityPacers (six of which were new to Taff Ely Transport) and 16 MetroRiders. The company's newest single-deck buses are 14 Volvo B6s with Marshall bodies, delivered in 1993. Three Leyland Lynxes were acquired in 1992 with the business of Miller of Foxton, and three Mark 2 Nationals are also owned. The Millerbus name is still carried on a small number of buses, including all those used on park-and-ride services in Cambridge.

One significant and old-established independent still serves Cambridge – Whippet Coaches of Fenstanton. The company's bus fleet includes double-deckers bought new – Atlanteans and Volvo Citybuses – and secondhand. The latter include some of the last remaining examples of the Scania-engined MCW Metropolitan still in regular use, as well as two ex-London Titans and a Willowbrook-bodied Atlantean which was intended for service in Baghdad. This bus had to be converted to right-hand-drive, and now sports a Plaxton Paramount front dash panel. Whippet's single-deckers are Volvos and Bedfords with Duple Dominant bus bodies, both new and second-hand.

Top **In the latter half of 1995 three new Northern Counties bodied Volvo Olympians joined the Cambus fleet. One of these is seen in Litlington Village.** Russell Upcraft

Centre **Most Volvo B6s are 9.9m models. Cambus is unusual in having the short 8.5m version. There are 14 and all have Marshall 32-seat bodywork. They were new in 1993.** Geoff Mills

Left **Omni have tried to broaden the appeal of their minibus by stretching it and adding a third axle. The prototype was unveiled in 1994 and a small number have been delivered in 1995. Whippet runs this one.** Geoff Mills

Viscount is a smaller operation than Cambus with just under 70 vehicles. The double-deck fleet composition is not dissimilar to that at Cambus, with a predominance of VRTs – there are 39. Again most are an Eastern Counties legacy, with a few second-hand vehicles from other operators. More modern 'deckers are 11 Olympians. There are six with Northern Counties bodywork and one bodied by Optare – all transferred from Cambus in 1989 when Viscount was created – plus three with Leyland bodies bought new in 1990. The 11th is a standard NBC-specification bus with ECW body, acquired from Selby & District in 1995. The only other vehicles in the Viscount fleet are minibuses – seven Optare MetroRiders and seven Marshall-bodied Iveco 59.12s. The purchase of Marshall bodywork by Cambus and Viscount supports local industry. The Marshall bus-building factory is in Cambridge. Viscount buses carry fleet number prefixes – B for big buses and S for small ones. Recent repaints in Peterborough operate in Peterborough Bus Company colours – red, cream and maroon.

Enterprise of Chatteris run from Ramsey to both Peterborough and Huntingdon, usually with an ex-London bus in the shape of either a Leyland National or a DMS-type Fleetline. The company also has one surviving ex-Lothian Atlantean which is used on schools work. A regular service is provided between Peterborough and Whittlesey by Morley's. Morley's bus fleet includes an interesting mix of types with three ex-Western Scottish Seddon Pennine VIIs, a couple of former London DMSs, a Titan, an ex-Reading VRT and a former Blackburn Atlantean.

Eastwards from Peterborough, Viscount has a depot at March. From March a service to Wisbech is run by Emblings of Guyhirn, generally using a Plaxton-bodied Reliance which was new to Premier Travel of Cambridge. At busy times the service is covered by Bristol VRTs which were new to various NBC operators. Wisbech is also served by Towler, running to King's Lynn and Christchurch, among other places. Towler runs a dozen vehicles including two ex-NBC VRTs and a number of Bedford coaches. The company's most modern bus is an ex-Cambus Optare CityPacer.

Top **The last Bristol VRTs entered service in 1981 with X-suffix registrations, with a significant number going to Eastern Counties. Some of these are now running with Viscount in Peterborough.** Mike Harris

Centre **Peterborough Bus Company is a trading name for Viscount, carried by a small number of buses including two new Optare MetroRiders.** Mike Harris

Right **There are three ex-London buses in the Enterprise fleet – two Fleetlines and this 1978 Leyland National. The National joined the Enterprise operation in 1991.** Richard Godfrey

Above **Still running for Morley's of Whittlesey is this distinctive ex-Reading Transport Bristol VRT with Northern Counties body. It is an uncommon long-wheelbase VRT/LL model. New in 1976, it moved from Reading to Cambridgeshire in 1990.** Geoff Mills

Left **Towler of Wisbech has a mixed fleet, ranging from 1974 VRTs to this 1988 Optare CityPacer seen on service in King's Lynn. All are second-hand. The CityPacer was new to Cambus and has been in the Towler fleet since 1993.** M G Doggett

SOUTH EAST ENGLAND

Top **Seamarks of Luton runs four MAN 11.190s with Optare Vecta bodywork.**
Three are ex-demonstrators and include this 1991 bus which was one of the original launch vehicles. Richard Godfrey

Above **Gem-Fairtax is a small subsidiary of London & Country. One of its Nationals is seen in Lindfield near Haywards Heath.** Richard Godfrey

The ownership of London's buses underwent its biggest upheaval in over 60 years during 1994, with the privatisation of London Buses Ltd (LBL). Despite the significance of this massive change in philosophy, from a publicly-owned service to privately-owned profit-making companies, the initial outward effects were minimal, especially when compared with 10 years of tendering which had seen the uniform red of London's buses being broken up by a veritable rainbow of new liveries on the vehicles of the private sector contractors who were winning a growing number of London Regional Transport (LRT) tenders. Now tendering is in the hands of a new London Transport Buses (LTB) organisation and all bus services in the capital are operated by private sector companies.

The Cowie Group (whose headquarters are in Sunderland) is in fact the biggest bus operator in London by virtue of its acquisition of two LBL subsidiaries – South London and Leaside and its ownership of Grey-Green. Between them the three companies operate over 1,000 vehicles.

Stagecoach owns two former LBL companies, East London and Selkent. It was quick to modify the livery – no, not to white with stripes, but by painting most types of bus overall red. A remarkable innovation by London standards was the application of fleet numbers to the fronts of buses, which is where most operators around the world have long accepted they should be... Routemasters have escaped the all-over-red rule and have a gold relief band between decks. There is a pleasant irony in Stagecoach, which almost 10 years ago played a key part in importing Routemasters to Scotland and provincial England, now owning its own fleet of the type in London. There is a further irony in the fact that one of the companies bought by Stagecoach – Selkent – was the only LBL subsidiary which did not have any Routemasters operating in its fleet

MTL Trust Holdings from Liverpool owns London Northern (the 'Northern' is being dropped from its trading style) and R & I Coaches, while the Go-Ahead Group from Newcastle owns London Central. The small Stanwell Buses operation in outer west London and Surrey is part of London United after a brief period in the ownership of the West Midlands Travel group, and an even briefer spell with a management buy-out team. The other four LBL companies are now in the ownership of management-led employee buy-outs – CentreWest, London General, London United and Metroline.

Above left **Stagecoach has adopted unrelieved red for its London fleets but makes an exception for East London's Routemasters, which have cream relief and gold (instead of white) fleetnames. A 1966 RML heads along Oxford Street.** Stewart J Brown

Left **MTL has adopted overall red for most types in its London Northern fleet, including Routemasters. They carry standard MTL-style fleetnames.** Stewart J Brown

So much for the ownership, what about the vehicles? So far there has been little change. Routemasters, mainly 30ft-long RMLs, still perform on many central area services. Most of those operated by ex-LBL companies remain in traditional London red, but variety is provided by Kentish Bus, with two dozen maroon and primrose RMLs on the 19 which links Battersea with Finsbury Park, and BTS with 22 RMLs in a brighter red (reminiscent of NBC poppy red) on the 13. This runs from Aldwych to Golders Green and is, incidentally, the only regular Sunday Routemaster operation apart from London Coaches' sightseeing tours. BTS is part of the Yorkshire-based Blazefield Holdings organisation, while Kentish Bus is a British Bus subsidiary. MTL London Northern has gone for unrelieved red on its Routemasters (and on all other types too).

Alongside the standard RMLs, East London still runs two one-time BEA forward-entrance Routemasters which perform frequently on the 15, from East Ham to Paddington. In addition East London has a green-liveried RMC which also takes turns on the 15. Cowie's South London company has standard RMs on the 159 running from Baker Street to Streatham and serving Oxford Circus, Piccadilly Circus, Trafalgar Square and Parliament Square on the way. The RMs on the 159 wear a red and cream livery, introduced at the start of 1994. The biggest Routemaster operators are London Central and Leaside, each of which has just over 100. London Central has gone in for modest route branding on the 12 and 36, with a vertical yellow ribbon motif .

At the other extreme from the 30-year-old RMs on the 159 are London Central's smart Optare Spectras on the 3, which also runs from Oxford Circus south through Piccadilly Circus and Parliament Square. The Spectras are the most stylish double-deckers in central London. They're also some of the rarest. With 24 London Central has the country's second-biggest Spectra fleet after Wilts & Dorset. London Central has the only East Lancs-bodied Darts in the capital (they run in Peckham) and it also has two batches of Volvo Olympians, nine with Alexander Royale bodywork and 10 bodied by Northern Counties.

Other modern types to be seen in the central area include smart Dennis Darts with Northern Counties bodies, operated by London Northern on the C2 Camden Link. An imaginative livery with a white roof makes them stand out from most other red buses. Full-size Northern Counties Paladin bodies are fitted to other single-deckers in the central area, including London General's 13 Volvo B10Bs running on the Clapham Omnibus (otherwise known as route 88) from Oxford Circus to, surprise, surprise, Clapham. They are the only B10Bs operated by an ex-LBL subsidiary.

Volvo's mid-engined Citybus was also bought by London General. The company has 39 with dual-door Northern Counties bodies and these can be seen mainly on the 133 which runs from London Bridge to Tooting Broadway. The only other Citybus operators in the capital are Grey-Green and Londonlinks. The Red Arrow network of central London limited stop services is operated by London General using East Lancs Greenway rebuilds of Leyland National 2s. They are Gardner-powered.

Among the most eye-catching buses in central London are London Northern's Dennis Darts on the Camden Link service. They have 34-seat Northern Counties bodies with a particularly attractive interpretation of London Buses' red, grey and white colours.
Colin Lloyd

BTS, now part of Blazefield Holdings, uses a bright red livery for its buses. The company operates Routemasters between Golders Green and Aldwych, with the route displayed on the upper deck side panels. A smart RML loads in Golders Green at the start of its journey.
Stewart J Brown

New Volvo Olympians have joined the London Central fleet, with bodywork by Northern Counties and, as seen here in Peckham, Alexander. They keep pre-privatisation colours, but with a new fleetname.
Stewart J Brown

Grey-Green serve central London with the 24 from Hampstead Heath to Pimlico, operated by Alexander-bodied Citybuses and new Northern Counties-bodied Scania N113s. Citybuses are also used by Grey-Green on the 168 which runs from Hampstead Heath to the Elephant & Castle. While the 24 and 168 are run by buses bought new, elsewhere Grey-Green's fleet includes rebodied buses. These are based on time-expired Volvo B10M coach chassis which were fitted with new East Lancs double-deck bodies in 1992 and operate on the 141 from Moorgate to Wood Green. Further north, Grey-Green has East Lancs-bodied B10M single-deckers operating to Brent Cross on the 210. Generally similar buses, but with 1992 bodies on mid-1980s coach chassis, operate between Debden and Walthamstow.

Grey-Green also operates in east London, with Leyland Lynxes and Ikarus-bodied DAF SB220s in the Ilford area. The company's 14 Leyland Olympians run on the 103 between Rainham and North Romford. This route was operated briefly by County Bus & Coach but was taken over by Grey-Green, with the vehicles, in 1991. Other types operated on LTB services include Dennis Darts and second-hand Metrobuses. The company also runs services in Kent, using Lynxes and Nationals.

The biggest of the established independent operators in east London is Hong Kong-owned Capital Citybus. Its services reach as far north as South Mimms, but with a strong concentration in Walthamstow and Romford. Capital Citybus is the successor to the London tendered operations of Ensign Bus. Ensign continues as a sightseeing tour operator – London Pride – with assorted open-top double-deckers.

Capital Citybus runs a fascinating mixture of new and second-hand types. The former include 48 Olympians, 26 Dennis Dominators, 16 MCW Metrobuses and 10 Volvo B6s; the latter more Dennis Dominators, MCW Metrobuses and Leyland Olympians from a variety of sources. The older Leyland-built Olympians have bodies by Alexander and Northern Counties while the newer Volvo-built chassis have Northern Counties Palatine II bodies.

Capital Citybus has a minimal presence in central London, on the 153 which runs from Finsbury Park to Smithfield. This is generally covered by Mercedes with Plaxton Beaver bodies. Similar vehicles can be found at the northern extremities of Capital Citybus's regular operations, on the 298 from Southgate to South Mimms. The other small buses in the fleet are Optare MetroRiders.

Top **Grey-Green's varied double-deck fleet includes MCW, Leyland, Scania and Volvo models. Most of the Leylands are long-wheelbase Olympians with 77-seat Northern Counties bodies which were new to County Bus & Coach in 1990. They were taken over by Grey-Green, along with part of County's operations, in 1991.** Colin Lloyd

Centre **Capital Citybus operates 13 Volvo B6s, 10 of which have Alexander Dash bodies. They entered service in 1994.** Colin Lloyd

Bottom **Capital Citybus has a substantial fleet of modern double-deckers which includes MCW Metrobuses, Dennis Dominators, and Leyland and Volvo Olympians. Further variety was added in 1995 with the acquisition of a DAF DB250 for evaluation. It has Northern Counties Palatine II bodywork.** Richard Godfrey

In Romford Capital Citybus vehicles outnumber those of East London, the ex-LBL company now owned by Stagecoach. Most East London services in the Ilford and Romford areas are operated by Leyland Titans, but there are also Dennis Lances (ex-Selkent), Optare Deltas and Dennis Darts. Wheelchair-accessible Scanias with Wright bodies are run on the 101 from North Woolwich to Wanstead. These are part of a 68-strong accessible bus fleet funded by LRT and introduced during 1994 across five London Buses subsidiaries prior to their privatisation. East London has the world's biggest fleet of Leyland Titans, with just under 300. The only other substantial Titan fleets are operated by London Central and Selkent. Indeed, from the 1,125 delivered new to the capital, there are fewer than 800 left in revenue-earning service. The MCW Metrobuses delivered at the same time have enjoyed a higher survival rate.

Most of London Buses' Scanias are with East London which runs 50, 42 bodied by Northern Counties and eight by Alexander. The only other Scanias with a former LBL company are 21 Alexander-bodied buses with London Northern. One small operator running into Romford is Blue Triangle. The company's regular services in the Romford area are usually run by Nationals. Transit Holdings, which tried unsuccessfully to run commercial services in the capital through its Docklands Transit operation, is still around with Docklands Minibus, running Mercedes on LTB tendered routes in Barking.

Selkent, on the south of the Thames, has no Routemasters in service, nor does it have any Metrobuses. Its double-deck operations are in the hands of ECW-bodied Olympians, from the last big order – for 260 – placed by London in 1985, and Titans. Major investment in new double-deckers is underway and 52 Volvo Olympians were delivered in 1995, with Northern Counties bodies. These break from London tradition by having fleet numbers, 301-352, without a type prefix. Selkent operates Dennis Lances with Plaxton Verde bodies. Small buses are mainly MetroRiders and Mercedes.

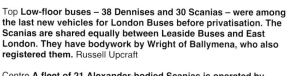

Top **Low-floor buses – 38 Dennises and 30 Scanias – were among the last new vehicles for London Buses before privatisation. The Scanias are shared equally between Leaside Buses and East London. They have bodywork by Wright of Ballymena, who also registered them.** Russell Upcraft

Centre **A fleet of 21 Alexander-bodied Scanias is operated by London Northern, some of which carry dedicated branding for the X43. From time to time they can be found on other duties, as this example in Enfield illustrates.** Peter Rowlands

Right **Stagecoach has been modernising the Selkent fleet and in 1995 added 52 new Volvo Olympians with Northern Counties bodies. Northern Counties has become a major supplier to Stagecoach, particularly in London and north east England.** Richard Godfrey

FirstBus has a strong presence in north-east London through Thamesway. Routes reach as far in as the City, with the 214 running between Liverpool Street and Highgate Village. It uses Plaxton-bodied Dennis Darts. Elsewhere most of the London area services provided by Thamesway, generally around Walthamstow, are operated by Reeve Burgess-bodied Mercedes, most of which were new to Eastern National. Thamesway was created shortly after Badgerline took over Eastern National and split the company in two. Outside London the main centres of Thamesway operation are Basildon (its headquarters) and on the Essex coast around Southend. The company is in the throes of a livery change. It started life in 1990 with an unusual combination of yellow and maroon. This was changed from mid-1994 to an even more unusual yellow and purple.

The last major operator running buses which aren't red in the north-east of London is County Bus & Coach. This is part of what was London Country North East, and can thus trace its roots back to the days of London General Country Services. When LCNE was privatised it was bought by AJS. It was soon split into two – County Bus & Coach and Sovereign Bus & Coach – and each went its own way. County was bought by Lynton Travel (in effect a management buy-out from AJS) in 1990, but in the autumn of 1994 was sold on to West Midlands Travel.

Lynton invested in new buses during its ownership of County. It bought Dennis Darts and Iveco Ford minis. These have replaced older types in the fleet. Its LT tendered routes include the 66 from Romford to Leytonstone which is usually run by Leyland Lynxes, and Walthamstow area services which are the preserve of Mercedes minis. Double-deckers are operated on a number of Essex and Hertfordshire routes and are generally vehicles inherited from LCNE – Atlanteans and Olympians. The company's newest buses are four Wright-bodied Dennis Lance SLFs. These were partly funded by Essex county council and operate between Harlow and Romford. The Lance SLF has a flat floor allowing access for passengers in wheelchairs.

County is unusual among major operators in running its vehicles exclusively with local branding – TownLink in Harlow, LeaValley in Hertford and ThameSide in Grays. Since its acquisition by West Midlands Travel each of these names has been given a WM prefix.

In Harlow the Buzz Co-operative was set up by former County drivers in 1988. It runs a fleet of 11 Mercedes, most being Reeve Burgess conversions of 609D vans, but there are also two Optare StarRiders. Reg's Coaches run local services in and around Hertford using Dennis Darts with Duple bodies, and Alexander-bodied Mercedes 709Ds. Routes are operated from Hertford to Welwyn Garden City and to Hatfield.

Top Romford area mobility routes are operated by Thamesway using Marshall bodied Darts. Keith Wood

Centre Four Wright-bodied Dennis Lance SLFs are operated by County Bus & Coach on a service between Romford and Harlow, which is supported financially by Essex county council. Note the WM prefix to the TownLink fleetname, indicative of the company's recent change of ownership. Geoff Mills

Left Reg's Coaches of Hertford run three early examples of the Dennis Dart with the short-lived Duple Dartline body. This bus, new in 1989, was a Duple demonstrator. It was acquired by Reg's in 1990 and is seen in Hertford bus station. Mike Harris

One small business provides services in outer north-east London – Wests Coaches of Woodford Green. Although the company has been in coach operation for almost 50 years, it only moved into buses with the advent of deregulation in 1986. It runs in the Epping and Loughton areas and has nine MCW Metroriders, four Wright-bodied Dennis Darts (uncommon in a small fleet) and two Optare Deltas. Many of West's buses have personalised BUS registration marks.

The other part of what was LCNE is Sovereign Bus & Coach, which since 1991 has been part of Blazefield Holdings. Sovereign is the major operator in Welwyn Garden City and has a strong presence in Stevenage, either in its own right or trading as Welwyn Hatfield Line. The big bus fleet is made up mainly of Nationals and Lynxes, with a few double-deckers. Small vehicles are Mercedes, many of which carry Welwyn Hatfield Line livery. Welwyn Hatfield Line was started in 1987 by a group of former London Country drivers. It was bought by Sovereign in 1990.

Watford is one of the main centres of operation of The Shires (formerly Luton & District) fleet, the former London Country North West operation. Services are provided by a mix of elderly ex-LCNW buses including B-series Leyland Nationals and Roe-bodied Olympians. More modern additions to the fleet have been MCW Metroriders and Olympians with Leyland bodies.

Lucketts also run Watford local services, mainly with Dennis Darts bodied by Plaxton and Marshall. These have BUS registrations. There are also Optare CityPacers. The company's first new full-size bus entered service in 1995, a rare Iveco TurboCity 50 with WS Coachbuilders body. WS was formerly Wadham Stringer and Luckett's TurboCity 50 is the first to be sold in England. Timebus Travel is a relative newcomer and provides two local services in Watford. What makes it interesting is the choice of vehicle, usually a smartly repainted ex-London Routemaster in LT red with grey lining.

Top **West's of Woodford Green have an interesting bus fleet. It includes nine MCW Metroriders, bought new in 1988, and four Dennis Darts with Wright Handybus bodies. The Darts all have BUS registrations.** Malcolm King

Centre **Sovereign Bus & Coach runs 19 Leyland Lynxes, most of which have come from other companies in the Blazefield group. This 1989 model came south from Harrogate & District in 1993.** Mark Bailey

Right **Mercedes-Benz minibuses with Reeve Burgess or Plaxton Beaver bodies are a Blazefield standard with over 70 in operation in the company's southern subsidiaries. Ten carry Welwyn Hatfield Line livery, including this 1989 709D seen in Welwyn Garden City. It has a Reeve Burgess-built body, produced in Pilsley, near Chesterfield.** Colin Lloyd

Above left **Lucketts of Watford operate this unusual Iveco TurboCity 50 fitted with WS Coachbuilders body. The TurboCity has a 9.5-litre Iveco engine, mounted vertically at the rear. This was originally an M-registered Iveco demonstrator; it was re-registered by Lucketts.** Richard Godfrey

Above right **American-built buses have never been common in Britain, and the Blue Bird doesn't look set to change that. Designed primarily for school bus use, it is being offered to British operators as a low-cost full-size bus. University Bus has four, delivered in 1994. The Blue Bird has a Cummins engine.** Tony Wilson

Below left **Timebus Travel operates local services in Watford using smartly repainted Routemasters. Routemaster operation outside London is becoming increasingly rare.** Mike Harris

Below right **Red Rose of Aylesbury operate mainly small buses. These include this Mercedes 811D with Optare StarRider E bodywork. It was originally used as an Optare demonstrator.** Mike Harris

Perhaps the most bizarre new buses to be found anywhere in Britain are the US-built Blue Birds run by University Bus of Hatfield. They are the only Blue Birds operating on a regular service in Britain – indeed the total number of Blue Birds in the country has barely reached double figures – and whatever plus points they have, style isn't one of them. University Bus also runs second-hand Nationals and two new Mercedes-Benz OH1416 with Wright Urbanranger bodies. These are the only examples of this model in service as yet. The company's routes serve Watford, Welwyn Garden City and St Albans. Red Rose Travel sounds as if it should be in Lancashire, but it isn't. It operates in Watford and Aylesbury with a mixed fleet which includes Iveco Ford minibuses.

The southern part of what was London Country North West, based in Slough, was taken over by Q Drive Buses in 1993 and has now been absorbed into Q Drive's Bee Line fleet. Bee Line serves Slough, Maidenhead, Windsor and Bracknell, with the area to the south of the Thames being part of what was Alder Valley North before it metamorphosed into the Bee Line. It was bought by Q Drive in 1987. Much of the fleet is still part of Q Drive's NBC inheritance, in particular large numbers of Leyland Nationals. Modern buses include Northern Counties-bodied Leyland Olympians, five of which were purchased in 1988 and are the fleet's newest 'deckers. The only other double-deckers are a handful of Bristol VRTs. Recent new deliveries have been Dennis Darts and Scania L113s. The former are bodied by Plaxton, the latter by Northern Counties.

The Scanias, which serve Bracknell and Reading, entered service at the start of 1995 and introduced a new livery with a different shade of yellow, a blue skirt and orange relief. This is replacing the original yellow and dark grey livery, and is a major improvement. Some buses carry branding for routes serving Heathrow Airport. In Windsor an old-established local service is run by White Bus, with a Y-series Bedford.

The Shires runs into Slough with a service from Amersham, typically using National Greenways, while a Slough town service is provided by Nightingale Coaches. Most of Nightingale's vehicles are Mercedes minibuses, but interest is provided by an Optare-bodied Leyland Cub which was new in 1985 to the West Yorkshire PTE. The front-engined Cub was built at Leyland's Bathgate factory and was developed from the Terrier light truck. It was a model with a short production life and Cubs in passenger service are rare.

Q Drive's other bus operation, London Buslines, operates services in north-west London using double-deckers bought new. These are 33 Leyland Olympians with bodywork by Alexander and Northern Counties. The company also has minibus operations, covered by Plaxton-bodied Mercedes and Renaults.

Top **The Bee Line adopted a new livery at the start of 1995 and among the first buses to carry it were new Scanias with Northern Counties bodies, one of which is seen in Bracknell bus station.** Stewart J Brown

Centre **Optare bodied 15 Leyland Cubs for the West Yorkshire PTE in 1985. They had short lives with their original owner and were soon dispersed to other operators around the country. One is now running in Slough for Nightingale, operating alongside Mercedes minibuses.** Stewart J Brown

Right **London Buslines operates tendered services in west London using Leyland Olympians. The oldest are 11 with Alexander bodies, which date from 1989. One heads through Stamford Brook for Richmond.** Mike Harris

North-west London is mainly Metroline territory, served largely by Metrobuses and Darts. Other Dennises in the fleet are 44 Lances. The majority have Northern Counties bodies (and are used on the 113 which runs in to Oxford Circus) but there are also 13 Wright-bodied SLF models. Repaints in the early part of 1995 were in unrelieved red as Metroline decided on a new post-privatisation livery, now settled as red with a blue skirt. Metroline expanded soon after its privatisation by buying Atlas Bus & Coach from London Coaches which had owned the company since August 1994. It was bought by Metroline in November 1994 and runs the 52 from Willesden to Victoria with a fleet of 27 Titans. Metroline also own Brent's Coaches of Watford, acquired in September 1995.

London Buslines isn't the only Olympian operator in north and west London. Another small operator running Olympians is Armchair Passenger Transport. It operates the 260 between North Finchley and Shepherds Bush and the 65 from Ealing to Kingston. Armchair's 29 Olympians are bodied by Alexander and Leyland. Second-hand Atlanteans are kept as spare buses. An unusual small-scale operation in the north-western suburbs is the 398, which is run by Blue & White Buses – formerly Scorpio Coaches – between Ruislip Station and Northolt, usually with a one-time Lothian Duple-bodied Leyland Cub or a three-axle Talbot. This is a commercial operation, run with LTB's agreement, but not part of the tendered route network.

The two main red bus fleets in this part of London are MTL London and Leaside Buses. Leaside has the biggest Metrobus fleet in London, with 334 in stock, and has recently started to refurbish some of the vehicles to extend their lives. It also has a fleet of 40 modern Alexander-bodied Olympians, delivered in 1992. Leaside operates north to the Enfield area. However London Northern has the most northerly depot of any ex-LBL company, at Potters Bar.

BTS Coaches started running LT tendered services in 1988. It currently has the Routemaster-operated 13, already mentioned, and the 114 which operates in the Harrow area, using 14 Northern Counties-bodied Leyland Olympians, purchased in 1991. Four ex-London Titans are used as spares. The company was taken over by Blazefield Holdings in 1994. Sovereign Buses (Harrow), another Blazefield company, runs a substantial network of minibus routes in the area. All 28 buses in the fleet are Mercedes, with Plaxton Beaver bodies.

Top **Since privatisation Metroline has introduced a new livery, adding a blue skirt and a new fleetname to the previous LT red. This is one of 31 Dennis Lances with Northern Counties bodywork. It is seen at Edgware station.** Tony Wilson

Centre **Armchair operate tendered services in London with 29 Olympians. The oldest have lowheight Alexander bodies and were new in 1990.** Capital Transport

Left **Thirteen Palatine II bodied DAFs arrived with Leaside Buses in October 1995 in the new Cowie livery. They were first used on a special service to Alexandra Palace, where one of the vehicles, DBS 12, is pictured.** Russell Upcraft

CentreWest serves the area to the south of Metroline. The company has been abandoning the use of CentreWest as a fleetname, and most vehicles carry alternative branding. Vehicles from Westbourne Park garage, including Routemasters, run under the Gold Arrow name, originally coined for Mercedes minibuses. Ealing routes carry Ealing Buses fleetnames, while in Uxbridge the name Uxbridge Buses is used. Buses on routes from Alperton garage carry Challenger names.

CentreWest was an enthusiastic buyer of Wright bodywork and operates 89 Wright-bodied Renault minibuses in and around Ealing. It also has 107 Wright-bodied Darts. In Uxbridge most local services are run by Alexander-bodied Mercedes. CentreWest is easily London's biggest minibus operator with almost 100 Mercedes in addition to the 89 Renaults.

The 607 Express service is operated by CentreWest between Uxbridge and Shepherds Bush with a fleet of dedicated single-deckers. Most are Leyland National 2s, rebuilt to single doorway layout and fitted with coach seats, but there are also six Lynxes and a National Greenway. The company has expanded westwards and runs a tendered service to Slough on behalf of Buckinghamshire county council. This is normally operated by National 2s. At the end of 1995 CentreWest established a base in Orpington, running Plaxton-bodied Darts on LTB tendered services.

Heathrow Airport is a major traffic generator. The main local operator is London United, running Dennis Darts and MCW Metrobuses. London United has the country's biggest Dart fleet, with just under 200. The company runs accessible bus services using Reeve Burgess-bodied Iveco Fords equipped with wheelchair lifts. They are funded by the local authority and are in a green and white livery.

London United made history at the start of 1994 by being the first British bus operator to introduce a fleet of wheelchair accessible buses when the 120 from Hounslow to Northolt was converted to Dennis Lance SLF operation. The SLFs have attractive Wright Pathfinder bodies and carry distinctive signwriting to highlight their special features. Similar buses are operated by Metroline and CentreWest. A new-style fleetname has been introduced since the management buy-out from LBL in 1994, and the red livery is being revised with grey and white relief.

London United operate the Airbus services from Heathrow to central London. These have traditionally been operated by a fleet of 24 Metrobuses with just 50 seats – 41 on top and nine inside, leaving plenty of space for luggage. They can also carry passengers in wheelchairs. Replacements for the Metrobuses started to arrive in 1995 in the shape of new Volvo Olympians, with air-conditioned Alexander Royale bodywork. Duple-bodied Darts are used on an Airbus Direct service which provides direct links to selected central London hotels.

Top CentreWest is one of the biggest users of Wright bodywork. It has over 200 Wright-bodied buses, half of which are Dennis Darts. Capital Transport

Centre London United's new livery adds bright white relief to the traditional London red, as shown by an MCW Metrobus in Kingston. Geoff Rixon

Right In 1995 London United augmented its established double-deck Airbus service between Heathrow and central London with an Airbus Direct operation, serving key hotels. This is run by Dennis Darts. Colin Lloyd

Stanwell Buses was set up by London Buses in 1986, with a base at Hounslow as a low-cost unit to win tenders which might have been lost to private sector companies if London Buses had submitted quotes which carried the full weight of the organisation's overheads. Trading as Westlink, the operation thrived and in January 1994 it was sold, with 119 buses, to its management. This made it the first bus-operating subsidiary of LBL to be privatised. Its independence was short-lived. Two months later, in March, it was taken over by West Midlands Travel who in September 1995 sold it on to London United.

Westlink operates Leyland Nationals and Titans, Dennis Darts, Optare Deltas and Vectas, MCW Metroriders and front-wheel-drive CVE Omnis. Six Omnis are operated in Hounslow and Richmond on services where wheelchair access is required. Westlink's operations are centred on Hounslow and Kingston, but include routes running out to Staines, Egham and Esher.

London Coaches (privatised in a management buy-out from LBL in 1992) operates the lengthy 726 service from Heathrow which serves London's southern suburbs and ends up at Dartford. Once part of the Green Line network, it is now operated by DAF SB220s with coach-seated Ikarus bodies. It runs through Croydon, a major population centre overshadowed by its proximity to London, and the headquarters of Cowie's South London company. South London fell foul of the traffic commissioner in 1994 over vehicle maintenance. This is widely seen as having sunk any chances of success for a planned management-led employee buy-out of the company. Since taking over Cowie has been working hard to raise maintenance standards and one visible sign of this is the number of buses which have been repainted and which look very smart indeed. South London inherited the bulk of London Buses' bulk order of Leyland Olympians. It has a fleet of 161. Its other 'deckers are Metrobuses and Routemasters.

Top **A new type for Westlink in 1995 was the Optare Vecta. The company already runs examples of the bigger Delta. The Vectas have MAN chassis; the Deltas are based on DAF's SB220.** Geoff Rixon

Centre **London Coaches run an orbital route from Dartford to Heathrow using DAF SB220s with Ikarus bodies. The 726 route number is a legacy of the route's history as part of the Green Line network.** C D Jones

Left **Attractive new buses to be seen at Heathrow Airport are the 30 Berkhof-bodied Dennis Lance SLFs being operated by Speedlink on behalf of BAA. These are accessible to passengers in wheelchairs.** Tony Wilson

London General, the biggest of the privatised LBL subsidiaries, serves an area stretching northwards from Sutton, which is another sizeable town in London's shadow. Here the livery has been revised and retains the grey skirt which was used by London Buses, but with the addition of a narrow band of yellow relief, which changes the character of the livery more dramatically than might be expected. Big buses carry London General fleetnames while small buses run under the Streetline banner. In Sutton a local service is run by Tellings Golden Miller with new Mercedes minibuses.

Back to Croydon, which is served by two British Bus subsidiaries, London & Country and Londonlinks. London & Country is the successor to London Country South West, and its fleet still contains NBC standard Atlanteans and Nationals, although many of the Nationals are now East Lancs Greenway rebuilds. However as an alternative to the Greenway L&C has carried out a National rebuild of its own, installing a Cummins B-series engine and Allison gearbox, which is the drivetrain used in the Dennis Dart. Soon after privatisation – Drawlane bought LCSW from NBC in 1987 – it took batches of Dennis Falcons, Dennis Dominators and Volvo Citybuses. Most of the Falcons are now elsewhere in the British Bus group, but the Dominators and Citybuses remain. Recent deliveries have been varied. and have included Volvo B6s, Dennis Darts, Volvo Olympians and Dennis Lance SLFs with Wright bodies which operate between Croydon to Guildford. The company is based in Reigate and its services cover much of Surrey.

Epsom Buses' vehicles can be seen in Croydon, although operations centre on Epsom and there are also routes to Kingston and to Weybridge. Dennis Darts are the most recent additions to this fleet, with bodies by Alexander, Marshall and Plaxton. The company's older buses are Bedfords.

Operations in the western part of Surrey are run by Guildford & West Surrey Buses, whose livery is identical to that used by London & Country. The fleet make up, not surprisingly, isn't too different either and there is some movement of buses between the two fleets. The creation of G&WS followed L&C's acquisition of Alder Valley's 48-strong fleet in the Guildford area in 1990. The company serves Guildford and Woking. An unusual addition to its fleet has been a Volvo B10M with Caetano Stagecoach bus body, acquired in 1995 with the Tellings Golden Miller operations in Staines. London & Country also took over the bus operations of AML of Hounslow in 1994.

Top **A 1980 London General Metrobus in Parliament Square shows the company's post-privatisation livery – a subtle and attractive modification of the old London Buses scheme.** Colin Lloyd

Centre **The London & Country fleet still has a large number of buses dating from NBC days. These include Roe-bodied Leyland Olympians, such as this 1983 bus seen picking up passengers in Epsom High Street.** R Godfrey

Right **Epsom Buses' operations are largely covered by Dennis Darts with bodywork by Plaxton, Alexander and, on this 1993 bus, Marshall.** Stewart J Brown

There are three established independent operators in Guildford. Safeguard has been running local services for almost 70 years and these are generally covered by two Leyland Lynxes bought new in 1988, or by more recent Dennis Darts with Plaxton Pointer bodies. The Dart chassis are, of course, produced in Guildford. The Tillingbourne Bus Co can trace its history back for a similar length of time. It is based in Cranleigh, and services work as far north as Reading and as far south as Horsham. Much of Tillingbourne's fleet was bought new, including such rarities as Dennis Dorchesters with Wadham Stringer bodies and the last Plaxton Derwent bodies to be built, supplied in 1993 on Volvo B10M chassis. The newest buses are two Northern Counties-bodied Volvo B6s. Blue Saloon is by comparison a relative newcomer with just over 20 years of bus operation. Its local routes are operated by ECW-bodied Bristol LHs, including three bought new. All three of the Guildford independents run 100 per cent single-deck fleets.

At the start of 1995 London & Country's operations on LTB tendered services were hived off to a new British Bus subsidiary, Londonlinks Buses, which is managed from the Kentish Bus offices in Northfleet, rather than from London & Country's Reigate headquarters. Londonlinks took over a fleet of 160 buses which includes Volvo Citybuses and Dennis Dominators with East Lancs bodies, ex-London Buses Titans, and East Lancs-bodied Volvo Olympians which were almost new. Its first new buses were four Plaxton-bodied Darts for operation between Croydon and Sutton. The livery is an adaptation of the two-tone green and red used by London & Country with the most obvious change being the use of light green rather than dark green for the roof. Londonlinks services are mainly to the south of central London, but its routes do penetrate north of the Thames, to Euston and to Oxford Circus. It also runs south from Croydon, to Caterham and to East Grinstead.

London & Country has two small subsidiaries. Gem Fairtax runs Leyland Nationals from Crawley and two minibuses in Edenbridge. Horsham Buses runs minibuses in L&C fleet livery.

Top **Locally-built Dennis Dart chassis form the basis of the two newest buses in the Guildford-based Safeguard fleet. They have Plaxton bodywork. The newer of the pair, which entered service in 1994, is seen in Guildford town centre.** Mike Harris

Centre **Tillingbourne of Cranleigh operate services in Surrey and into Berkshire. Most of the company's buses were bought new and these include two Volvo B6s with 40-seat Northern Counties bodywork.** Colin Lloyd

Right **Blue Saloon's local services in Guildford are operated by Bristol LHs, the oldest of which is this 1975 example. Like most LH buses it has ECW bodywork.** Stewart J Brown

Right The Tillingbourne Bus Company run a summer Sunday heritage service on a circular route from Guildford via Godalming and Cranleigh. Among the vehicles used is this rare Bristol SUL4A with ECW body which was new to Western National in 1982. Only 181 SUs were built – and of these 133 were new to the associated Southern and Western National companies. Russell Upcraft.

Below Nostalgiabus of Mitcham operate jointly with London & Country on another summer Sunday circular based on Guildford, which runs through Polesden Lacey and Dorking. Seen at Dorking is a former London Transport GS-class Guy. LT bought 84 of these neat little buses for its Country Area operations in 1953. They had Perkins P6 engines and 26-seat ECW bodies. Russell Upcraft.

Left **London & Country pays tribute to its heritage in this Routemaster painted in the dark green livery originally worn by London Transport's country area buses. It carries the company's name in LT-style lettering and came from Southend Transport.** Russell Upcraft

Below **Also operating in London & Country's heritage fleet is this former London Transport RF-class AEC Regal IV with Metro-Cammell body, smartly restored in LT Country Area green.** Russell Upcraft

Kentish Bus – London Country South East as was – has been part of British Bus since the sell-out by its previous owners, Proudmutual, in 1994. Kentish Bus has expanded quite dramatically since its formation in 1987, winning an increasing number of London tendered services which take its buses into the heart of the capital. Most of its central London routes are run by Northern Counties-bodied Olympians, while in outer south-east London and in north Kent midibuses predominate. These too are Northern Counties-bodied and comprise 45 Darts and 12 Volvo B6s delivered during 1994. These were accompanied by 12 Volvo Olympians, with Northern Counties Palatine II bodies, which operate in the Woolwich area.

Kentish Bus took over the London operations of Boro'line Maidstone when that closed down in 1992. That brought more variety to the fleet, including Leyland Lynxes and Alexander-bodied Volvo Citybuses. In November 1993 it took over the bus operations provided by Transcity in the Greenwich and Dartford area, along with Transcity's fleet of nine Dennis Darts and assorted minibuses. The company is a major provider of bus services in the Dartford and Gravesend areas but has recently lost a number of its LTB-tendered services in Kent to Metrobus of Orpington.

Metrobus runs both tendered and commercial routes in Kent and in outer London, running as far west as Croydon. In the late 1980s and early 1990s it was buying new Leyland Olympians. It has 15, plus a number of second-hand examples, most of which came from the West Yorkshire PTE. Full-size single-deckers are Leyland Lynxes, both new and ex-Merthyr Tydfil, but since the launch of the Dennis Dart it has bought little else for its single-deck requirements.

Further into Kent, and Maidstone & District is the main operator. This former NBC business was bought by its managers in 1986 and sold to British Bus in the spring of 1995. During its period under management control the company bought a fair number of new buses. The first were Mercedes 609Ds, but between 1988 and 1994 it bought 30 Olympians with lowheight Northern Counties bodies.

Single-deckers have been Plaxton Pointers, nine on Dennis Darts followed by 10 on Volvo B6s. Older vehicles include just over 60 ECW-bodied Bristol VRTs delivered in NBC days, plus some similar buses acquired from other fleets. There are a few Nationals and just under 40 first-generation NBC minibuses, Mercedes L609D vans which were converted to buses locally by Rootes, whose body works were in Maidstone.

Top **In 1994 Kentish Bus won new tenders in south-east London and to operate these ordered 57 midibuses with Northern Counties bodies. These comprised 12 Volvo B6s and 45 Dennis Darts. A Dart is seen in Lewisham.** Colin Lloyd

Centre **Metrobus has been a regular customer for Plaxton-bodied Dennis Darts. Recent deliveries are allocated to the Orpington to Crystal Palace service, operated under contract to London Transport.** Colin Lloyd

Right **Maidstone & District was taken over by British Bus in 1995. Among its last new buses before the change of ownership were 15 Volvo Olympians with Northern Counties bodies.** Mike Harris

More interesting vehicles among the company's NBC legacy are seven long-wheelbase Olympian commuter coaches which were originally used on the Invictaway services to London but now run between Maidstone and Gillingham. There are also 10 MCW Metrobus IIs delivered in 1984 for evaluation by NBC. Four Leyland Lynxes in the fleet were acquired in 1991 with local bus services being run by Shearings. M&D still runs commuter services, using Leyland Tigers.

The company has expanded by acquisition. It took over New Enterprise Coaches of Tonbridge in 1988 and this continues as a separate operation with a fleet which is made up mainly of Bedford coaches but includes three double-deckers for school contracts. When Boro'line Maidstone shut down in 1992, M&D covered most of its local services. It further consolidated its position in the town in 1994 by taking over competing services operated by Bygone Buses. There are few small companies serving Maidstone. One which does is Farleigh Coaches, with a couple of Leyland Nationals on a local service. Another is Nu-Venture, also running a National and Talbot Pullman minibuses. Turners of Maidstone operate to Coxheath with Nationals or a former Maidstone Borough Transport Bedford YMT.

To the south, East Surrey has built up a network of services in the East Grinstead, Oxted, Caterham, Croydon and Tunbridge Wells area. It's a smart operation with a number of new buses, mostly Dennis Darts with Plaxton bodies. There's also a couple of Optare MetroRiders. Older vehicles include R-series Ford buses, and assorted Bedfords. Search back through the mists of time and you'll find that the East Surrey name has been used before – it was a subsidiary of London General in the 1920s, and a predecessor of what eventually became London Country. Also serving the Tonbridge and Tunbridge Wells area is Wealden Beeline. Leyland Leopards are favoured here, most with Alexander and Duple bus bodies. There are also a few Omnis, and recent new purchases have been three Dennis Darts with Wadham Stringer bodies. One is the standard Portsdown – rare enough in itself – but the other two are the only Winchester coach-style bodies to have been built on Darts. One was an exhibit at Coach & Bus 93 in the colours of Thames Transit.

Sittingbourne, on the eastern edge of M&D's territory, has local services being run by M&D and by Smith's. This company started running commuter coaches to London in 1980, and since 1986 has run local bus routes too. The standard vehicles are Leyland Nationals. Another Sittingbourne-based company, Chalkwell, runs services in north Kent. Most are operated by minibuses, including five Optare CityPacers which were new to London Buses.

Top **East Surrey operates four Dennis Darts, the three newest of which are 9.8m models and have Plaxton Pointer bodies. The company's first Dart was an ex-Wadham Stringer demonstrator.** Russell Upcraft

Centre **Turners operate in Maidstone with a couple of Leyland Nationals. This one, seen in the town centre, started life with Bristol Omnibus.** Mike Harris

Left **Wadham Stringer's steel-framed Portsdown body was not a high-volume product and most were sold to operators in the South East. Wealden Beeline operate this, an ex-demonstrator. It is seen in Tunbridge Wells.** T S Blackman

Beyond M&D country lies East Kent, since 1993 part of Stagecoach South whose territory covers a broad swathe of southern England from Margate in the east right through to Portsmouth in the west. As the most recent addition to the Stagecoach South empire, East Kent's conservative but attractive maroon and cream livery has not quite disappeared under corporate Stagecoach white. But it will do so soon. The buses acquired from East Kent included NBC-style VRTs along with some distinctly unusual VRTs with highbridge Willowbrook bodies. There are also the inevitable Leyland Nationals. Following privatisation in 1987, East Kent first bought MCW Metrobuses, taking 22 in 1988-89. Metrobuses are an unusual type to find in a Stagecoach fleet. Then followed a pair of Alexander-bodied Scania 'deckers, before the company standardised on Northern Counties-bodied Olympians, ordering 24 in the period from 1990 to 1993. The last were delivered in Stagecoach livery, while the earlier examples have since been repainted white.

There are a few small operators in East Kent country. In Ramsgate Eastonways operate Leyland Nationals, ex-London Fleetlines and a Titan, with some services being run in conjunction with the local port authority. It also has Iveco Ford minibuses for local services. Thanet Bus of Margate has operations to Ramsgate and Canterbury, generally run by Mercedes minibuses. Town & Around of Folkestone operate to Hythe and have a local service in Dover. The fleet includes Nationals, but of more interest are a couple of ex-Northern Scottish Fords with Alexander bodies and the company's only new bus, a 1991 Wadham Stringer-bodied Leyland Swift. From Ashford, Kent Coach Tours operate to Faversham and to Aldington, with smart Leyland Nationals on a route previously covered by Westbus who pulled out of bus operation in 1993 to concentrate on coaches. Poynter's of Ashford run to Canterbury, and between Faversham and Whitstable. The fleet is made up mainly of Nationals, of which there are seven. Fuggles of Benenden run in the Tenterden area and down to Rye. The fleet includes elderly Leyland Nationals and Leopards, and a 1994 Wadham Stringer-bodied Dart. You'll search in vain for a Mr Fuggles. Fuggles is a Kentish hop and this, of course, is traditional brewing country. Also serving the Rye and Hastings areas is Rambler of St Leonards, which runs one of the area's smartest coach fleets. Its bus operation has some unusual vehicles, including three Bedford Y-series with Wright TT bodies, a Lex-bodied Bedford YMQ-S, and one of the handful of Bedford JJL rear-engined midibuses built in a joint venture between Bedford and Marshall in the late 1970s – 10 years before the Dennis Dart.

Top **There are very few Metrobuses in Stagecoach livery. East Kent bought 22 in 1988-89 and these are now being repainted. They are Mark II models.** Russell Upcraft

Centre **The Canterbury park-and-ride service is run by East Kent, using Dennis Lance SLFs with Berkhof bodies. These were the first low-floor buses in the Stagecoach group.** Mike Harris

Right **Thanet Bus runs 10 minibuses, mainly in the Margate and Ramsgate areas, but also to Canterbury where this Mercedes is seen. New to Kelvin Central in 1986, it is an L608D with Alexander conversion. It was purchased by Thanet Bus in 1992 and is one of four similar vehicles in the fleet.** David Harman

Above left **Kent Coach Tours** operate a smartly-liveried fleet and use Leyland Nationals and Mercedes minibuses on local services in and around Ashford. This 1988 609D has Made to Measure bodywork. Richard Godfrey

Above right **Town & Around of Folkestone** have a small fleet of six buses including two Alexander bodied Ford R1014s from Northern Scottish, one of which is seen on a Kent county council service. Richard Godfrey

Left **Leyland Leopards and Nationals** are used on most of the services operated by Fuggles of Benenden. This short PSU4 Leopard was new in 1976 to the West Yorkshire PTE. It has been with Fuggles since 1992. David Harman

A small number of short-wheelbase Bedford YMQ-S chassis were fitted with Lex Maxeta bus bodies in the early 1980s, primarily for NBC subsidiaries. United Counties had three, one of which is now with Rambler. It is seen in Hastings. A P Gainsbury

Moving west, what was once Southdown territory is now shared between South Coast Buses, with its main depots in Hastings and Eastbourne, and Sussex Coastline, broadly serving the area westwards from Brighton. Hastings & District has vanished without trace – it was a relatively short-lived NBC subsidiary formed in 1983 to take over the Hastings area operations of Maidstone & District. It was sold to its management in 1987 and bought by Stagecoach in 1989.

A rather more substantial operation to have vanished without trace is Southdown Motor Services, whose green and cream buses once covered most of Sussex. In the 1960s the fleet numbered almost 1,000 buses and coaches. Now it has been absorbed by the two new companies created by Stagecoach South in April 1992. There has been substantial investment in new buses for both companies, initially with Dennis Darts, and then with Volvo B10Ms. There have also been Alexander-bodied Leyland Olympians. The newest double-deckers are Volvo Olympians with Northern Counties bodies. More unusual Northern Counties-bodied buses are five B10M single-deckers delivered in 1994, using chassis which were originally intended for one of Stagecoach's African fleets.

There has also been an influx of Alexander-bodied Mercedes minibuses which have generally replaced first-generation van conversions. Other odd small buses are MCW Metroriders, most of which came from Cedar of Worthing in 1989, and two Wadham Stringer-bodied Leyland Swifts which are operated on behalf of East Sussex county council and are in dark green County Rider colours.

Southdown was owned by its management after being sold by NBC and during this time, from 1987 to 1989, it bought one batch of new vehicles, 12 Volvo Citybuses with Northern Counties bodies. Most are still running for Stagecoach South. The remainder of the pre-Stagecoach fleet is made up of standard NBC types – Bristol VRTs and Leyland Nationals.

There are areas on the south coast where Stagecoach South is not the only operator. Eastbourne is served by Eastbourne Buses, the world's first municipal bus operator (back in 1903) and still local authority owned. Eastbourne has an interesting fleet, with a mix of new and used buses. Until 1994 the most modern double-deckers were 12 Northern Counties-bodied Olympians delivered in 1988. That distinction now goes to a solitary DAF DB250 delivered at the end of 1994 which was the first DAF/Northern Counties 'decker to enter service. Earlier double-deck types are seven East Lancs-bodied Dominators and an assortment of Atlanteans including ECW-bodied examples acquired from Ipswich and Colchester.

New purchases in the 1990s have in the main been Dennis single-deckers, with Darts, seven rare Javelin buses, and Lances. Four of the Javelins have Duple bodies; one has a Plaxton body, while the remaining two have Wadham Stringer bodywork. Wadham Stringer also supplied the bodies for the company's five Darts and three Lances. Modern single-deck buses which are not of Dennis manufacture include two 1986 Volvo B10Ms with Duple bodies which came from Hutchison of Overtown, and two Ikarus-bodied DAF SB220s, bought new in 1994.

Eastbourne Buses is one of the country's biggest users of Wadham Stringer-bodied buses – not counting the Ministry of Defence. It has 10, including five Portsdowns on Dennis Dart chassis. This is the newest, delivered in 1992. Malcolm King

South Coast Buses has five Volvo B10Ms with Northern Counties bodies, delivered in 1994. The chassis were originally intended for operation in Africa and have front-mounted radiators, hence the grilles in the front panel. The bodies also differ in other respects from later Stagecoach orders for generally similar buses, notably in having square-cornered glazing.
Stewart J Brown

Southdown bought 12 Volvo Citybuses during its short period as a management-owned company. Nine remain with South Coast Buses. They have Northern Counties bodies.
Stewart J Brown

Along the coast in Brighton, the main local operators are Brighton Transport and Brighton & Hove, both of which have undergone recent changes in ownership. Brighton Transport is the former local authority fleet, which was bought by its management in December 1993 and now trades as Brighton Blue Bus. An unusually high proportion of the fleet carries overall advertising.

Brighton Transport runs 66 buses including 25 double-deckers. The latter are a mixture of 1978 Leyland Atlanteans and 1980s Dennis Dominators, all with East Lancs bodies. The single-deck fleet is made up primarily of Leyland National 2s, Dennis Darts and Leyland Lynxes, but there are also some Leopards with Willowbrook's Lynx-look-alike Warrior body. Renault minibuses with Alexander bodies play a small part in the operation.

Brighton Transport also has a base in Lewes and buses stationed there carry the Lewes Coaches fleetname. This operation reaches as far inland as Crawley and East Grinstead. RDH Services (the initials of the owner, R D Hunnisett) operates tendered services in the Lewes and Tunbridge Wells areas. The company's bus fleet includes two Cubs and a Lancet, all with Reeve Burgess bodies. They were new to East Sussex county council. Most services are run by rather more mundane Sherpas with Carlyle bodies. Lewes is one of the towns served by Autopoint of Herstmonceux, which lies midway between Lewes and Bexhill. It has routes from Lewes to Newick, Alfriston and Hailsham. Autopoint's bus fleet is made up of second-hand Nationals and new and second-hand Mercedes. In Bexhill local services are run by the Bexhill Bus Company, which started in the early 1980s, before deregulation. Its fleet is single-decked and is made up mainly of Nationals. Bexhill's operations extend to neighbouring Hastings.

Brighton & Hove, a former NBC subsidiary bought by its management in 1987, has since the end of 1993 been part of the Newcastle-based Go-Ahead Group. The first sign of the changed ownership has been the arrival in Brighton on long-term loan of two Roe-bodied Atlanteans from the Group's north-eastern operations. These join standard NBC Bristol VRTs (including some dual-door examples) and a fleet of 34 Scania double-deckers with East Lancs bodies which were Brighton & Hove's preferred choice after privatisation. The Scanias include four former Leicester Citybus vehicles.

Brighton & Hove also runs Leyland Nationals. Its minibus fleet is made up largely of Wadham Stringer-bodied Mercedes which came from Bournemouth Transport in 1990, when they were just one year old. New in 1995 were its first midibuses, Dennis Darts with Marshall bodies. The company was previously part of the Southdown operation, having been formed as a separate unit in 1986 as part of the process of splitting up NBC's biggest subsidiaries in readiness for privatisation.

Top **Brighton Transport last bought double-deckers in 1985. In the late 1980s it ordered Leyland Lynxes and currently has 12 with both Gardner and Cummins engines. The newest date from 1990 and are Cummins-powered.** Stewart J Brown

Centre **A new era at Brighton & Hove has been ushered in with fleet numbers commencing at 1 for a batch of Marshall-bodied Dennis Darts delivered in 1995. They are the company's first new buses since 1990.** A P Gainsbury

Left **Leyland Nationals have ousted Bristol REs from the Bexhill Bus Company's operations. This bus was new to Western National.** P R Gainsbury

Chichester is Sussex Coastline country, but local services are also provided by Sussex Bus, a company set up in 1985. These are run by Iveco Ford minibuses, acquired from a variety of sources, and by Leopards which have been re-bodied with Willowbrook Warrior bus bodies. There are also two Duple Dominant buses in the fleet, a Reliance ex-Tillingbourne, and a Leopard from Graham's of Paisley. A Chichester town service is run by Blue Lake whose buses are early rear-engined models – two London-style AEC Swifts and a former Southdown Marshall-bodied Bristol RE.

The Portsmouth area effectively marks the western edge of Stagecoach South's coastal operating territory, although services run west to Southampton. Inland the company trades as Stagecoach Hants & Surrey in and around Aldershot, and as Hampshire Bus in Basingstoke, Andover and Winchester. The Hants & Surrey operation was taken over from Q Drive in 1992. It had previously been part of Alder Valley. Hampshire Bus was Stagecoach's first acquisition in England, being bought from NBC in March 1987.

There are Dennis Darts in both divisions, along with Mercedes minibuses and former NBC VRTs. Older minibuses are mainly Ivecos, some of which have gravitated here from elsewhere in the Stagecoach group. Indeed Ivecos are widely spread throughout Stagecoach South's operations, building on the fleet which East Kent was operating when it was taken over.

Stagecoach did for a short time have control of services in Portsmouth, when it acquired Portsmouth City Transport in 1989 from its previous owners, a consortium formed by Southampton Citybus and employees of PCT. There is a theory that every time Stagecoach takes over another operator an alarm bell sounds at the offices of the Monopolies & Mergers Commission. The Portsmouth takeover was one of this mythical bell's first soundings, and ultimately Stagecoach was forced to sell its Portsmouth business to Transit Holdings. This happened in 1991 and Transit quickly converted services in the town and its environs to minibus operation, claiming remarkable increases in ridership. Services in the city are run by Blue Admiral, while those running further out trade as Red Admiral. Blue Admiral runs Mellor-bodied Transits, but these are increasingly being replaced by Transit Holdings' unusual two-door minibuses, Iveco Fords bodied by Mellor. Red Admiral services are run mainly by Carlyle-bodied Mercedes 811Ds. These are the biggest buses in regular service with Transit Holdings in Portsmouth.

Top **The most numerous type in the Sussex Bus fleet is the Iveco Ford 49.10 with Robin Hood bodywork. The company runs six, the newest of which is this 1989 bus seen in Chichester. All are second-hand.** Richard Godfrey

Centre **Orders from Stagecoach have made Alexander a major force in the minibus business. The standard Stagecoach minibus is the Mercedes-Benz 709D with Alexander's AM Sprint body, as seen here with Stagecoach Hants & Surrey in Farnborough.** E C Churchill

Right **Minibuses provide most of the local services in Portsmouth. Among the most modern are Blue Admiral's Iveco Fords with two-door Mellor Duet bodies. Colour-coded destination displays help passengers identify which of the city's main corridors the bus serves.** Mike Harris

An interesting small operator running in Havant is Hants & Sussex (not to be confused with Hants & Surrey – or even Hants & Dorset for those with long memories). This company is based in Emsworth and its main claim to fame is that its front-line buses are former London Transport and London Country AEC Merlins and Swifts, now on average 25 years old. Who said they wouldn't last?

Across Portsmouth harbour lie Gosport and Fareham, the main centres of operation for People's Provincial, which was unique among ex-NBC companies in being owned by its employees through a co-ownership scheme. It was taken over by FirstBus in the autumn of 1995. The company has services running into Portsmouth, inland to Petersfield, and to Southampton. Its fleet has been built up around two main types – Mark 1 Nationals and Iveco Ford minibuses. It has around 50 of the former (mostly second-hand) and just over 66 of the latter. It also runs a unique ACE with Wadham Stringer body. Double-deckers re-appeared in quantity in 1993-94. Most are ECW-bodied VRTs from Western National and Bristol City Line.

Two major operators run local services in Southampton. The bigger is Southampton Citybus, which was privatised at the end of 1993 when it was sold by the local authority to its management and employees. The standard Southampton bus in the 1970s was Leyland's Atlantean with East Lancs body and there are 60 in operation, the newest dating from 1982. Atlanteans dedicated to school services carry Schoolbus fleetnames and a band of yellow relief above the lower deck windows.

The end of Atlantean production brought an end to standardisation and Southampton tried both Leyland Olympians and Dennis Dominators in the mid-'80s. Most of these have in fact been sold, and just one Dominator and two Olympians survive in the bus fleet, although there are four long-wheelbase Olympians in the company's Red Ensign coach fleet.

In 1990 the company was among the first Dennis Dart operators, although it hedged its bets on the midibus front by running the Darts alongside Atlanteans which were rebodied as single-deckers by East Lancs. These are now allocated to services working around Southampton airport. Southampton Citybus's Darts have bodywork by Duple, Wadham Stringer and Plaxton, and one has been converted to operate on compressed natural gas. Full-size single-deckers are 11 Leyland Lynxes and two Volvo B10Bs. Most of Southampton's buses are named after ocean liners which once sailed from the city.

Top **In 1993-94 People's Provincial reintroduced regular double-deck operation using Bristol VRTs from Bristol Omnibus and, as seen here in Fareham bus station, Western National. People's Provincial was taken over by FirstBus in 1995.** Graham Jones

Centre **Southampton Citybus operates some 70 Atlanteans, most of which have East Lancs bodies and represent the city's standard type from the late 1960s to the early 1980s. Most carry the names of ocean-going ships which have served the city's port.** Gerald Mead

Left **There is growing interest in alternative fuels to cut urban pollution. Southampton Citybus, working in conjunction with Hampshire county council, is among the front-runners in trials of gas-powered buses and this Duple-bodied Dart has been converted to run on compressed natural gas. The gas is stored in roof-mounted containers. New CNG-powered Darts are to be delivered in 1996.** Gerald Mead

Southampton's other main operator is Solent Blue Line, which is the trading name of the strangely-titled Musterphantom Ltd – you'll find that on the legal lettering – which is a subsidiary of Southern Vectis. It started operations in 1987 and runs a selection of Bristol VRTs. Some of these came from Hampshire Bus, whose Southampton operations were taken over by Solent Blue Line when Hampshire Bus was bought by Stagecoach. There are also a number of relatively rare highbridge buses which were new to Ribble. More modern double-deckers are Leyland Olympians, bodied by Leyland, while the newest buses in the fleet are East Lancs-bodied Volvo Olympians. Minibuses are mainly Iveco Fords.

Not all Solent Blue Line buses are owned by Musterphantom. Unusually the company's livery is also carried by buses operated by Marchwood Motorways, running routes under franchise. The buses used on this operation include Carlyle-bodied Darts, Leyland Nationals, and four DAF SB220s bought new. Marchwood also runs a sizeable fleet of modern coaches.

Across the Solent lies the Isle of Wight, home of Southern Vectis, a former NBC operation which was privatised in a management buy-out in 1986. The company's newest buses are Olympians with Northern Counties bodies. These followed earlier deliveries of similar buses but with Workington-built Leyland bodies. Older double-deckers are conventional NBC Olympians and VRTs with ECW bodies. An unusual feature on recent double-deck deliveries is the use of alternate pairs of rearward-facing seats on the top deck so that four people travelling together on popular tourist routes can chat to each other without one couple getting a crick in their necks.

Top Most of Solent Blue Line's operations in Southampton are operated by double-deckers. These include Leyland-bodied Olympians delivered in 1989. Mark Bailey

Centre Only the legal lettering reveals that this Solent Blue Line bus is in fact operated by Marchwood Motorways. It is one of four DAF SB220s in the Marchwood fleet and was new in 1993. It has an Ikarus Citibus 480 body. Malcolm King

Below left Summer services operated by classic buses are becoming increasingly widespread. Southern Vectis has a fleet of six Bristol Lodekkas, which includes two FS6Gs with 60-seat ECW bodies. They wear Tilling green livery. Steve Warburton

Below right Southern Vectis is adopting a revised livery, still using green and cream, but applied in a different style. One of the company's newest Olympians, delivered in 1995, illustrates the latest livery. It has a Northern Counties lowheight body. Richard Godfrey

Back on the mainland, the area north of Stagecoach South's operations is served by Reading Transport. This company, still in local authority ownership, trades as Reading Buses or, in Newbury, as Newbury Buses. The Newbury operations were taken over from Q Drive's Bee Line business in 1992. Reading Transport has also taken over the Bee Line operations in Reading, as well as some of its commuter coach operations to London. Reading Transport already operated London coach services, which it still does with both double-deck and single-deck coaches. The double-deckers are Olympians and DAF DB250s, which carry quite different styles of Optare bodywork. The Olympians have Titan-derived Roe-style bodies, while the DAFs have the Alusuisse-type Spectra body, built using aluminium extrusions.

There are eight Spectras in the Reading fleet – six buses and two coaches. Optare has also supplied the company's most modern single-deckers, MAN-based Vectas (some of which run in Newbury) and DAF-based Deltas. There are also Optare MetroRiders, StarRiders and even a couple of ex-Lancaster CityPacers, to give Reading Transport a pretty comprehensive selection of Optare products. Earlier generations of buses which pre-date the Optare association include ECW-bodied Olympians, MCW Metrobuses and 12 Leyland Titan integrals. Few Titans were sold to operators outside London and these are the only provincial Titans still running for their original owner.

Competition for Reading Buses appeared in the summer of 1994 with the launch of Reading Mainline, which is the trading name of the grandly-titled Greater Reading Omnibus Co. Reading Mainline's initials are RM, and it's no coincidence that this is a Routemaster operation, running cross-town services. Chiltern Queens of Woodcote operate to Reading and Mercedes minibuses share the work with altogether more interesting Plaxton-bodied buses bought new in the early 1970s – one Reliance and one Leopard. Tappins, a respected Oxfordshire coach operator, runs a service between Reading and the Thames Valley business park, using a Dennis Dart.

The acquisition of Bee Line's operations in Reading and Newbury added a number of unfamiliar types to the Reading Transport fleet. These included Leyland Nationals (more of which have been purchased subsequently from other operators) and ECW-bodied VRTs. These were, of course, standard NBC types which Bee Line inherited when it was privatised in 1987. The maroon and cream livery is re-lieved by a turquoise band on Reading buses and a green band on Newbury buses. Bennetts of Newbury, best known for its high-quality coach fleet, runs a service into Newbury from West Ilsley, normally using a Leyland National.

Top **Reading Transport never bought a new Leyland National. Since acquiring some of the type with the Bee Line operations in 1992, a few more secondhand examples have been purchased. This 1979 National started life with the Greater Glasgow PTE.** Malcolm King

Centre **Competition appeared on the streets of Reading in 1993 with the launch of Reading Mainline, running a fleet of smart Routemasters.** Gerald Mead

Left **Chiltern Queens operate a Reading service and also run a local route in Henley-on-Thames. Operating on the latter is a Mercedes-Benz 811D with Alexander body.** Mark Bailey

Oxford's buses have undergone an identity change, following the sale of City of Oxford Motor Services to the Go-Ahead Group. This former NBC subsidiary was bought by its management in 1987 and adopted a new identity, trading as the Oxford Bus Company. It then took over the Bee Line operations in High Wycombe in 1990, which were re-branded as the Wycombe Bus Company, in the same red, white and black livery as was used in Oxford. Minibuses in Oxford carried Oxford City Nipper names on a predominantly green livery.

Now all that has changed, and the company's new owners have introduced a fresh identity to the operations in Oxford. These are now branded as Cityline, with all vehicles in red, white and blue, in a layout which maintains continuity with the previous colour scheme. The green livery formerly used on minibuses has been adapted for application to the company's park-and-ride double-deckers. Coaches running to London retain the Citylink name with a blue, yellow and white colour scheme. Competition on this service is provided by the Oxford Tube, run by Thames Transit.

The fleet which the Go-Ahead Group took over was ageing. During the first seven years of the company's life in the private sector, new vehicles were five Alexander-bodied Olympians, 33 Metroriders (from both MCW and Optare) plus a fair number of coaches for the busy London services. The company also bought 25 Titans from London Buses, which were used to replace slightly older Bristol VRTs. Most VRTs have now gone from Oxford, with the arrival of new Marshall-bodied Dennis Darts in 1995. This will soon leave ECW-bodied Olympians from 1982-83 as the fleet's oldest buses. They are unusual in that they are two-door layout – and are lowheight to boot. The most unusual Olympian is an ex-Singapore demonstrator, which has Alexander bodywork and was purchased in 1987. It was an exhibit at the 1980 motor show.

Some of the MetroRiders are of interest. The 15 G-registered buses were bought for an attack on Exeter which never materialised because the buses were too long to be allowed in Exeter's High Street and incumbent operator Devon General fought any proposals for a relaxation of the length limit. The four newest MetroRiders are unique in that they are battery-powered, the first buses of this type in Britain since the 1970s when optimists were forecasting an imminent breakthrough in battery performance which would overcome the problems of high weight and limited range. Twenty years on that breakthrough is still awaited, and the four electric MetroRiders are so heavy that they can only carry 18 people within their gross vehicle weight. At 7 tonnes unladen they are over 50 per cent heavier than a diesel-powered MetroRider.

Top Under Go-Ahead Group control, City of Oxford has adopted a new image. Local buses trade as Cityline, and the livery has been modified to include a blue skirt – it used to be black. The company operates Leyland Olympians with ECW bodies which are unusual in having two doors. They were new in 1982-83. Peter Rowlands

Centre The Oxford park-and-ride services run by City of Oxford also have a new identity. Among the buses used on the dedicated car park services are Alexander-bodied Olympians bought in 1988 after the company's privatisation. Mike Harris

Right Electric buses solve the problem of urban pollution – but at a cost. City of Oxford is running four battery-powered Optare MetroRiders on the City Circuit which links the railway station with the central shopping area. Peter Rowlands

In High Wycombe, COMS continues to trade as the Wycombe Bus Company, by and large running the fleet which was taken over from Bee Line. This includes types not to be found in Oxford - Nationals and Lynxes. Unusual among Wycombe's VRTs are two which were new to an independent, Mayne of Manchester. They moved south in 1991. Recent additions to the Wycombe fleet – now in the same red, white and blue livery as used in Oxford – have included ex-London Central Mercedes 811Ds, and Olympians transferred from the main Oxford operation. There are 40 vehicles in the Wycombe operation, compared with around 150 in Oxford. Bee Line still run in to High Wycombe, with an hourly service from Heathrow Airport.

City of Oxford's main competition in Oxford comes from Thames Transit, set up in 1987 by Devon General with a fleet of some 50 Ford Transits. Devon General had in 1986 been the first NBC bus-operating company to be privatised. It soon took over South Midland which had been an NBC subsidiary based in Witney running a predominantly rural service network. South Midland had been sold to two of its managers at the end of 1986, and was quickly absorbed by the expanding Thames Transit operation. As Thames Transit has matured so its buses have got bigger, and many services in Oxford are now run by Darts with dual-door Plaxton Pointer bodies. Out-of-town services are operated by Mercedes 709Ds. Small operators serving Oxford include Charlton Services, with Leopard coaches running in from the company's home town, Charlton-on-Otmoor, and Regis of Faringdon, whose services run in south Oxfordshire and across to Swindon. Regis runs two ex-London Fleetlines, a National 2, and a one-time Eastern Scottish Seddon. The National was new to the Atomic Energy Authority. It doesn't glow in the dark. Worth's of Enstone operate from Oxford to Chipping Norton, and also serve Banbury and Witney generally using coaches or ex-London Titans.

Both Oxford and High Wycombe were served by Yellow Bus from Aylesbury until July 1995 when The Shires took over the Yellow Bus operations which had been started by Mott's Travel in 1991. Some of the newest buses were taken into The Shires stock – two Northern Counties-bodied B6s, a Lynx, two Mercedes minibuses and a Northern Counties-bodied Olympian which started life with the London Borough of Lambeth. Mott's continues as a coach operator.

Top **When City of Oxford took over the Bee Line operations in High Wycombe in 1990 it acquired a number of types which were non-standard. These included three Olympians with ECW coach bodies. The appearance of this one has been marred by the fitment of a standard bus-style front dome and upper deck windows; as built it has stylish curved screens on both decks.** Malcolm King

Centre **Transit Holdings, pioneer (and sole user) of two-door minibuses, has moved up to two-door midis for some of its Oxford services. They are Dennis Darts with Plaxton bodies. The first entered service in 1994. By late 1995 there were 48.** Tony Wilson

Left **Former London Transport Titans have been finding their way into a surprising number of small fleets. Worths of Enstone have two.** David Harman

The Shires covers a broad swathe of the country from Aylesbury round to Luton. As Luton & District, it was bought from NBC by its managers in 1987 and expanded by taking a share in Derby City Transport and Clydeside 2000, and by buying London Country North West in 1990. Luton & District was itself a young company, having been created in January 1986 to take over the southern part of United Counties' operations.

At the start of 1995 Luton & District had two liveries, green and grey for the former London Country North West operations and red and cream for the rest of the fleet. Green buses carried local identities – Chiltern Bus, Hemel Bus and Watford Bus while red buses traded as Aylesbury Bus, Dunstable Bus, Hitchin Bus, Luton Bus, and Stevenage Bus. The Stevenage operations included services taken over from Sovereign Bus & Coach in 1990.

These identities can still be seen, but they are being phased out as The Shires adopts a new blue and yellow livery. With the new colours come new names: Network Watford, Luton & Dunstable, Aylesbury and the Vale, Chiltern Rover (in High Wycombe), Gade Valley (for Hemel Hempstead), Hitchin & District and The Stevenage Line. And if you've never heard of the Gade Valley, fear not – you're not alone.

The Shires operates a substantial fleet of Leyland Nationals, inherited from both Luton & District and LCNW. It also runs VRTs, generally ex-L&D, and Atlanteans, generally ex-LCNW. In what was L&D's green bus area it has 22 Leyland-bodied Olympians, bought by LCNW between 1989 and 1991 when it was management owned. Other purchases at that time included Carlyle-bodied Dennis Darts for a London tendered service in the Harrow area, and four two-year-old long-wheelbase Olympians with Northern Counties bodies which came from Ensign Bus.

In the red bus area there are 11 Lynxes (two of which are ex-Sovereign) and a couple of batches of Alexander-bodied Olympians, running to 25 in all. Other buses from the Sovereign fleet include London Country specification Olympians with Roe bodies. L&D's biggest single investment in new buses came in 1994, with 32 Northern Counties-bodied Volvo B6s, allocated to both the red and the green areas of the fleet, although some have already been repainted in the company's new colours. In 1994 there was also expansion with the take-over of Stuart Palmer of Dunstable, which ran elderly double-deckers. These are still running, with no obvious clues to the change in the company's ownership. Luton & District itself underwent an ownership change in 1994, becoming part of British Bus.

Further expansion in 1995 following the acquisition of Mott's bus services saw The Shires take over the bus operations of Buffalo of Flitwick. Modern buses acquired included Plaxton-bodied Darts, Volvo B10Ms with Plaxton Derwent bodies, and a Volvo B10B with Alexander body. There were also three B10M coaches which had been re-bodied as buses by East Lancs. Vehicles are being repainted in The Shires colours with appropriate area names – most being in Luton & Dunstable territory. Buffalo continues to run coaches. Cedar is now the main small operator in Bedford. It has a mixed double-deck fleet, used mainly on schools work. The most modern are also the most unusual – two Y-registered Dennis Falcon Vs which were new to Nottingham. Single-deckers include an ex-SBG Seddon, a Dennis Lancet and, rare on service work, a Leyland Swift with Portuguese-built Elme bodywork. New in 1990, it is Cedar's most modern vehicle.

Facing page top **In 1994 Luton & District took delivery of 32 Volvo B6s with Northern Counties bodies. Just over half were allocated to what had been London Country North West territory and carried that operation's green and grey livery.** Mike Harris

Facing page centre **Luton & District's other livery was red and cream, applied in LCNW style. This Olympian – originally part of the London Country fleet – was acquired in 1990 with the Stevenage operations of Sovereign Bus & Coach. Roe built the body.** Mark Bailey

Facing page bottom **Luton & District is now LDT and trades as The Shires, but with a variety of local fleetnames. An Alexander-bodied Olympian illustrates the Luton & Dunstable name.** Gerald Mead

Right **Luton & District owns Stuart Palmer Travel, which continues to operate in its own livery. Most Stuart Palmer buses are ex-London Fleetlines with sound encapsulation – the B20 model. Park Royal bodied this 1977 bus.** Phillip Stephenson

Centre **Rare buses in the Cedar Coaches fleet are two Dennis Falcon Vs with East Lancs bodies. They were new to Nottingham City Transport. The only other Falcon V double-deckers in regular service are with GM Buses South.** Geoff Mills

Bottom **Double-deck operation in Milton Keynes is in the hands of Bristol VRTs operated by Buckinghamshire Road Car, a Stagecoach subsidiary. Road Car, and sister operation Milton Keynes City Bus, also run Mercedes minibuses.** Stewart J Brown

Luton is the headquarters of Seamarks, a coach operator which has since deregulation been operating tendered bus services, with routes in the St Albans and Harpenden areas. Its bus fleet comprises four Optare Deltas, four Optare Vectas and an East Lancs-bodied Scania K92 which came from Boro'line Maidstone. There are also two Optare minibuses – a CityPacer and a MetroRider. In Hitchin, which is in The Shires territory, Myall of Bassingbourn operate to Steeple Morden using a Dennis Dart.

To the north the new city of Milton Keynes hosts another part of what was United Counties. Milton Keynes City Bus was formed at the same time as Luton & District – January 1986 – and pursued a policy of running minibuses, in an unfortunate and nondescript grey livery which, it is hard to believe, was recommended by design consultants. The minibuses were generally Mercedes van conversions. Just as full-sized buses had virtually vanished, MKCB was bought by Cambus Holdings in November 1992, and there has since been a rethink with second-hand VRTs appearing on a number of services. MKCB had an offshoot, the Buckinghamshire Road Car Co, and that has been enlarged to a considerable extent at the expense of MKCB. Cambus introduced a new red and cream livery and Citybus fleetnames to the MKCB fleet. Buckinghamshire Road Car's buses are green and cream and carry Road Car fleetnames. Most of the VRTs and other big buses – a few National 2s – run for Road Car. Citybus – now known as MK Metro, although without any change of livery or fleetname, continues as a minibus operation. Competition in the city, from London-based R&I Buses, has come and gone, leaving Challenger of Luton, with former Bee Line Buzz Sherpas, as the main rival operator. Johnson's of Hanslope was taken over by MKCB in 1990, and the former Johnson's operation has been absorbed by Road Car. The Shires run to Milton Keynes with Mercedes minibuses.

SOUTH WEST ENGLAND

Top **East Devon** started operating in 1994 and its original fleet included two ex-Busways Bristol LHs which had been new to Bristol Omnibus. The newer of the pair, a 1980 bus, is seen in Exeter on the service from Sidmouth. Graham Jones

Above **Damory Coaches** is a subsidiary of Wilts & Dorset, and its fleet is made up largely of former Wilts & Dorset buses. These include two 1978 ECW-bodied Bristol VRTs, one of which is seen in Salisbury. Graham Jones

The south west of England is a deceptively large and varied region. As an illustration of its size, Penzance, for example, is further from Bristol than Sheffield is from London. Much of the area is rural, but there are significant population centres in Bristol, Swindon, Bath, Bournemouth, Exeter and Plymouth. FirstBus has a strong presence throughout the region through companies which were part of the Badgerline group. Stagecoach can be found mainly in what might be described as the north east of the south west, through its acquisition of Western Travel at the end of 1993. There are local authority owned fleets serving Swindon, Bournemouth and Plymouth.

Bristol is the region's biggest city and is served by the Bristol Omnibus Co, trading as City Line and with one of the brightest liveries around. Bristol Omnibus was once one of NBC's biggest subsidiaries, but in the 1980s its operating area was cut right back, with services in Gloucestershire being taken over by the newly-formed Cheltenham & Gloucester Omnibus Co, while those in rural Avon passed to Badgerline. Which leaves the present-day Bristol Omnibus Co serving the city and its environs with a fleet of some 350 modern vehicles.

Bristol Omnibus was privatised in 1987, being sold to Midland Red West in partnership with the company's management. Badgerline bought Midland Red West in 1988, and the two major parts of the old Bristol company were thus re-united in common ownership. Much of the fleet has been replaced since the Badgerline takeover. The most common type is the Mercedes-Benz 709D with Plaxton Beaver bodywork; there are 74 in service, delivered in 1993-94. Older generations of minibuses are a handful of 1986 Mercedes L608D van conversions, and a large fleet – 48 – of Iveco Ford 49.10s with unusual angular Dormobile Routemaker bodies.

The Badgerline group's standard midibus combination, Dennis Dart/Plaxton Pointer, is represented by 48 buses delivered in 1994-95. There is also one B6 with a Pointer body, on loan from Volvo for long-term evaluation. The only full-size single-deckers in the City Line fleet are 62 Leyland Lynxes. Three Bristol VRTs remain – the end of Bristol bus operation in the city where they were made is now just a matter of time. The only other signs of NBC's legacy to the company are 46 Olympians with Roe bodies. These feature the Park Royal-style windscreen which was also specified by London Country Bus Services, rather than the BET screen which was NBC's standard. The 1990s have seen new investment in double-deckers, in the shape of Northern Counties-bodied Olympians. The first 30, delivered in 1992-93, have Leyland-built chassis and Northern Counties' traditionally-styled Palatine body. But the second batch of 24 are altogether more eye-catching Palatine IIs, on Volvo-built chassis. The last six carry a striking silver livery for operation on the busy Bath Road park-and-ride service.

Top City Line is the name used by Bristol Omnibus. The colourful livery suits the company's fleet of Plaxton-bodied Mercedes minibuses. This is one of 74 delivered in 1993-94. Richard Godfrey

Centre City Line operates 48 Plaxton-bodied Dennis Darts – and this solitary Volvo B6. The Plaxton Pointer body on the B6 is easily identifiable by the raised window line behind the rear wheels. Malcolm King

Left A high-profile park-and-ride service in Bristol is operated by City Line using six specially-liveried Volvo Olympians. They have Northern Counties Palatine II bodies and come from a batch of 24 delivered in the winter of 1993-94. They are the company's newest double-deckers. Mike Harris

There is little sign of competition in Bristol. Durbin of Patchway, which had been running a few tendered and commercial services, was taken over by Bristol Omnibus in October 1994. The Durbin fleet, which numbers almost 50 vehicles, retains its own identity. Most Durbin vehicles are coaches, but for its bus operations the company has eight ECW-bodied Bristol VRTs and ex-Cityline Mercedes L608Ds, the Mercedes were added to the fleet following the takeover by Bristol Omnibus. Sky Blue is the trading name for the bus operations of another FirstBus subsidiary, Wessex. It was set up in 1993 to counter competition from a small operator which has since ceased running. The Sky Blue fleet numbers nine Leyland Nationals transferred from Brewers in South Wales and from Badgerline.

One of the few genuine independents running into Bristol is A Bus, with a service from Keynsham. This was started in 1991 using an ex-Thamesdown Fleetline which is still owned. A Bus also runs a VRT, an unusual long-wheel-base PDR2 Atlantean which was new to Plymouth and, perhaps indicative of an upturn in business, a brand new DAF DB250 with Northern Counties Palatine II body which is running in overall white – the colour it wore when it arrived from Hughes DAF, the dealer who had it in stock. A recent arrival on the Bristol bus scene is Valley Travel, which has won a number of Avon county council tenders. Valley runs second-hand Dodge S56s and Ford Transits. The Dodges include examples which were new to South Yorkshire Transport, Plymouth Citybus and two SBG companies, Central and Fife. A rather different minibus operator is Swiftlink of Filton, operating six modern Mellor-bodied Mercedes in the Bristol area on Avon tendered routes. Mercedes-Benz minibuses adapted to carry wheelchair lifts are operated on Avon tenders by Buglers of Brislington. Buglers also run Bristol VRTs on school contracts. Another small operator in Brislington is Silver Wing, running schools contracts and a service to the University of the West of England. The bus fleet includes two VRTs, a former London Transport National, and one of the ever-popular ex-SBG Leopards with Alexander body-work. Bristol is served by the smallest National Express coach in current operation. A Talbot Pullman provides a shuttle service between the city centre and the airport. This is promoted as part of the National Express network and the Talbot carries full National Express livery. It is run by Wessex.

Top **Durbin Coaches of Bristol was taken over by Badgerline in 1994 and is now in effect a subsidiary of Bristol Omnibus. Its double-deckers are all ECW-bodied VRTs, one of which is seen in central Bristol.** Richard Godfrey

Centre **Sky Blue was set up by Wessex to counter competition in Bristol. It runs Leyland Nationals transferred from other Badgerline group companies.** Mike Harris

Right **A Bus has a small but varied fleet with four double-deckers from four different manufacturers. This ex-City Line VRT is in fact owned by Crown Coaches, but is operated by A Bus.** Mike Harris

The newest bus operated by Buglers of Bristol is a Mercedes-Benz 711D with Marshall body. It is one of a number of vehicles in the Buglers fleet fitted with a wheelchair lift. Note the Easyrider name in the windscreen, used for accessible services in Avon.
Allan Macfarlane

The Swiftlink fleet includes six Mercedes-Benz with Mellor bodywork. The newest are a pair of 27-seat 709Ds which entered service in 1995.
Richard Eversden

Silver Wing operates both tendered and commercial services in the Bristol area. The company's buses are mainly small vehicles, but two double-deckers are owned and both are 1974 Bristol VRTs with ECW bodies. This one was new to Maidstone & District. Richard Godfrey

Services outside Bristol are in the main operated by Badgerline, set up at the start of 1986 to take over the Bristol Omnibus operations in Bath, Wells and Weston-super-Mare, along with country services radiating out from Bristol and running as far north as Gloucester. As the Badgerline group grew, so badgers could be seen adorning the sides of buses from Cornwall to Yorkshire. But since the creation of FirstBus, the only place with badgers on its buses is the Avon-based operation where it all started. FirstBus was quick to turn the clock back by re-uniting Badgerline with City Line in October 1995. Badgerline's fleet is roughly the same size as that of City Line, at just under the 350 mark, but its composition is more varied.

For a start, there are more older vehicles, including 55 Bristol VRTs. A fair number of these have come from elsewhere in the Badgerline group – Thamesway in particular – and there are some open-toppers for use in Bath and Weston. Two of Badgerline's VRTs run on liquified petroleum gas and carry special liveries. Other double-deck types are Olympians inherited from Bristol Omnibus, 15 Volvo Citybuses with Alexander bodies (three of which were new to Western National), 10 Leyland-bodied Olympians, and two unusual long-wheelbase Olympians with striking East Lancs coach bodies which were new to Rhymney Valley District Council in 1985. The single-deck fleet includes a fair variety too. The first new single-deckers supplied to the company after privatisation were 14 Volvo B10Ms with Alexander P-type bodies, not a common combination. Earlier types are Leyland National 2s, while more modern types are seven Lynxes and 16 Dennis Lances with Plaxton Verde bodywork. The ubiquitous Dart/Pointer is also to be found running for Badgerline. There are 36, with more on the way. Minibuses are in the main Plaxton-bodied Mercedes 709Ds, but there is a substantial fleet of Robin Hood-bodied Iveco Fords, which date back to 1986-87, and a few even older Mercedes L608D van conversions. The Mercedes fleet includes five buses acquired in mid-1994 when Badgerline took over the bus operations of Clapton Coaches of Radstock. One of these was an Optare StarRider and it joined 20 similar buses bought new by Badgerline in 1988.

The first new-generation low-floor buses in the South West entered service with Badgerline in Bath in July 1995, running every 10 minutes between the bus station and Whiteway. They are six Dennis Lance SLFs with Wright Pathfinder bodies. At some stops on the route special platform islands have been built to ensure that the bus can pull up with its entrance level with the kerb. These are the first low-floor buses in the Badgerline/First Bus group and have been partly funded by Avon County Council which works in partnership with key local operators.

Top **Since the creation of FirstBus in the summer of 1995 the only buses which now correctly carry badger logos are those run by Badgerline in Avon. This 1976 VRT was one of those acquired from Bristol Omnibus when Badgerline was created in 1986. VRTs are the company's oldest buses.** Stewart J Brown

Centre **The Dennis Lance with Plaxton Verde bodywork was the Badgerline group's standard full-size single-decker. Badgerline has 16 of the type.** Mike Harris

Right **The first low-floor buses for an operator in the South West were six Dennis Lance SLFs with attractive Wright Pathfinder bodies. They are operated by Badgerline on a Bath city service.** Russell Upcraft

Competition in Bath is most evident on open-top city tours, where Ryan operates red-liveried VRTs and DMSs in competition with Badgerline's VRTs. Local services are run by Streamline Faresaver using Mercedes minis. It has six with Plaxton Beaver bodies and four bodied by Marshall – all delivered new in 1993-94. On the northern edge of Badgerline's territory school services are run by Westward Travel of Wotton-under-Edge. The bus fleet includes a couple of Fleetlines, a VRT, a National and an ex-A1 Dennis Dominator.

Gloucester has seen considerable change over the last two years following the purchase of Western Travel by Stagecoach in December 1993. Western Travel was the main operator in the city and in neighbouring Cheltenham, operating buses in four distinctive and fast-disappearing liveries. In Gloucester the dark blue livery and City of Gloucester fleetname survive on only a handful of buses, while the silver minibus livery has disappeared.

There are two reasons for this. The obvious one is the re-painting of the buses which Stagecoach had taken over, but more significantly there has been a substantial influx of new buses to the city's services – the first since the intro-duction of minibuses in the mid-1980s – and these, naturally enough, are in corporate Stagecoach white. The new vehi-cles are Volvo B6s and B10Ms, and Mercedes 709Ds, all bodied by Alexander. Leyland Nationals and Olympians and a few Bristol VRTs represent the old order, but most have been repainted since the Stagecoach takeover.

Western Travel also owned Red & White, and that fleet too is succumbing to corporate Stagecoach white, although the buses which reach Gloucester are often still in red and include elderly Mark 1 Nationals and modern Marshall and Wright-bodied Mercedes minibuses. Double-deckers run in too, usually ECW-bodied Olympians and VRTs and, more interestingly, ex-Selkent Leyland Titans which were new to the West Midlands PTE. Coaches, usually Plaxton-bodied Tigers, cover some of the Red & White services into Gloucester.

Smaller operators running into the city include locally-based Bennetts with a Duple bus-bodied Tiger, an Optare Delta acquired from Walls of Manchester, or one of five ex-Yorkshire Woollen VRTs which are used mainly on school runs. Bennetts buses are turned out to the same high stan-dard as the company's smart coach fleet. The Optare Delta is of interest as it was the first of the type to enter service, with Wigmore of Dinnington, in 1988.

Top **Streamline Faresaver run Mercedes minibuses on a number of routes in the Bath area. The newest are four 811Ds with 31-seat Marshall bodywork.** Stewart J Brown

Centre **Most buses in the Cheltenham & Gloucester fleet are now in corporate Stagecoach colours. A 1978 B-series National loads in Gloucester city centre. It was inherited from Bristol Omnibus.** Stewart J Brown

Left **Bennetts of Gloucester operate a smart coach fleet and maintain their buses to a similarly high standard. The company's oldest vehicle is this 1978 Bristol VRT seen heading through Gloucester on its way to Newent. Coach-style polished wheeltrims are fitted.** Stewart J Brown

Cottrells of Mitcheldean operate interesting double-deckers on services from the Forest of Dean to Gloucester. The oldest is a T-registered Fleetline which was bought new. Then there are two early MCW Metrobuses which came from Greater Manchester Transport. Metrobuses are rare in small fleets. The company's newest double-decker is even rarer, a mid-engined Leyland Lion with Alexander body. The Lion, manufactured in Denmark by DAB, was Leyland's answer to Volvo's Citybus, but only 32 were built. Cottrells is one of six which were new to Clydeside Scottish in 1987. Cottrells fleet also includes a Tiger with unusual Duple 300-series bus body, another rarity in the shape of a Wadham Stringer-bodied Leyland Swift, and a few coaches which also appear occasionally on the company's bus services. Another Forest of Dean firm is Geoff Willetts with services in the Lydney area. These are run by two smart Leyland Nationals, one of which has been the subject of an East Lancs Greenway conversion.

Swanbrook operate services from Gloucester, north to Tewksbury and south to Quedgley and Arlingham. These are run by a mixture of vehicles including elderly Bedford coaches, on occasion a Duple 425 integral, and – particularly on the short Quedgley run – a choice of buses. These include a former West Midlands Fleetline, an ex-London DMS and an ex-London Titan (both acquired from Kinch of Loughborough), or recently acquired Leyland Nationals. Swanbrook has been a late convert to the second-hand National and has introduced both Marks 1 and 2 to its fleet during 1995. The company's original partners were a Mr Swan and a Mr Brook. Swanbrook runs 30 vehicles. In Tewksbury Warners run a local service trading as The Boomerang Bus Co. The Boomerang fleet comprises five Carlyle-bodied Sherpas and two Optare CityPacers. All are second-hand.

Top **There are very few Leyland Lions in service with small operators. Cottrells of Mitcheldean have one, a 1987 model which was acquired from Clydeside 2000 in 1994. It has 86-seat Alexander bodywork.** Stewart J Brown

Centre **Geoff Willetts operates in an unusual livery, as shown by this National Greenway which was rebuilt by East Lancs in 1993 using an N-registered Mark 1 as a base. It is seen loading in Coleford, on the service from Monmouth to Lydney.** Allan Macfarlane

Right **Swanbrook's bus fleet includes two ex-London types – one Titan and three DMS-type Fleetlines. This is a 1976 FE30AGR with Park Royal body which has been with Swanbrook since 1992. It carries advertising for the company's holidays.** Richard Eversden

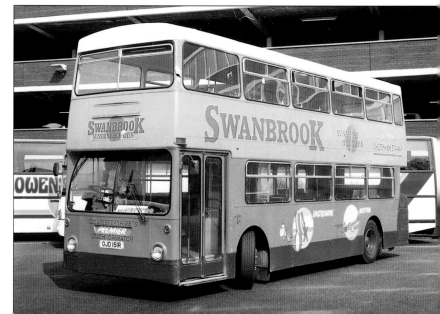

Mike's Travel run south from Gloucester to Thornbury. The fleet is a smart one and the service is usually operated by AEC Reliance coaches. AECs are becoming increasingly rare on local services. The newest coach in the Mike's Travel fleet is a Leyland Tiger with Duple Dominant body and this too appears on service. Another type which it is unusual to find on bus operations is the Bedford PJK, or VAS as it was originally known. Ebley Coach Services run an N-registered Plaxton bodied example and this can be seen from time to time on the service from Gloucester to Painswick. Circle Line of Gloucester is a Stagecoach subsidiary which has retained its own identity and operates a few tendered bus services, mainly with green-liveried Bristol VRTs. Circle Line also runs school contracts in Gloucester and the Saturday park-and-ride service in Cheltenham. The company's ownership by Stagecoach arises from a minority shareholding which was held by Western Travel.

In Cheltenham, the silver Metro livery used by Cheltenham District (since August 1993 a separate company, rather than part of Cheltenham & Gloucester) is still in evidence on a few minibuses, including MCW Metroriders. But as in Gloucester, Stagecoach corporate white is rapidly replacing both the Metro colours and the red livery which was used on full-size vehicles.

Among the small operators serving Cheltenham is Castleways of Winchcombe. The company's services are usually operated by Leyland Leopard coaches, but in 1995 it bought a Plaxton-bodied Dennis Dart. In keeping with the high-standards set by Castleways the Dart even has polished coach-style wheeltrims. Another interesting bus in this smart fleet is a three-axle Talbot Pullman, used mainly for schools services. It is the only second-hand vehicle in the company's 14-strong fleet. And if anyone wonders why shamrocks adorn the front corners of Castleways' buses – they give a clue to the origins of the company's owner. Pulham's of Bourton-on-the-Water run services in the Cotswolds and to Cheltenham using Plaxton-bodied Leopard and Tiger coaches.

Top **The Bedford VAS – or PJK as it was later termed – was once widely used on rural services. Few survive. Ebley Coach Services run this Plaxton-bodied example, seen in Gloucester bus station on the service to Painswick.** Stewart J Brown

Centre **This Leyland National, named Rocket Ron, entered the Circle Line fleet in 1995 from Swindon & District, the two companies now sharing the same parent company, Stagecoach.** Malcolm McDonald

Left **Cheltenham District's red livery is fast disappearing. This bus is one of those which were refurbished by the company and repowered with DAF engines before being badged as National 3s.** Richard Eversden

South-east from Cheltenham lies Swindon, which saw rapid growth in the 1980s. Two operators serve the town. Thamesdown Transport is owned by the local authority and in the main runs urban services, although its buses can be seen as far away as Marlborough, Newbury and Cirencester. Swindon & District is owned by Stagecoach (it was part of Western Travel) and its roots can be traced back to the Bristol Omnibus Company's operations in the area.

Thamesdown Transport's bus fleet is made up largely of Dennises. It runs Lancets, Falcons, Dominators and Darts – it just needs a few Lances to give it a full set of Dennis's recent bus models. There are eight Lancets in the fleet. Seven are short-wheelbase models of which four came from Merseyside Transport and three were new to Portsmouth City Transport. The eighth is a 10m bus which was originally a Dennis demonstrator. The ex-Merseyside vehicles have unusual short Duple Dominant bodies while the remainder have Wadham Stringer Vanguard bodywork. Further ex-Merseyside Lancets are being acquired to replace the ex-Portsmouth vehicles.

The company's Dominators include examples bought new and second-hand. The new ones, bought between 1982 and 1990, have bodywork by Northern Counties and East Lancs. The second-hand Dominators came from East Staffordshire and Derby, the former with East Lancs bodywork; the latter with Northern Counties. The oldest Thamesdown double-deckers are ex-GM Buses Fleetlines with Northern Counties bodies, new in the late 1970s and acquired in the late 1980s, and a few ECW-bodied Fleetlines. The fleet's Falcons are seven with Duple Dominant bodies which were new to Leicester City Transport.

Minibuses, mainly Northern Counties-bodied Dodges, were introduced to the company's operations soon after deregulation in 1986, but more recently Thamesdown has standardised on Dennis Darts with Plaxton Pointer bodies. It now has 28. Most of the recent additions to the fleet carry names, generally of railway locomotives with a Swindon association. Thamesdown Transport runs a small coach fleet and also owns Kingston Coaches of Winterslow.

Top **Thamesdown Transport's newest buses are Dennis Darts with Plaxton Pointer bodies. The first batch, delivered in 1993, are of the relatively rare 8.5m-long model. All of the Darts carry Dartline fleetnames.** Richard Godfrey

Centre **Fleetlines and Dominators make up the Thamesdown double-deck fleet. The first Dominators were five with Northern Counties bodies and they were delivered in 1982.** Mike Harris

Right **Northern Counties produced a stylish body for the Renault S56 and Thamesdown was among the first customers. This vehicle was originally a Northern Counties demonstrator.** Richard Godfrey

The Swindon & District fleet was part of Cheltenham & Gloucester until 1991 when it was set up as a separate company. Evidence of its Bristol Omnibus roots remains in the shape of a few ex-Bristol Omnibus VRTs, Olympians and National 2s. Additions to the fleet during its period as a Western Travel subsidiary included five long-wheelbase Olympians with low-height Alexander bodies – prophetic perhaps, with their similarity to the then standard Stagecoach double-decker – and five former Greater Manchester Titans which were purchased from Thames Transit in 1990. One of the big Olympians is now with Cheltenham & Gloucester, but the others remain in Swindon, as do the Titans. The last new buses delivered before the Stagecoach takeover were two Wright-bodied Mercedes 811Ds, which joined a minibus fleet made up mainly of MCW Metroriders. Stagecoach has put a number of new Alexander-bodied 709Ds and Volvo B6s into service with Swindon & District. Here as elsewhere in what was Western Travel territory the company's old livery – red and cream – is giving way to Stagecoach white.

Andy James Coaches of Malmesbury operate to Swindon, as well as to Chippenham, Tetbury and Cirencester. Services are run by Leopard coaches which although generally in the region of 15 years old are smartly turned-out, which is more than can be said for many operators running old Leopards. They have bodywork by Duple and Plaxton. New additions to the fleet have been Mercedes minibuses which carry ARJ registrations – Andy James' initials. Alex Cars of Cirencester run between there and Tetbury, and also link with some trains at Kemble Station, generally using a Mark 1 National.

Fosseway of Chippenham operate a minibus service in Swindon using some of its sizeable fleet of second-hand Ford Transits. Bigger buses in the fleet include an Optare StarRider and a short-wheelbase Bedford YMP with unique Imperial bodywork. Fosseway's minibuses work tendered services in the Chippenham area, and also run as far afield as Yate, in Avon.

Top **Swindon & District's livery is another of those which is disappearing in favour of Stagecoach white. Among the more unusual buses in the fleet are five Leyland Titans which were new to Greater Manchester Transport. They joined the Swindon fleet in 1990, coming from Thames Transit who had acquired them with the South Midland company's operations.** Mike Harris

Centre **The last buses to be delivered to Swindon & District in the company's red and cream livery were two Mercedes 811Ds with Wright bodywork.** Richard Godfrey

Left **Andy James of Tetbury operates local services with Leyland Leopards. This is a 1981 example with Duple Dominant body and was new to West Yorkshire Road Car. It has been with Andy James since 1994.** P J Chancellor

South of Swindon lies Salisbury, the headquarters of British Bus, but served by one of the few large ex-NBC subsidiaries to remain independent, Wilts & Dorset. Wilts & Dorset runs just under 300 buses in an area which extends north to Marlborough and south to Bournemouth. A service runs east from Bournemouth to Southampton. The company was privatised in a management buy-out in 1987 and since then has invested in a large number of new Optares. It has the country's largest fleet of Spectras, which also means the largest fleet of DAF double-deckers since few DAFs have as yet been bodied as 'deckers by any other builders. There are 47, delivered in three batches between 1993 and 1995. They can be seen throughout the company's operating area. It also has six Optare Deltas and 41 Optare MetroRiders. The MetroRiders followed on from 75 MCW-built buses delivered in the late 1980s, to which have been added a few second-hand examples, including 15 from Yorkshire Rider.

This significant intake of new buses doesn't mean that the fleet is devoid of interesting older types. Wilts & Dorset in its present form was created in 1983, having previously been part of Hants & Dorset, and there are still some pre-1983 buses in the fleet including around 50 ECW-bodied VRTs, a few Mark 1 Nationals and half-a-dozen Bristol LHs. The company also runs a varied Olympian fleet. As well as having standard NBC-style models with lowheight ECW bodies, it runs ex-West Yorkshire Roe-bodied buses. Some of both types are convertible open-toppers and are used on a coastal service which runs across the Sandbanks Ferry to the Isle of Purbeck (which is in fact not an island). To allow for operation across the chain-hauled ferry the air suspension on the Olympians has a ferry lift device, more commonly fitted to coach chassis, which allows the body to be raised to give extra clearance on the ramp. Also unusual are a trio of East Lancs-bodied Olympians which started life with Plymouth City Transport.

Wilts & Dorset has expanded in the Blandford Forum area through a series of takeovers. In the summer of 1993 it acquired Damory Coaches, following that at the end of the year with Oakfield Travel and the associated Stanbridge & Critchel operations which had for the previous nine months or so been owned by British Bus through its Guildford & West Surrey company. One odd side effect of this was the appearance in Dorset of buses carrying Guildford & West Surrey legal lettering and, in a few cases, Guildford & West Surrey fleetnames too. Damory Coaches now runs a fleet made up largely of ex-Wilts & Dorset vehicles including Metroriders, Nationals, two VRTs (the fleet's only 'deckers) and a pair of LHs. Local services are run in Blandford Forum, but most of the company's routes are rural, generally under contract to Dorset county council. The Damory Coaches fleet numbers 36 vehicles. Shaftsbury & District runs schools services with a fleet which shows obvious enthusiast involvement. It includes two ex-London Transport RF-class AEC Regal IVs, an ex-London Bristol LH, and a forward-entrance Routemaster.

Warminster lies on the western edge of Salisbury Plain and also marks the end of Wilts & Dorset territory. Here old-established Beeline operates a number of tendered services using either new Plaxton-bodied Mercedes minibuses or some of its fleet of Y-series Bedfords, two of which have Duple bus bodies.

In Bournemouth the main provider of local services is Bournemouth Transport, which trades as Yellow Buses and is still in local authority ownership. The Yellow Buses operation has traditionally been mainly double-decked. All pre-1992 buses are double-deckers, of four different types. However post-1993 fleet additions have seen a switch to single-deckers. Yellow Buses has no minibuses – although a fleet of 20 Mercedes was run for a short time in 1989-90.

The oldest buses are Alexander-bodied Fleetlines, the last of which are V- and W-registered 1980-81 models with Gardner engines; all earlier Fleetlines are Leyland-powered. The combination of Alexander's alloy-framed AL-type highbridge body and Fleetline chassis is an unusual one. Most Alexander-bodied Fleetlines in the late 1970s had lowheight AD-style bodywork. When Fleetline production ceased Bournemouth Transport ordered 20 Olympians, which are unique in being fitted with Marshall bodies. All are still in service. Next came three batches of Volvo Citybuses, totalling 15 in all. The newest double-deckers are Dennis Dominators, the change in vehicle policy being marked by the arrival of a new managing director. The last of these, all bodied by East Lancs, were delivered in 1992.

Now Yellow Buses has gone single-deck. First came six Dennis Lances with East Lancs bodies in 1993. These were followed by a dozen 9.8m Darts, also East Lancs-bodied, in 1995. Bournemouth Transport runs coaches – not surprisingly trading as Yellow Coaches – and since 1992 has owned Dorset Travel Services, which is a major contractor to National Express. Still in the fleet but out of use are four former London DMSs which were purchased in 1993-94 to combat competition from Bournemouth Heritage Transport running Routemasters in the town. The BHT services have been withdrawn, leaving Yellow Buses and Wilts & Dorset as the only significant operators in Bournemouth and its environs.

The combination of Leyland Olympian chassis and Marshall body was unique to Bournemouth Transport. The company has 20, delivered in 1981-82. They are the only Olympians in the fleet. Gerald Mead

The Dennis Dart finds new customers every year. Among 1995's converts was Bournemouth Transport which took 12 with 40-seat East Lancs bodies. Richard Godfrey

Heading to the far west, Plymouth is the last major city in the South West and is served by Plymouth Citybus and Western National. Plymouth Citybus is the successor to the city's municipal transport department and is still owned by the local authority. Plymouth Citybus runs around 170 buses and coaches, with the emphasis since deregulation being very much on small vehicles. Part of the company's strategy at deregulation was the widespread introduction of minibuses to city services, using a fleet of 85 Reeve Burgess-bodied Dodges, the last of which were scheduled to come out of service in the autumn of 1995. The 1990s have seen the company standardise on Mercedes 709Ds, of which there are now 85. Most have Beaver-style bodies, built by Reeve Burgess on the first batch and by Plaxton on more recent deliveries, but there are also two with Wadham Stringer bodies. Since 1992 Plymouth Citybus has added 34 Plaxton Pointers to its fleet. Most are on 9.8m Dennis Dart chassis but the 1994 intake included three on Volvo B6s for comparison. No doubt both Dennis and Volvo are waiting to see who gets the next order.

The older vehicles in the fleet are Leyland Atlanteans. There are 37, most of them with dual-door East Lancs bodies. The newest are X-registered buses delivered in 1981. The only other double-deckers are four East Lancs-bodied Volvo Citybuses, two of which are long-wheelbase coaches and carry Citycoach fleetnames. The company also runs 10 Volvo B10Ms in its Citycoach operation. The fleet livery is being modified and brightened with grey and red relief replacing the rather sombre black which was used previously. Grey was first tried on the original 1992 batch of Plaxton Pointers.

Western National, whose headquarters are in Truro in Cornwall, also operates in and around Plymouth, although head-to-head competition with Plymouth Citybus is a thing of the past. Western National runs 400 buses and coaches and carries on the name of a long-established operation which, prior to restructuring by NBC in 1983, had a fleet which was over 1,000-strong. The 1983 changes saw a new slimmed-down Western National serving Cornwall and south Devon, while a new North Devon company took over services in north Devon, a revived Southern National operation became responsible for operations in Somerset and parts of Dorset, and Devon General was reformed to run in the Exeter and Torbay areas.

So much for the history. More recently Western National was privatised in 1987, being sold to a consortium headed by Plympton Coachlines and Badgerline. Subsequently control passed to Badgerline, and then in the summer of 1995 to FirstBus. Minibuses account for almost half of the fleet with just over 190 in use. These range from small coaches such as the Toyota-based Caetano Optimo to standard Badgerline group Plaxton-bodied Mercedes. There are 79 Plaxton Beavers spread throughout the company's operating area which stretches down to Lands End. NBC Mercedes L608D van conversions are also still widely used. Other Mercedes include four Optare StarRiders acquired from Badgerline in 1991 and 26 811Ds with Carlyle bodies.

Bigger single-deckers include six Leyland Lynxes, bought new in 1988 and the company's first post-privatisation big buses, and 29 Dennis Darts with Plaxton bodies, yet another example of the Badgerline group standard midibus. The most south-westerly low-floor bus is a solitary Lance SLF used by Western National for specific journeys on the service running from Plymouth via Tavistock and West Dartmoor to Oakehampton. Bristol VRTs figure strongly in the double-deck fleet. Most were delivered new in the late 1970s and early 1980s, but under Badgerline control a few have moved in from elsewhere in the group and in particular Thamesway and South Wales Transport. As in most other NBC companies, the VRT was succeeded by the Olympian, and Western National has eight with ECW bodies. Its newest 'deckers are four Volvo Olympians with Northern Counties bodies. These were among the first of the Scottish-built Olympians to enter service – in July 1993 – and are unusual in having K-prefix registrations. The only other K-registered Volvo Olympians are running for East Midland; volume deliveries of Volvo-built Olympians really only started after the change to L-prefix registrations. Much of Western National's territory is rural and on some routes Leopard coaches can still be found.

Cornwall is a county with a fair number of small operators. In Truro itself Truronian run Mercedes minibuses as well as a few Bristol LHs and VRTs. Unusual double-deckers are a one-time SELNEC PTE Mancunian – a rare survivor of a trend-setting design – and an experimental Leyland Atlantean with Alexander bodywork, used as a development vehicle by Leyland from 1970 to 1980 before being sold to Rennie of Dunfermline. Truronian serves Helston, Falmouth and Perranporth. Hopley's of Mount Hawke run in to Truro from Redruth, normally with a Bedford YRT with Duple bus body. Cornishman Coaches of Wadebridge run a Truro to Newquay service, while Prout of Port Isaac run a Port Isaac to Wadebridge service, generally with Bedford coaches.

Right Wheal Briton is the trading name of Palmer of Blackwater and derives from an old Cornish tin mine. Old mine names are also used for the vehicles. This AEC Reliance is one of two similar buses bought from the Ministry of Defence and seats 54 passengers. It has Marshall bodywork. Steve Warburton

Below The Truronian fleet contains a number of quite elderly double-deckers including this 1973 VRT which started life with Yorkshire Traction. Truronian bought it from Lincolnshire Road Car in 1991. A somewhat younger Western National bus waits behind it in Helston. Graham Jones

For many the Devon General name recalls a company with a proud heritage and shiny Regent Vs. The present-day reality is rather different and the new Devon General company has been in the van of progress when it comes to small bus operation. Devon General was the first NBC bus company to be sold, being bought by its management in August 1986. This was the genesis of Transit Holdings, which now has operations in Oxford, Portsmouth and London, and is expanding into Australia, where bus service deregulation is becoming an issue.

Minibuses were in fact introduced to Exeter in NBC days, in 1984, and it is a remarkable tribute to both the Ford Transit and Devon General's engineers that a few of the pioneering 16-seaters remain in the fleet more than 10 years later. Some NBC engineers forecast a life of as little as three years for Transit buses in urban operation. Devon General provides services in and around Exeter. A sister company, Bayline, serves the Torbay area. Most types of vehicles are operated by both companies, and in a bewildering variety of liveries, most of which are route-specific.

The first-generation Transits, most of which have Carlyle bodies, were succeeded from 1987 by the new Transit, with its smoother bonnet profile. Most of the post-1987 Transits have bodywork by Mellor and are operated by Bayline. More recently Transit Holdings has been buying bigger minibuses for most of its operations, based on the Iveco Ford 59.12 chassis. What makes them particularly noteworthy is that they have dual-door bodywork, by Marshall, Mellor or WS Coachbuilders. Two Ivecos delivered in 1994 were Britain's first hybrid buses. These feature a 997cc Fiat Uno petrol engine which provides power to a generator which drives an electric motor. The generator also charges storage batteries which provide additional power for acceleration and hill climbing. During deceleration the electric power is regenerated and returned to the storage batteries. In busy shopping areas the petrol engine can be switched off, and the bus runs solely on battery power. There is also a batch of Mercedes 709Ds delivered in 1995 which have dual-door Marshall bodies. Earlier F-registered 709Ds with Reeve Burgess Beaver bodies are also owned and are used mainly on rural routes. There is one big bus in the fleet: an open-top VRT used by Bayline for a summer seafront service. Wallace Arnold also operate an open-topper in Torbay. It is an ex-Southdown PD3.

Top **On many of its rural routes Devon General runs 25-seat Mercedes-Benz 709Ds with Reeve Burgess bodies. One leaves Exeter bus station for Tiverton.** Richard Eversden

Centre **Growing concern about urban pollution has seen a small number of operators evaluating alternatives to diesel power. Devon General is running two dual-mode Iveco Ford 49.10s with Mellor bodies.** Steve Warburton

Left **Urban services operated by Transit Holdings companies in Portsmouth, Oxford and Exeter are generally being converted to two-door vehicles to speed the flow of passengers at busy stops. The most recent deliveries to Devon General have been Mercedes 709Ds with Marshall bodywork.** Richard Eversden

Transit Holdings might be Exeter's best-known minibus operator, but it isn't the only one. Dartline operate a number of tendered services, both in Exeter and west towards Dartmoor. The fleet is made up of Mercedes, with both van conversions and coachbuilt buses. All carry girls' names. Devon Services of Paignton operate in Torbay and Totnes. The company's bus fleet includes three Bristol LHs and a couple of Leopards with Alexander Y-type bodies. One, as might be expected, started life with the Scottish Bus Group, but the other is unusual in being an ex-NBC vehicle. It was new to West Riding. To the north of Exeter, East Devon is a new operator based in Crediton running to Exeter and Sidmouth. The company has three ECW-bodied LHs and in 1995 bought its first new buses, two Marshall-bodied Iveco Fords. Red Bus Services, based at Clyst Honiton, to the east of Exeter, is run by an enthusiast, which explains why the fleet has what must be the only Albion Nimbus licensed for public service. More normal buses in the fleet include two ex-SBG Seddon Pennines and a Mercedes-Benz 811D which was bought new in 1991. It is a 33-seater – two seats bigger than the venerable Nimbus. Red Bus Services operate tendered routes for Devon County Council and in the summer run an Exeter city tour using a smart open-top ex-Devon General AEC Regent V.

Above right **Dartline of Exeter operate services using in the main new Mercedes minibuses, all with girls' names. This is Claire Marie, a 1994 811D with 33-seat Marshall body.** Mark Bailey

Below **Most of the Bristol LH buses in service with small fleets started life with either NBC or London Transport. This Devon Services bus in Paignton is unusual in that its first operator was Greater Manchester Transport. It was new in 1974, by which time the use of flat-glass windscreens had generally been abandoned by ECW in favour of the curved BET screen.** Malcolm McDonald

Few ex-Scottish Bus Group Seddons have travelled as far from their original haunts as the pair owned by Red Bus Services. New to Eastern Scottish in 1978, they were bought from Lowland Scottish 10 years later. They have Alexander Y-type bodies.
Richard Godfrey

Red Bus Services run an Exeter city tour using this former Devon General AEC Regent V, smartly repainted in traditional Devon General colours. It was new in 1957 and has MCW bodywork.
Richard Godfrey

In Kingsbridge and the surrounding area Tally Ho! operate regular local services as well as less frequent long-distance routes which take the company's buses as far as Exeter. A large number of schools services are run too. ECW-bodied Bristols predominate in the Tally Ho! fleet, with REs, LHs and VRTs.

The other two companies formed out of Western National, North Devon and Southern National, are both now part of Cawlett, set up by the managers of both businesses in a joint buy-out from NBC in 1988. The two fleets are managed from Taunton, which is in Southern National country. Southern National's operations extend coast-to-coast from Weymouth in the south to Minehead in the north. The fleet has a large number of small buses. The oldest are Transits, bought in NBC days. The newest are Mercedes, generally with bodywork by Alexander and Wright. Double-deckers are standard NBC VRTs, of which there are 22, and ECW-bodied Olympians, of which there are just four (all ex-Devon General), plus a couple of Roe-bodied examples acquired from West Yorkshire PTE. Full-size single-deck buses are Mark 1 Nationals, but Bristol LHs with Plaxton coach bodies are used on service and there are a couple of LHS buses, one of which was new to London Transport, and three Dennis Darts.

Right **The Tally Ho! fleet is made up largely of second-hand ECW-bodied Bristols – REs, VRTs and LHs. There are 15 LHs, all of which were new to London Transport in 1976. Their 7ft 6in wide bodywork makes them ideally suited to narrow Devon lanes.** Mark Bailey

Below **The oldest double-deckers in the Southern National fleet are ECW-bodied Bristol VRTs. This bus was new to Yorkshire Traction in 1976 and moved to Western National in 1982, passing to the new Southern National company in the following year.** Geoff Mills

The bulk of Taunton area services are provided by Southern National, generally with minibuses. Local coach operator Berrys run to Wellington using an ECW-bodied VRT. There are four in the fleet. Near the eastern edge of Southern National's operating area, Safeway Services of South Petherton operate to Yeovil from Ilminster and Crewkerne. Safeway's routes also run west to Taunton. The company has been running for almost 70 years and its current bus fleet is made up of Leopards. These range from a Willowbrook-bodied bus bought new in 1973 to a 1992 Willowbrook Warrior rebody of a 1977 chassis. The company's fleet is 100 per cent British made. Its newest coaches are Leyland Tigers. Another operator serving Yeovil is Wake's of Sparkford with a route to Shepton Mallett. Wake's also run schools services and infrequent rural routes. The fleet is made up mainly of Duple-bodied Bedfords but there is one 1983 Leyland Tiger with a 1995 East Lancs body and an ex-military Marshall-bodied Tiger. On the south coast Smith's of Portland run four ECW-bodied Bristol REs on a service to Weymouth. Local services in the town are run by Weybus using ex-Red & White Freight Rover Sherpas.

Top **Recent deliveries to Southern National have comprised Mercedes minibuses and Dennis Dart midibuses. Wright Handybus bodywork is fitted to this 9.8m-long Dart which entered service in 1993.** Richard Godfrey

Left **Smith's of Portland operate four Bristol REs on a service between Weymouth and Southwell, which involves a steep climb up Portland Hill. They were new to Bristol Omnibus but came to Smith's from Western National, whose livery they still carry.** Graham Jones

Below **Safeway Services are fond of the Leyland Leopard, a chassis upon which all of its buses are based. This Duple Dominant bodied example was bought new in 1980. It seats 59.** Barry Spencer

Back to Cawlett and the North Devon fleet – which is numbered in a common series with Southern National – has a generally similar make-up. Its operations extend southwards from the north Devon coast, reaching as far as Exeter. It is the main operator in Barnstaple and Ilfracombe. None of North Devon's buses carry North Devon fleetnames. Most trade under the Red Bus brand, but there are local identities and liveries too – Atlantic Blue, South Western and Tiverton & District.

Here again the small bus fleet is made up mainly of NBC-era Transits and more modern Mercedes, the newest of which have Marshall and Alexander bodies. Big buses include Nationals, five VRTs and just one ECW-bodied Olympian, along with Leopard and LH coaches which are used on service. North Devon runs eight Darts, five with Wright bodies plus two Carlyles and one Marshall. Two of the Wright-bodied buses have wheelchair lifts built into the stepwell and operate in Devon County Council blue and cream colours. They are in fact owned by Devon CC. Added interest among the double-deck fleet is provided by a pair of ex-Blackpool Atlanteans (which are among the 12 buses running in South Western red and cream) and Cawlett's newest big buses, three L-registered Volvo Olympians with Northern Counties bodywork. These run as part of the 12-strong Tiverton & District operation. There are also 12 buses in Atlantic Blue colours – six minis and six Nationals. Atlantic Blue buses operate around Ilfracombe and to Bideford, while South Western's operations are in the Exeter area. The scope of Tiverton & District's operations ought to be self-evident. South Western operate one green-liveried bus, an 11.3m National which has been converted from single door to dual door – the opposite of what most people do – and fitted with racks to carry bicycles. It is in traditional Southdown-style colours and serves the users of a cycle trail between Barnstaple and Okehampton.

Top **North Devon trades as Red Bus, although its minibuses are in fact yellow. The company still runs a large number of first-generation 16-seat Transits with Robin Hood bodywork. They date from 1985-86.** Stewart J Brown

Centre **South Western livery is worn by North Devon's latest Dart, the only one in the fleet with Marshall bodywork. It was new in 1994.** Malcolm King

Right **Three Volvo Olympians with lowheight Northern Counties bodies were bought by North Devon in 1993. They are in Tiverton & District livery.** Richard Godfrey

A number of local services are provided in the Ilfracombe area by Filers, running a varied fleet which includes Leopard coaches, assorted minibuses and three ex-Hull Atlanteans with 1986 Northern Counties bodies on 1970 chassis. They were rebodied while in the ownership of Cleveland Transit. However the star of the fleet is the only Iveco double-decker in Britain (and possibly in the world). This is an Alexander-bodied TurboCity 100, launched in the UK by Iveco in 1991 – and perhaps one of the greatest flops of modern times. After serving for a period as an Iveco demonstrator (and failing to notch up one single order) it was advertised for sale by a dealer for almost 12 months before being bought by Filers. Flop or not, it's an impressive-looking bus and currently carries an overall advertisement for a local radio station. Filers run from Ilfracombe to Bideford

Cawlett also operate in the Dorchester area, following the take over in the autumn of 1994 of the bulk of the bus operations of Bere Regis & District. These are now run by West Dorset Coaches, which trades as Dorchester Coachways. Most of the fleet is made up of Bedford and Volvo coaches acquired from Bere Regis.

In rural south Devon there are a number of small bus operators. Axe Valley serve the coast between Lyme Regis and Sidmouth where the company also runs a local service. Dodge S56 minibuses are generally used, including three with Reeve Burgess bodies which came from Plymouth Citybus. Inland, the Honiton area sees Kilmington Coaches running tendered services with minibuses acquired from a number of operators. These include relatively rare East Lancs-bodied Dodge S56s. The only big bus run by Kilmington Coaches is a short Ford R-series with Wadham Stringer body.

This is a region where there are also many rural bus services which operate only once or twice a week, generally being run by local coach operators working under contract to the appropriate local authority.

Top **An Atlantic Blue Leyland National leaves Bideford for Barnstaple. New in 1989 it is a late V-registered example of the Mark 1 version; the first National 2s were also V-registered. Atlantic Blue is one of North Devon's trading names.** Richard Godfrey

Centre **The only Iveco double-decker in Britain is this ex-demonstration TurboCity 100. New in 1991, it has an 83-seat Alexander body which incorporates a standard Iveco windscreen layout. It was bought by Filer's in 1994 and given this overall advertisement in 1995.** Barry Spencer

Left **Axe Valley runs three ex-Plymouth Citybus Dodge S56s with Reeve Burgess bodies. They were new in 1986 and are 23-seaters. This one is seen in Sidmouth.** Richard Godfrey

WALES

Top **The Brewers fleet, part of FirstBus, has expanded in recent years by taking over operations formerly run by its sister SWT operation. This Leyland National is among the many ex-SWT buses now running for Brewers.** John Jones

Above **When cutbacks in the Scottish Bus Group led to large numbers of serviceable Leopards being sold, they found ready buyers among small operators around the country. Henley's of Abertillery bought two 1978 models from Kelvin Scottish in 1987. They have 53-seat Alexander Y-type bodies.** John Jones

Cardiff City Transport's oldest buses are Alexander-bodied Bristol VRTs, the survivors of 71 delivered between 1979 and 1980. John Jones

The Welsh bus business has gone through much the same changes as have happened elsewhere in Britain. It has perhaps seen more established operators disappear than has happened elsewhere, with the demise of Cynon Valley, Inter Valley Link, Merthyr Tydfil Transport, Taff Ely and National Welsh – all established operators who might have been expected to have had reasonably secure futures at one time.

It also has the big groups taking a growing interest. FirstBus owns South Wales Transport and Brewers, both having previously been part of the Badgerline group. British Bus owns Crosville Wales. Stagecoach owns Red & White, acquired when it bought the Western Travel business at the end of 1993. This means that all of the former NBC operations in Wales are in the control of major groups, apart from the Porth operations of National Welsh, now run by Rhondda – and even here the big groups have an interest.

One of the country's biggest bus operators is, perhaps not surprisingly, to be found in the capital – Cardiff City Transport Services which trades as Cardiff Bus. This operation is still in the ownership of the local authority, and its fleet is 280-strong. This represents quite considerable growth. Ten years ago, before deregulation, the figure was just under 200. The growth has come about partly by the replacement of big buses with minibuses, and partly by expansion, particularly west to Barry Island following the collapse of National Welsh in 1992, and more recently into the Vale of Glamorgan with operations taken over from Golden Coaches.

The company's small buses are mainly MetroRiders, with almost 60 built by Optare having been added to 46 MCW-built examples. There is still a significant double-deck operation in the city, although only 10 double-deckers have been added to the fleet since deregulation – these are two batches of Scania N113s with Alexander R-type bodies. The oldest double-deckers are also Alexander-bodied – some 50 Bristol VRTs dating back to the late 1970s. In the early 1980s Cardiff placed orders with Volvo for 36 Ailsas, and Leyland for 36 Olympians, and these are the only other 'deckers in the fleet. The Ailsas have Northern Counties bodies, and are the only examples of the Scottish-built chassis to be supplied new to a Welsh operator. The Olympians have bodywork by East Lancs.

Post-deregulation big bus purchases have in the main been single-deckers. There are 41 Lynxes of both Marks I and II, and including a former demonstrator which is the only second-hand bus in the fleet. When the Lynx died, Cardiff took 14 Scania N113s with Plaxton Verde bodywork in 1992, and followed this up in 1994 with a further seven N113s, but this time with Alexander Strider bodies. The first midis in the fleet, Alexander-bodied Dennis Darts, were delivered in 1995. Cardiff last bought Dennis buses in 1929. The fleet has for many years carried both English and Welsh names – Cardiff Bus on the nearside; Bws Caerdydd on the offside.

Centre **Since deregulation in 1986 most of Cardiff City Transport's new vehicles have been single-deckers or minibuses. There are 41 Leyland Lynxes in operation with Cardiff, the biggest fleet of the type in Wales.** Mike Harris

Left **In recent times Cardiff has returned to Alexander for its bodywork. Seven Striders on Scania N113 chassis were taken into the fleet in 1994; Dashes followed at the end of 1995.** Richard Eversden

Competition on local services comes from Cardiff Bluebird, which runs a number of routes in the city. Its fleet is mainly made up of second-hand vehicles including eight Atlanteans and eight Metrobuses which were new to Midland Scottish. It also runs 17 Metroriders, eight of which were new to London Buses and has two Plaxton-bodied Dennis Darts, its first new buses. Cardiff Bluebird started bus operations in 1993. Golden Coaches, who ran into Cardiff from Llantwit Major have withdrawn from bus operation. The service is now run by Cardiff City Transport. Thomas Motor Services operate between Barry and Cardiff using second-hand Nationals.

Out-of-town services are run by a number of large operators including Red & White, South Wales Transport, Rhondda, Shamrock, Islwyn and Newport Transport. The last-named is also local authority owned and its big bus fleet is 100 per cent Scania. Newport was one of the first British operators to buy Scania buses back in 1981, when it took a batch of Marshall-bodied BR112 double-deckers, five of which are still in use. These followed earlier deliveries of Scania-engined MCW Metropolitans and Metro-Scanias. Since then Scania has supplied all of Newport's full-size vehicles and there are at present double-deckers with Marshall, East Lancs and Alexander bodies in operation, the newest dating from 1989. Single-deckers are 1983 BR112s with Wadham Stringer bodies (a combination unique to Newport) and more recently N113s with Alexander Strider bodies. There are 18 Striders in the fleet, the newest being 1995 deliveries. Where small buses are needed Newport runs G- and H-registered Optare MetroRiders and a few older MCW-built examples. Services are provided in and around Newport, west to Cardiff, and north to Cwmbran.

Top The varied fleet of Cardiff Bluebird provides competition for Cardiff City Transport. Its double-deckers are mainly Atlanteans. This one was new to Nottingham City Transport. *John Jones*

Centre Newport has standardised on Scanias for its full-size bus fleet. Most of the double-deckers have Alexander R-type bodies, or similarly-styled bodies built by East Lancs. This is a genuine Alexander body on a 1989 N113, representing the newest double-deckers in the fleet. *John Jones*

Below Most of the single-deckers operated by Newport also have Alexander bodies, but the oldest have Wadham Stringer Vanguard bodywork – a combination unique to Newport. They are BR112s, and they entered service in 1983. *Stewart J Brown*

Phil Anslow Travel of Pontypool has a large number of services in and around the town. For a time it was competing head-on with Red & White in and around Cwmbran. That competition has eased, but the company still has a substantial fleet and as well as serving Pontypool runs a number of Gwent County Council tendered routes. A trunk service runs north from Newport to Brynmawr, while another links Abergavenny, Monmouth and Hereford. The changing pattern of operation has seen the company withdraw its Sherpa fleet and replace them with bigger buses, including 18 Ivecos acquired from Badgerline and Bristol Cityline. Phil Anslow also runs seven Mercedes 709Ds with Dormobile Routemaker bodies, bought new in 1993, and a couple of 25-seat Iveco Fords, also bodied by Dormobile. Glyn Williams is another Gwent-based operator buying new Mercedes minis, but with Plaxton Beaver bodies. These join a 27-strong fleet made up of a mixture of Mercedes, bought new and second-hand, and 18 Leyland Nationals drawn from a variety of sources. The company's main service connects Blackwood and Newport, but it also serves Tredegar and Abertillery, and runs a number of tendered routes. Harris Coaches of Blackwood operate locally and also run a service between Bargoed and Caerphilly. The company's fleet includes Sherpas and MCW Metroriders – five of each – and two ex-London Nationals.

South Wales at one time had a fair number of municipal fleets. Now there are just three, the third being the small Islwyn Borough Transport operation, which serves the area around Blackwood, Tredegar and Caerphilly, and south to Cardiff. IBT's newest buses are second-hand Mercedes minis, while its oldest are 20-year-old Leopards bodied by Willowbrook. There are also Marshall- and Duple-bodied Leopards, and five East Lancs-bodied Tigers delivered in 1985-86 which are the newest full-size buses. Unusual vehicles operated by IBT are three 1987 Dodge Commandos with East Lancs bodies. IBT also runs coaches under the Kingfisher name and these include a rare (in Britain) Mercedes-Benz O303 acquired in 1991 with the business of Paul Diaper.

Top **A large fleet of Iveco Fords is operated by Phil Anslow, most having come from Badgerline and Bristol City Line. This 49.10 is ex-Badgerline and has a Robin Hood body.** John Jones

Centre **Leyland Nationals and Mercedes minibuses are the main types operated by Glyn Williams. A 1977 National arrives in Newport on the service from Blackwood. It was new to National Welsh, but reached Glyn Williams in 1992 by way of Cynon Valley.** Stewart J Brown

Left **Islwyn Borough Transport has been updating its fleet with modern second-hand minibuses. Dormobile bodywork is fitted to this Mercedes 811D which came from Patterson of Birmingham in 1995 following Patterson's withdrawal from local bus operation.** John Jones

Red & White's head office is in Cwmbran. The company was part of National Welsh until it was sold to Cheltenham-based Western Travel in 1991, owners of Cheltenham & Gloucester, on the other side of the English border. In 1992 Red & White took over the operations of Cynon Valley Transport, along with a number of Bristol REs, Leyland Lynxes and Renault minibuses. Although operating as Red & White Services, the Cynon Valley fleet is in fact run by the Aberdare Bus Company, a Red & White subsidiary. Similarly the Valleys Bus Company operates services in and around Pengam and the Rhymney Valley but also trades as Red & White. Red & White passed to Stagecoach with the Western Travel business at the end of 1993, giving the Scottish group its first Welsh operation.

Under both National Welsh and Western Travel control there had been a distinct lack of investment in new buses for Red & White. The most modern double-deckers were Bristol VRTs. These are still running but Western Travel added four ECW-bodied Olympians transferred from its Midland Red South fleet, while Stagecoach have added some late-model VRTs and three Leyland Titans transferred from Selkent but new to the West Midlands PTE. Both the Olympians and the Titans are used on routes running to Gloucester. The A-registered Olympians are Red & White's most modern 'deckers.

The picture was little different on single-deckers, with Western Travel taking over a fleet made up of Mark 1 Nationals, with Leopards for use on longer-distance services. The Cynon Valley take-over added six Lynxes – although even these were already second-hand, having been new to Merthyr Tydfil Transport. Stagecoach quickly injected a supply of 12 new B6s, 21 B10Ms and 12 Plaxton-bodied Dennis Javelin Interurbans. Where Red & White had spent some money was on minibuses, most of which were Wright-bodied Mercedes. Stagecoach has since added over 40 Alexander-bodied 709Ds. It has also transferred 17 National 2s from Fife Scottish to help update the fleet. Red & White is the main operator in Aberdare and in Merthyr Tydfil, where Parfitts have withdrawn their commercial services. It is also the principal operator to the north and east of its Cwmbran headquarters with services in Abergavenny and Chepstow, and through the Forest of Dean to Gloucester. Red & White's livery is quickly giving way to Stagecoach white with stripes.The Red & White name is one whose history can be traced back to the late 1920s, but which vanished after the formation by NBC of National Welsh in 1978.

Small operators in Abergavenny are Gavenny Bus, running a local service using either Sherpas or a Bedford CFL. Rees Travel of nearby Llanelly Hill operate infrequently to Brynmawr using one of their Duple-bodied Bedford Y-series coaches. Abertillery, to the south of Brynmawr, is the base of Henley's Bus Services, an established small operator which still runs an AEC Reliance bus with Plaxton Derwent body which was bought new in 1973. The company's other buses are an ex-SBG Y-type Leopard, a Bristol LH which was new to London but reached Wales by way of Aberdeen, a new Alexander-bodied Mercedes mini and a 1961 Reliance with Willowbrook body which was new to Western Welsh.

Henley's of Abertillery bought this Plaxton-bodied AEC Reliance in 1973, when bus services were strictly regulated and the government was subsidising investment in new buses with a 50 per cent capital grant. Almost 25 years later it is still in regular use. John Jones

Above **The number of Leyland Lynxes in Stagecoach ownership grows slowly as the Scottish-based group expands. There are five in the Red & White fleet which were acquired with the Cynon Valley Transport operations in 1992. This one started life with Merthyr Tydfil Transport.** John Jones

In Merthyr Tydfil the main operator running alongside Red & White was Parfitt's Motor Services, which started running local bus services in 1989 and was a major beneficiary of the collapse of Merthyr Tydfil Transport. In April 1995 the Parfitt's business was taken over by Rhondda. Earlier Stagecoach had reportedly been interested in buying it. Under Rhondda ownership the fleet has been cut dramatically. The Nationals which operated the bulk of services have mostly gone. Four Darts remain, and Rhondda has added three Nationals and a Tiger from its fleet, along with three second-hand Leyland Swifts. Parfitt's retains its identity, but its livery is being modified and the fleet is now numbered in the Rhondda series.

Two small operators serve Merthyr Tydfil. John's Travel runs minibuses locally with a couple of Sherpas, and three Alexander-bodied Renault S56s. All are second-hand. In sharp contrast Silverline, with routes from Brecon to Merthyr Tydfil and to Swansea, has bought mainly new buses. The current fleet comprises two Optare CityPacers, two Wadham Stringer-bodied Leyland Swifts (one of which spent a year on Jersey), a Wadham Stringer-bodied Dennis Javelin bus (a type operated only by Eastbourne and the Ministry of Defence), and a Marshall-bodied Dennis Dart.

Rhondda is the only solid reminder of National Welsh. National Welsh was privatised when it was sold by NBC to its management in May 1987. At that time it had 410 buses and coaches. By 1990 its fleet stood at 626 vehicles and it was easily the biggest bus company in Wales. It closed down in 1992 when no buyer could be found for what was left of its operations. By that time it had revived the Rhondda name for its Porth-based operations and that part of the company was successfully sold. Its ownership is complex, but now includes interests which involve British Bus, FirstBus and Stagecoach among others.

Top **Competition in Merthyr Tydfil is no longer as fierce as it once was. John's Travel provides a local service with second-hand minibuses. These include this 1987 Alexander-bodied Dodge S56 which was new to Go-Ahead Northern. It has been with John's Travel since 1994 after a short time in the Red & White fleet.** John Jones

Centre **Silverline of Merthyr Tydfil has found a niche running long-distance services and has a modern fleet with which to do this. New in 1994 was the company's first Dart, with bodywork by Marshall. It has 37 high-backed seats to provide extra comfort for long-distance travellers.** John Jones

Below left **Rhondda's fleet includes East Lancs-bodied Leyland Tiger buses which were new to Rhymney Valley in the early 1980s. There are four.** Stewart J Brown

Below right **Harris of Blackwood runs a number of minibus types, including this MCW Metrorider which was new to Cardiff City Transport.** John Jones

Right **A number of modern second-hand double-deckers have been added to the Rhondda fleet in recent times, including Volvo Citybuses and Leyland Olympians. The latter include this former Rossendale Transport East Lancs-bodied coach.** John Jones

Below **Rhondda has also been buying second-hand Lynxes. This one was new to Chesterfield Transport.** John Jones

Bottom **Most new additions to the Rhondda fleet have been midibuses, with both Dennis Darts and Volvo B6s being taken into stock. This is a Volvo, with Plaxton Pointer body. Marshall and Wright-bodied midibuses are also operated.** Peter Rowlands

The fleet which Rhondda started off with was pretty mixed. It included Tigers with East Lancs bus bodies and Duple and Plaxton coach bodies. There were older Leopards and Nationals. And there were a few Olympians and some Metroriders. In 1993 it took over the bus services of Cyril Evans, which added four more ex-London Metroriders and five ex-London Nationals to the fleet. Cyril Evans operated in the Caerphilly area and services there and down to Newport run as Caerphilly Busways, with Nationals, Metroriders, two new Marshall-bodied Darts and five new Plaxton-bodied B6s. Rhondda has in fact bought quite a number of new midibuses with 16 Darts bodied by Marshall, Plaxton and Wright, and nine B6s bodied by Plaxton. There are only four double-deckers in the 82-strong fleet – a VRT which was originally with National Welsh, two ex-Great Yarmouth Volvo Citybuses and an ex-Rossendale Olympian with East Lancs body. Other recent additions to the fleet have been the company's first Leyland Lynxes, bought from Chesterfield Transport, an East Lancs rebodied Tiger and a Volvo B10M with Van Hool bus body.

Shamrock's services are run mainly by Mercedes minibuses, but the company does have bigger vehicles including Dennis Darts and a pair of Iveco's short-lived TurboCity 50s with WS Coachbuilders bodywork. John Jones

A bus service is provided in Pontypridd by Bebb using six 1994 Volvo B6s with Marshall bodies. They were the first B6 buses to enter service in Wales. Trevor Jones

Pontypridd, until 1988 served by Taff Ely Transport, now has the rapidly-expanding Shamrock as its main operator. Shamrock also operate in Aberdare, and run services to Cardiff. For the Cardiff route the company has six Plaxton-bodied Dennis Darts and, more recently has added six Northern Counties-bodied Darts and a pair of Iveco TurboCity 50s with WS Coachbuilders bodies from a small batch built for stock. The only other TurboCity 50 to have found a home so far is running for Lucketts of Watford. Ten Leyland Nationals are operated on school services. Most of Shamrock's 100-plus fleet is made up of small vehicles. There are almost 60 Mercedes minibuses, most of which were bought new. A couple of CVE Omnis are owned. The coach fleet contains unusual types too, in the shape of two rugged-looking US-built Bluebird Q Buses.

Bebb of Llantwit Fardre, best known for its modern coach fleet, runs between Pontypridd and Beddau with a fleet of six Marshall-bodied Volvo B6s, not a common combination. The only other Welsh operator of B6 buses is Rhondda. The Beddau service has been operated since the company's early days, back in the mid 1920s. An express service to Cardiff is run by some of the company's Volvo B10Ms with Plaxton Premiere bodies.

To the west is FirstBus country. It was originally South Wales Transport territory, and in 1987 the company was sold by NBC to its management. They sold out to Badgerline in 1990. In 1988, while still management-owned, SWT bought the business of Brewers of Caerau, at that time a family-owned company with around 30 vehicles. After Badgerline took control there were major changes at SWT, with much of the company's eastern operations passing to a much expanded Brewers operation. This left SWT serving Swansea and areas to the west. Brewers also took over some of the operations of National Welsh. The Brewers fleet now numbers some 150 buses and coaches (some of the latter trade as United Welsh Coaches) from depots in Port Talbot, Maesteg and Bridgend.

None of the vehicles now running for Brewers were in the fleet when Badgerline took over in 1988, such has been the pace of change. Its minibuses are Mercedes, with some elderly C-registered van conversions transferred from SWT and a smaller number of newer 811Ds with coachbuilt Plaxton Beaver bodies. These, like many recent deliveries to Brewers, have BMS registration marks from the DVLA's select series. All of the company's double-deckers – there are 17 – are standard NBC-style ECW-bodied Bristol VRTs. There is more interest among the single-deckers with six Leyland Lynxes. Three were bought new in 1992 and are among the few K-registered Lynxes about. Two are J-registered ex-demonstrators. The sixth is the only Mark I Lynx in the fleet and was transferred from Yorkshire Rider in 1994 shortly after Rider acquired it with the bus business of Rhodes of Yeadon. Rather more interesting is the other bus transferred from Rhodes at the same time, the only Van Hool A600 in the UK. It was built as a demonstrator in 1989 when Van Hool thought it might try to sell buses in Britain. It can often be seen on the Swansea to Cardiff service. There are also 25 Nationals, most transferred from SWT, and eight Dennis Darts to standard Badgerline group specification with Plaxton Pointer bodywork. Brewers services run inland to Aberdare and west to Swansea.

This bus, unique in the UK, is a Van Hool A600 rear-engined integral. It was an exhibit at the 1989 show at the NEC and served as a demonstrator before being sold to Rhodes of Yeadon in 1992. It joined the Brewers fleet in 1994. Richard Eversden

In Swansea the slimmed-down SWT runs most of the city services, and generally does so with minibuses operating under the City Mini name. These are mainly Mercedes-Benz, including some 608Ds transferred from Bristol Cityline to replace MCW Metroriders. These retain Cityline livery. SWT defines minibuses as vehicles with 31 or fewer seats, this being the break point in terms of drivers' pay rates. The company's Darts might look much the same as others for Badgerline group companies, but count the seats in the Plaxton Pointer body and you'll find there are only 31 instead of the customary 35 to make them minibuses rather than big buses. SWT runs 50 Darts. The only full-size single-decker buses are two Leyland Nationals and 10 Dennis Lances with Plaxton Verde bodies. The Lances – the only ones in Wales – are used on Timecutter limited stop services running from Swansea and have high-backed seats.

Double-deck bus operation is restricted to one regular service in Swansea and to schools and contract work. There are 19 – seven Olympians and 12 VRTs, all standard NBC buses with ECW bodies. There are also a couple of long-wheelbase Olympian coaches which were originally part of Eastern National's London commuter fleet. Named after two famous Welshmen, Dylan Thomas and Sir Harry Secombe, they operate the Swansea to Cardiff shuttle. They have Leyland TL11 engines; the only other Leyland-engined buses in the fleet are the two Nationals and the 510-powered VRTs. Away from Swansea minibuses cover much of SWT's services in Dyfed. In Llanelli the buses carry Sosban Link as a fleetname, while in Haverfordwest the town's river gives rise to the Cleddau Mini name.

Top **South Wales Transport's fleet includes minibuses with roof-mounted advertising boards, as shown by a 1986 Mercedes-Benz L608D with 20-seat Robin Hood conversion.** John Jones

Centre **Double-deckers play a small part in SWT's operations. Twelve Bristol VRTs remain. They have ECW bodies. The company also has a few Leyland Olympians.** Cliff Beeton

Below **Plaxton-bodied Dennises account for most of SWT's newest vehicles. There are 10 Lances, but the majority are Darts as seen here in Swansea.** Stewart J Brown

Bridgend is served by the Porthcawl Omnibus Co. It runs Leopards, including two rebodied with East Lancs bus bodies and a couple of ex-Maidstone & District Willowbrook-bodied examples. On its Cardiff service a Volvo or Leyland Tiger coach is often used. One double-decker is kept for contract work – a former Nottingham Fleetline.

Hawkes Coaches of Waunarlwydd to the west of Swansea run into the city centre from Gorseinon, trading as City Connection. Two Leyland Nationals are used. From Morriston, north of the city, Brian Isaac Coaches run minibuses on local services, including one to Neath. These are Mercedes L608D vans, converted to buses by Alexander and originally operated by Kelvin Scottish, and two Iveco Fords. There is also a National, while four Fleetlines are owned for contract work. Merlyn's of Skewen, primarily a coach operator, runs a Leopard with Duple Dominant bus body between Neath and Birchgrove. It's a 1981 model, and was purchased from Merthyr Tydfil Transport in 1989. Slightly further north, services from Pontardawe to Swansea are run by Glantawe Coaches using Reeve Burgess-bodied Dodge minibuses which were new to Plymouth Citybus. Glantawe was taken over by D Coaches in 1995, but has retained its identity. The name comes from the River Tawe which flows down to Swansea – or Abertawe in Welsh.

Top **The newest additions to the Porthcawl Omnibus Co fleet are a pair of Leyland Leopards which had been rebodied by East Lancs for D Coaches of Swansea. A change in D Coaches' operations rendered the vehicles surplus to requirements and they were bought from East Lancs by Porthcawl Omnibus in the summer of 1995.** John Jones

Left **Merlyn's only bus is a 1981 Leyland Leopard with Duple Dominant body. It came from Merthyr Tydfil Transport in 1989.** John Jones

Below left **Glantawe Coaches operate in the Swansea area and the fleet includes four 1986 Dodge S56s purchased from Plymouth Citybus in 1993. They have Reeve Burgess bodies of a short-lived style supplied principally to Plymouth and South Yorkshire Transport before being replaced by the popular Beaver.** John Jones

Below **Brian Isaac run between Neath and Swansea using Mercedes L608D vans which were converted to 22-seat buses by Alexander. They were originally operated by Kelvin Scottish.** Richard Godfrey

With a fleet of 70 vehicles the business of Swansea-based D Coaches and its Rees & Williams subsidiary is the biggest family-owned bus and coach operation in West Glamorgan, although many of its services are in Dyfed, operating from the Ammanford area under the Rees & Williams name. Rees & Williams was an independent operation which was taken over by D Coaches in 1987. The company's country routes are run by a mixture of Leyland Leopard buses and Dennis Darts. There are five Darts in the fleet, four with Plaxton bodies and one Alexander Dash. They carry Dyfed Diamonds fleetnames. Leopard coaches are also used on service, while in Swansea minibuses are operated on a small scale under the D Coaches name. Double-deckers, mainly ex-London DMSs, are used mostly on school work.

Ystradgynlais-based D&N runs to Ammanford and to Swansea. The company's newest bus is a 1992 Mercedes 709D, bought new. It also has two Sherpas and an Iveco Ford, and two Ford coaches which are used on the Swansea service. Llandeilo, north of Ammanford, is the base of Thomas Bros, whose fleet includes Bristol LH buses and coaches. The buses are bodied by ECW, while the coaches have Plaxton bodies and are also used on service. A unique bus in the fleet is a Cummins-engined Dennis Lancet with Duple Dominant bus body, an exhibit at the 1986 Motor Show in the livery of Northumbria Motor Services. It was seen by Dennis as a possible replacement for LHs in the Northumbria fleet, which makes its arrival in this LH-based fleet particularly apposite. It was used briefly as a Dennis demonstrator and joined Thomas Bros in 1988.

There are two sizeable operators based in Dyfed. In the east of the county Davies Bros has a fleet of some 80 buses and coaches running from depots in Carmarthen, Pencader and Trimsaran. In the west Richards Bros (also trading in Welsh as Brodyr Richards) has around 50 vehicles at Cardigan, Newport and Solva, the last named being not far from St David's Head, the western tip of Wales. Nearby St David's, incidentally, is Britain's newest – and smallest – city, having been granted this status by the Queen in 1995. Davies routes cover a wide area, and a number of services connect Carmarthen with Llanelli by a variety of routes. Most of the company's full-size buses are examples of that trusty workhorse, the Leyland Leopard. There are Leopard buses (bodied by Alexander, Duple, Plaxton and Willowbrook) and Leopard coaches. The Willowbrook buses are mainly rebodies, with Warrior bodies fitted to earlier chassis. There are also a couple of Tiger buses, one ex-National Welsh (but new to Rhymney Valley and a very rare example of a 10m Tiger); the other a 1984 Leyland prototype chassis which was built with left-hand drive and is now fitted with a 1990 Willowbrook Warrior body. Minibuses are used on some services and these are mainly Mercedes-Benz bought both new and used and allocated primarily to Dyfed contracted services. An East Lancs-bodied Dennis Dart was purchased in 1994.

Top **D Coaches operate services in Dyfed under the Rees & Williams and Dyfed Diamonds names, both of which are carried on this Plaxton-bodied Dennis Dart, one of three purchased in 1992.** Malcolm King

Centre **Thomas Bros of Llandeilo operate Bristol LHs with Plaxton coach bodies and ECW bus bodies. All are second-hand; this bus came from Devon General in 1985.** John Jones

Right **Davies Bros operate seven Leylands which have been rebodied by Willowbrook – six Leopards and a Tiger. This bus has a 1973 Leopard chassis and a 1988 Warrior body.** John Jones

Carmarthen is, of course, served by SWT, but it also attracts other, smaller, operators. Indeed SWT's presence is in decline following the loss of a number of tendered service contracts. One of the smaller operators is Ffoshelig Motors with a particularly smart fleet which includes two Leopard buses, a couple of Bristol LHs and three minibuses – two Mercedes bought new and an ex-GM Buses Dodge S56 with Northern Counties body. The Ffoshelig business is run by Jones of Newchurch. Some buses carry Jones rather than Ffoshelig names. Gwyn Williams serves Carmarthen from Llandarog, using 1970s Ford and Bedford coaches, and also runs minibuses on contracted services for disabled travellers. Jones of Login runs a Login to Carmarthen service, generally with a Plaxton-bodied Bedford coach. The company also has a fleet of service buses – Leopards and Bedfords which are used on school contracts. Meyers run from their home base in Llanpumsaint, usually with Freight Rover Sherpas or an Iveco Ford, but occasionally with a full-size coach.

The Richards Bros fleet is noteworthy for the large numbers of Bedfords it contains. With 37 full-size examples it can lay claim to being the country's biggest Bedford user. Over half are buses, mainly with Duple Dominant bodies, but there are also a few early 1970s Willowbrooks, including some rare surviving SB5s and an SB3. Bedford's demise has seen some quite remarkably different types of bus appear on Richards Bros services. Its three Optare Deltas are about as far removed from the utilitarian SB5s as it's possible to imagine. The first was bought new in 1990 while the others are an ex-demonstrator and a former Gatwick Airport bus. The company also has three Darts, one with Carlyle body, the other two bodied by Plaxton, and one MAN with Optare Vecta bodywork. Services are operated as far south as Haverfordwest, as far west as St David's and stretch north to Aberystwyth.

South of Haverfordwest is country served by another old-established operator, Silcox of Pembroke Dock. This is also a sizeable business – almost 75 vehicles – and another with Leopards forming the backbone of its bus fleet. These include Alexander-bodied buses which were new to SBG companies and some Willowbrook Warrior rebodies. More unusual are two Bristol LHs with Duple Dominant bus bodies, bought new in 1976 and still going strong. Conventional ex-NBC ECW-bodied LHs are operated too. The fleet also contains Mercedes minibuses and a few double-deckers, the oldest of which are Series 1 Bristol VRTs used mainly on school journeys but also from time to time on regular services. The Silcox business has a long association with the Bristol marque, going back to the days of the front-engined K and L models. The most modern double-decker in the Silcox fleet is a V-registered Leyland Titan which was new to Greater Manchester Transport. The most modern single-deckers are four Dennis Darts bodied by Marshall (three) and East Lancs. The Marshall-bodied Darts have SMC – Silcox Motor Coach registrations.

Top Ffoshelig operate a smart fleet with an interesting mix of vehicles. London Transport was the original operator of this Bristol LH, now leading a much quieter life in Carmarthen. Richard Godfrey

Centre Richards Bros of Cardigan operate one of Britain's biggest fleets of Bedfords with some 40 still in use. Most are mid-engined Y-series models including this 1977 YMT which was fitted with a new Willowbrook Warrior body in 1988. John Jones

Left A recent addition to the Silcox bus fleet is this Dennis Dart with Marshall body. John Jones

Inland, Rees of Crymych, who trades as Midway Motors, runs a Crymych to Cardigan service. Three Ford buses are available for this. Two are R1014s with Duple Dominant bodies which came from the Isle of Wight county council, the third is an R1014 with unusual Plaxton Bustler body, acquired in 1993 from University Bus of Hatfield. The company also has half a dozen Ford R-series coaches. Further north, but still in Dyfed, James Brothers of Llangeitho runs local tendered services with Mercedes minibuses. In nearby Tregaron Crosville Wales has its most southerly outpost.

Powys is the biggest of the eight Welsh counties, and also the least densely populated, with the Cambrian mountains running the length of the county. The two main towns in Powys are Llandrindod Wells and Builth Wells, just seven miles apart. In the former, Cross Gates Coaches runs a fleet made up entirely of coaches which range from AEC Reliances to a Van Hool Eos. Services are operated to Newtown and to Rhayader. There is also a route running to Cardiff. In Builth Wells, Browns run north to Llandrindod Wells and south to Brecon. Bedford coaches are used. The company also runs a Sherpa minibus on a market day service in Crickhowel.

Below **The most common double-deck type in service with Crosville Wales is the standard NBC-style Bristol VRT with ECW body. This is a 1981 example.** John Jones

Above **Rees of Crymych operate a service using three Ford buses. RDL671S is one of two purchased from Isle of Wight county council.** John Jones

The major operator in north Wales is Crosville Wales with a fleet of 300 vehicles, half of which are minibuses. It is now part of British Bus although it started life in the private sector as a management buy-out from NBC and was then owned by National Express for a period. Crosville Wales was created in 1986 when NBC split the Crosville company in two. The English operation, run from the company's traditional headquarters in Chester, retained the Crosville name which is now nothing more than a fleet-name for the PMT operations in the Chester and Wirral areas following some rapid changes in the company's ownership in the period up to 1990.

Crosville Wales was, like Cardiff City Transport, a believer in having fleetnames in both English and Welsh. However the English language version of the company's name is disappearing and most buses now carry only Crosville Cymru fleetnames. It has also retained Crosville's alpha-numeric fleet numbering scheme, since adopted in England by PMT following its acquisition of the Crosville operations on the other side of the border.

New vehicles in recent years have been minibuses, apart from a pair of Optare Deltas in 1989 and four Optare Vectas in 1995 for use on the Rhyl to Chester service. All of the minibuses are Mercedes, apart from seven Iveco Fords.

There are no midis in the fleet, but apart from the two Deltas there are other modern single-deckers in the shape of 14 Leyland Lynxes acquired from Colchester Borough Transport in 1994, after Colchester was bought by British Bus. To these it has added four Lynxes displaced from the Atlas Bus operations in London in 1994 and five from Chesterfield Transport. The other single-deck buses are 25 Nationals, and a further two which have been rebuilt as Greenways by East Lancs, and repowered with Gardner engines at the same time. There were 11 Greenways, but the remainder have been transferred to sister British Bus company The Shires (alias Luton & District Transport). Leopard and Tiger coaches are used on some longer services and there are second-hand Volvo B10Ms which are normally to be found on the Traws Cambria service running from Aberystwyth to Cardiff.

Crosville Wales has a substantial double-deck fleet – 84 including 11 open-toppers which come out in the summer months. The vast majority are ECW-bodied VRTs, but the newest are 10 Olympians dating from 1985. Crosville Wales covers a large area, which includes the major towns of Bangor and Aberystwyth, and covers much of three Welsh counties – Clwyd, Gwynedd and Dyfed as well as areas of Powys. As part of Gwynedd's promotion of public transport, many buses operated in the county by Crosville and other significant operators have red fronts and carry Bws Gwynedd names, although the practice is less widespread now than it was in the early 1990s.

Top **British Bus owns both Crosville Wales and Colchester Borough Transport. Changes at CBT have provided Crosville Wales with a fleet of relatively young Leyland Lynxes, transferred from the Essex company. This bus was new to CBT in 1987 and moved to Crosville Wales in 1994. It is seen in Chester.** Tony Wilson

Centre **Four Optare Vectas were bought by Crosville Wales in 1995 and are used mainly on the service between Rhyl and Chester. The Vecta is based on a rear-engined MAN underframe.** John Jones

Left **Open-toppers are a feature of the Crosville Wales operation during the summer months. Most are Fleetlines, including two long-wheelbase CRL6-33 models which were transferred from Southend Transport in 1993. They have Northern Counties bodies.** John Jones

Cut-backs by Crosville Wales have led to considerable expansion by smaller operators, particularly in Gwynedd where there are over 25 small bus companies providing services, very often after winning tenders from the county council. Crosville Wales' headquarters are at Llandudno Junction, just three miles inland from the renowned Victorian resort town. In Llandudno Aberconwy Borough Council still provides a service aimed at visitors, although using rather less glamorous vehicles than the attractive small Guys which figured for so long in the fleet of its predecessor, Llandudno Urban District Council. Now the fleet comprises four second-hand Bedford VAS5s, two each bodied by Duple and Plaxton. The oldest dates from 1971 while the newest is a 1984 vehicle which must have been one of the last VASs to enter service in Britain. They carry Great Orme Tours fleetnames. Aberconwy also runs the Great Orme Tramway with four Hurst Nelson cars built over 90 years ago.

Alpine of Llandudno sold its commercial services to Crosville Wales in July 1995. No vehicles were involved, but the Alpine name and livery has been applied to 10 vehicles in the Crosville Wales fleet to run the ex-Alpine services. Alpine continues to operate contracts. Prestatyn Coachways of Dyserth operate a Prestatyn town service using a Sherpa minibus. Blythin of Llandudno Junction trades as both Empire and Goldstar International. It operates from Llandudno to Ton-y-Bwlch and also has a substantial number of contracts. All of Blythin's vehicles are second-hand and the bus fleet includes four ECW-bodied LHs and a couple of Leyland Cubs with Wadham Stringer bodies which started life as school buses in London. A number of double-deckers – including five Bristol VRTs and six ex-Merseyside Fleetlines – are owned and are used principally on school services. Three of the LHs and three of the 'deckers were acquired in 1992 when the company took over Shearings' operations in the area which ran under the Gwalia Coaches name. Shearings had taken over the Gwalia business in 1990 when it was in expansionist mode. But it soon decided to retrench and to concentrate on its core holiday coach touring business. Sel's Mini Travel of Llanrwst operate to Betwys y Coed and Cwm Penmachno and have a number of contracts with Gwynedd County Council. Seven Iveco Ford 49.10s are owned, including two bought new with Elme Orion bodies, made in Portugal. Infrequent services in the Bala and Llanrwst areas are operated by Williams of Bala. Bedford or Leyland coaches are used.

Top **The commercial services operated by Alpine of Llandudno were taken over by Crosville Wales in 1995. For these Crosville use buses in Alpine livery, including this B-series Leyland National.** John Jones

Centre **Blythin of Llandudno Junction operates a mixture of second-hand buses and coaches. These include six 1973 Daimler Fleetlines with Metro-Cammell bodies. These were new to the Merseyside PTE, whose fleet number is still carried on this bus.** John Jones

Right **The red and white livery of Williams of Bala has been adapted to provide a Bws Gwynedd red front on this PMT-bodied Mercedes 709D. This was for a time a requirement on tendered services being run on behalf of Gwynedd county council, although it is not now being rigorously enforced.** John Jones

Anglesey, separated from the mainland by the Menai Strait, is the base for no fewer than five small operators running local bus services. Goodsir of Holyhead runs three local services, generally using a Mercedes 709D with Reeve Burgess body. Carreglefn Coaches is based in the village from which it takes its name and runs school services using Bedford coaches and also serves Kwiksave at Amlwch. Similarly, Ellis of Llangefni runs three local services, but with former NBC ECW-bodied VRTs running alongside the company's coaches and a 1973 Bristol RELL. Jones of Llanfaethlu is another operator with a mixture of local and schools services. Jones has three VRTs with Northern Counties bodies. These were new to Cleveland Transit and represent a rare combination which was built only for Cleveland and Reading. Jones also has a number of Nationals, some of which are in B&I Line colours and operate a free shuttle service in Holyhead between the ferry terminal and the railway station. The newest bus owned by Jones is a Mercedes with a Reeve Burgess Beaver body. Lewis Y Llan (which means Lewis of Llan – short for Llanerchymedd) is based in Amwlch and runs from there to Holyhead and from Cemaes to Llangefni. The company has three buses – two Optare StarRiders bought new in 1990 and, in sharp contrast, an ECW-bodied Bristol LH which was new to Bristol Omnibus. Lewis Y Llan runs five coaches, one of which is a comparatively rare Leyland Royal Tiger Doyen integral.

Services are operated between the mainland and Anglesey – over the Menai Bridge – by Padarn of Caernarfon, who run from Bangor to Llangefni, normally with one of two Carlyle-bodied Dennis Darts in London Buses red or with a one-time South Midland Bristol VRT. Other services are operated around Bangor with minibuses – either a Carlyle-bodied Iveco, new to the company in 1990, or a 1987 Sherpa which came from Busways in 1989. Padarn takes its name from Llyn Padarn, a lake near Llanberis. There are two small fleets running from Bangor to Bethesda. Purple Motors has done so for many years and currently runs either an ex-Tayside Alexander-bodied Ailsa, which is the company's only 'decker, or one of five single-deck buses owned. One of these was bought new in 1982, a Duple-bodied Bedford, while the others are second-hand Leopards. Three have Dominant bus bodies similar to that on the Bedford while the fourth has a Willowbrook Warrior body which was fitted in 1991. D&G of Llanllechid operate a little way beyond Bethesda to Gerlan using either a one-time Hills of Tredegar Leopard with Duple Dominant bus body similar to those in the Purple fleet, a Volvo B9M or a minibus.

Top **Jones of Llanfaethlu operate services on Anglesey, including a connecting service between the B&I ferry terminal and Holyhead town centre. For this the company has Leyland Nationals in a dedicated livery. The newest is this 1976 bus, which came from London Country North West in 1990.** John Jones

Centre **The oldest vehicle operated by Purple Motors of Bethesda is a 1975 Leyland Leopard with Duple Dominant bus body. It was originally operated by Safeguard of Guildford from whom it was purchased in 1982.** John Jones

Left **D&G Coaches operate in Gwynedd using Leyland Leopards and a few smaller buses. The latter include this Freight Rover Sherpa with Dormobile body which was new in 1987 to Yorkshire Rider.** John Jones

Above **Silver Star run a number of Bristols including LHs, a VRT and this RE. It was originally a Crosville bus. Note the Bws Gwynedd name on a red rectangle above the door.** John Jones

Right **Only two of the vehicles in the 34-strong Express Motors fleet were bought new. One is a 1981 Ford R-series coach; the other this 1990 Mercedes-Benz 609D with Made-to-Measure body.** John Jones

Williams of Deiniolen operate two routes from Bangor, one running to Llanberis and the other to Dinorwic. These are often worked by double-deckers in the shape of either a Roe-bodied Fleetline which came from Grimsby-Cleethorpes Transport, or an ex-Tees & District VRT. Williams Deiniolen (which is how the company trades) has a couple of Leyland Nationals and one bus bought new, a Mercedes 811D with Dormobile body.

Caernarfon is an important transport centre, served by Crosville Wales and a number of smaller companies. Silver Star of Upper Llandwrog operate five services from Caernarfon running to Cesarea and Carmel, Nantlle, Bethel and Waunfawr, Dinas Dinlle and Cae Gwyn. Three ECW-bodied Bristol REs are used on service. All originated with other Welsh operators – Rhymney Valley and Crosville although they came via Catch-A-Bus in north-east England. Silver Star also has ECW-bodied Bristol LHs and a Plaxton-

bodied Dennis Dart. Arvonia of Llanrug operate a Caernarfon town service normally using a Carlyle-bodied Mercedes. Express Motors of Bontnewydd have a service from Caernarfon to Blaenau Ffestiniog via Porthmadog and also run to Porthmeirion, Beddgelert and Bangor. An unusual bus in this fleet is an East Lancs Greenway rebuild of a Leyland National, a type more often found in bigger fleets. It has a Volvo engine. Another rebuild, or more accurately a rebody, is a Leopard with Willowbrook's neatly-styled Warrior bodywork. There are five standard Nationals, while double-deckers are two VRTs, a former West Midlands Ailsa, and an East Lancs-bodied Atlantean. KMP of Llanberis operates in to Caernarfon every half hour, normally with ex-NBC VRTs. The letters are the initials of the first names of the owner's three daughters. The company also runs four Leyland Nationals and two minibuses, one of which is a three-axle Talbot Pullman.

Clynnog & Trefor, based in Trefor on the Lleyn Peninsula, operate primarily from Caernarfon to Pwllheli, a route they have covered for many years. Indeed with a history going back to the period just before World War I, Clynnog & Trefor is one of the oldest bus operators in Wales. Double-deckers are used and the company has five VRTs. Berwyn of Trefor also operates from Caernarfon, running in competition with Clynnog & Trefor, and generally using minibuses. These include a tri-axle Talbot Pullman complete with Bws Gwynedd red front, three Mercedes, three Iveco Fords and a couple of Sherpas. Caelloi, based in Pwllheli, has two mid '70s VRTs with ECW bodies and two YMTs, one bodied by Duple, the other by Plaxton. School services are operated, along with a commercial service between Pwllheli and Pothmadog which uses ex-Bebb Iveco Fords. Nefyn Coaches operate from Nefyn to Pwllheli and from Pwllheli to Dinas and Pencaenewydd. The company has two front-line buses, both bodied by Reeve Burgess and both bought new. One is a Mercedes 709D with the popular Beaver body while the other is an altogether more unusual Leyland Swift with Harrier-style bodywork. Not that many Harriers were built, and most were coaches rather than buses. Lithfaen Motors run between Lithfaen and Pwllheli. The company only owns four vehicles. The oldest is a 1970 Willowbrook-bodied Bedford YRQ and the newest an ex-GM Buses Iveco Ford. In the middle are a 1981 YMQ with Duple Dominant bus bodywork and a 1983 VAS5 with Dominant coach body.

Wrexham is the busiest town in Clwyd. Wrights, who provided services in and around the town, closed down at the start of 1994. The town's smallest operator provides a local service with just one bus. The operator is Chaloner and the bus a Reeve Burgess-bodied Mercedes 811D. Edwards of Bwlchgwyn run into Wrexham, using two Bedford YMTs with Duple Dominant bus bodies, both second-hand. A Duple-bodied Bedford is also operated on services to Wrexham by E Jones & Sons of Ponciau. Jones also has an ex-Lothian Cub, with a scaled-down version of the Dominant bus body, and two Wadham Stringer-bodied Dennis Lancets, as well as a more unusual Dennis in the shape of an ex-South Yorkshire Optare-bodied Domino. Williams also run from Ponciau to Wrexham, and they too have a Duple bus-bodied Bedford. They also have a YMT with a Plaxton Bustler body, which was a Plaxton demonstrator, and a Ford R1014 with Plaxton Derwent body, bought new in 1976. Vale of Llangollen, a company best known for its coach fleet, run to Wrexham from Cefnmawr using ex-Tayside Ailsas with Alexander bodies.

Top **Clynnog & Trefor operate Bristol VRTs on schools and regular services. All have ECW bodies and were first operated by NBC subsidiaries – PMT in the case of this bus waiting to take up a schools run.** Michael Fowler

Centre **Carlyle bodywork is fitted to this Iveco Ford 49.10 operated by Caelloi of Pwllheli. It was new to Bebb in 1992.** John Jones

Right **Nefyn Coaches operate to Pwllheli using small buses including this Mercedes with Reeve Burgess Beaver body.** John Jones

Acton Coaches link Wrexham with Mold, using either a Transit, a Sherpa or a Duple-bodied Bedford YNT. P&O Lloyd, based at Bagillt, run a Holywell local service and also provide scholars' services which take the company's double-deckers to Mold and to Flint. The company has 12 'deckers. All are Fleetlines and they were new to a variety of operators – Chester, Midland Scottish, Nottingham, South Yorkshire and West Midlands. The ex-South Yorkshire buses have London DMS-style Metro-Cammell bodies. Local services between Mold and Holywell are run by Phillips of Holywell with a Bristol LH bus, an LHL coach, an ex-SBG Seddon Pennine VII and a couple of Sherpas.

Bryn Melyn Motor Services operates between Llangollen, the company's base, and Wrexham as well as providing local services in the Llangollen area and running two days a week to Oswestry. Ford R-series coaches and Mercedes minibuses are operated. Further south, in Oswestry (which is actually in England), lengthy services are run by Tanat Valley of Llangedwyn. Leopards which started life with Ribble and Trent are normally used. An ex-South Yorkshire Atlantean and a former Merseyside Atlantean are used on schools work and occasionally on regular service. Oswestry is also served by Midland Red North, which took over some of the Crosville Wales operations in the area. Midland Red North runs cross-border services which take its vehicles south to Welshpool and north to Wrexham.

Devaway of Bretton, which is only just inside Wales, is a growing operator. It was started in 1987 by ex-Crosville employees. It now runs just over 30 buses. All are second-hand and they range from Mark 1 Nationals to Optare CityPacers. There are eight of the former and five of the latter. The CityPacers came from Lancaster City Transport when that operation closed down in 1993 and one has been repowered with a Sherpa engine. Its double-deck fleet consists of 11 ECW-bodied VRTs, five of which are dual-door buses from the City of Oxford fleet. Recent expansion has been made by acquiring a particularly odd batch of buses from another failed municipal operation: six Ward Dalesman GRXIs from Darlington Transport. These are the only GRXIs built and they have Wadham Stringer bodies. The model designation is in two parts. The letters GR indicate Gardner Rear-engined. The second part of the type code is the overall length in Roman numerals: XI metres. Devaway serve Mold and Denbigh and have a number of routes running in to Chester, including one from Connah's Quay on the north side of the River Dee. Also linking Mold and Denbigh is M&H using either Duple-bodied Ford coaches or a Sherpa minibus.

Top **Jones of Rhos, near Wrexham, operate a bus fleet which features Dennis Lancets, Y-series Bedfords and this ex-Lothian Leyland Cub. It has 31-seat Duple Dominant bodywork.** John Jones

Centre **Most of the double-deckers in the Vale of Llangollen fleet are ex-Tayside Ailsas with Alexander bodies and they date from 1976-77. Almost all of the vehicles in the fleet carry VT or VLT registrations.** John Jones

Left **The rear-engined Ward Dalesman GRXI was built for just one operator, Darlington Transport. There were six, and all are now with Devaway. New in 1983, they were bought by Devaway in 1994. They have Wadham Stringer bodies.** John Jones

BUSES IN BRITAIN – THE MAJOR GROUPS

Blazefield Holdings
BTS Coaches
Cambridge Coach Services
Harrogate & District Travel
Ingfield Northern Rose
Keighley & District Travel
Rover Coaches
Sovereign Bus & Coach Co
Sovereign Buses (Harrow)
Welwyn Hatfield Line
Yorkshire Coastliner

British Bus
Bee Line Buzz Co
Clydeside Buses
Colchester Borough Transport
Crosville Wales
Derby City Transport
Frontline, Tamworth
Gem Fairtax
Guildford & West Surrey Buses
Horsham Buses
Kentish Bus & Coach Co
Liverline Travel
London & Country
Londonlinks Buses
Maidstone & District
Midland Fox
Midland Red North
North Western Road Car Co
Northumbria Motor Services
Selby & District Bus Co
South Yorkshire Road Transport
Southend Transport
Star Line, Knutsford
Stevensons of Uttoxeter
The Shires (LDT)
West Riding Automobile Co
Yorkshire Woollen District Transport Co

Cowie Group
Grey-Green
Leaside Bus Co
South London Transport

FirstBus
Badgerline
Brewers
Bristol Omnibus Co
District Bus, Wickford
Durbin Coaches, Bristol
Eastern Counties Omnibus Co
Eastern Scottish Omnibuses
Eastern National
Grampian Transport
Kirkpatrick of Deeside
Leicester Citybus
Lowland Omnibuses
Mainline Group (part)
Mairs Coaches

Midland Bluebird
Midland Red West
Northampton Transport
Oban & District (part)
PMI
Quickstep Travel
Rider York
South Wales Transport
Thamesway
Wessex Coaches
Western National
Yorkshire Rider

Go-Ahead Group
Brighton & Hove Bus and Coach Co
City of Oxford Motor Services
Gateshead & District Omnibus Co (Go-
   Ahead Gateshead)
Langley Park Motor Co (Gypsy Queen)
London Central Bus Co
Low Fell Coaches
Northern General Transport Co
Northern National Omnibus Co
OK Motor Services
Sunderland & District Omnibus Co (Wear
   Buses)
Tynemouth & District Omnibus Co
   (Coastline)
Tyneside Omnibus Co (VFM Buses)
Venture Transport (Shaws)
Visitauto (Metro Taxis)

MTL Trust Holdings
Fareway Passenger Services
Heysham Travel
Liverbus
London Northern Bus Co
London Suburban
Merseyrider
Merseyside Transport
R&I Buses

Stagecoach Holdings
A1 Buses
Aberdare Bus Co
Bluebird Buses
Buckinghamshire Road Car
Busways Travel Services
Cambus
Cheltenham & Gloucester Omnibus Co
Cheltenham District Traction
Chesterfield Transport
Circle Line, Gloucester
Cleveland Transit
Cumberland Motor Services
East Kent Road Car Co
East London Bus & Coach Co
East Midland Motor Services
Fife Scottish Omnibuses
G&G Travel

Grimsby-Cleethorpes Transport
Hampshire Bus
Hartlepool Transport
Kingston-upon-Hull City Transport
Midland Red South
Milton Keynes City Bus
Premier Travel Services
Red & White Services
Ribble Motor Services
South Coast Buses
South East London & Kent Bus Co
Stagecoach (South)
Stagecoach Hants & Surrey
Sussex Coastline
Swindon & District
United Counties Omnibus Co
The Valleys Bus Co
Vanguard Coaches
Viscount Bus & Coach Co
Western Scottish Buses

Transit Holdings
Bayline
Blue Admiral
Devon General
Docklands Transit
Red Admiral
Thames Transit

West Midlands Travel Group
County Bus & Coach Co
Tees & District Transport Co
Teesside Motor Services
United Automobile Services
West Midlands Travel

Yorkshire Traction
Andrews, Sheffield
Barnsley & District Traction Co
Lincolnshire Road Car Co
Meffan, Kirriemuir
Sheffield Omnibus
South Riding
Strathtay Scottish Omnibuses
Yorkshire Terrier
Yorkshire Traction Co